POSITIVE DISCIPLINE

FOR PRESCHOOLERS

ALSO IN THE POSITIVE DISCIPLINE SERIES

POSITIVE DISCIPLINE
FOR PRESCHOOLERS

For Their Early Years—
Raising Children Who Are Responsible,
Respectful, and Resourceful

Completely Revised and Expanded 3rd Edition

JANE NELSEN, ED.D., CHERYL ERWIN, M.A., AND ROSLYN ANN DUFFY

HARMONY

BOOKS · NEW YORK

Published in the United States by Harmony Books, an imprint of the Crown Publishing Group, a division of Random House LLC, a Penguin Random House Company, New York. www.crownpublishing.com

Harmony Books is a registered trademark, and the Circle colophon is a trademark of Random House LLC.

Earlier editions were published in 1994 and 1998 by Prima Publishing, Roseville, California. Subsequently published in paperback by Three Rivers Press, an imprint of the Crown Publishing Group, a division of Random House LLC, New York, in 2007.

Library of Congress Cataloging-in-Publication Data

Nelsen, Jane.
Positive discipline for preschoolers : for their early years—raising children who are responsible, respectful, and resourceful / Jane Nelsen, Cheryl Erwin, and Roslyn Duffy.—Rev. 3rd ed.
1. Preschool children. 2. Toddlers. 3. Child rearing.
4. Discipline of children. 5. Parent and child. I. Erwin, Cheryl.
II. Duffy, Roslyn. III. Title.
HQ774.5.N45 2007
649'.122—dc22   2006028849

ISBN 978-0-307-34160-0

Printed in the United States of America

Design by Cynthia Dunne

Interior illustrations by Paula Gray

14 13 12 11 10

Third Edition

To my nineteen grandchildren: Joshua, Amber, Trey, Ken, Drew, Woody, Kristina, Mac, Scotty, Kelsie, Katie, Riley, Kara, Melissa, Gibson, Andrew, Emma, Sage, and Greyson.

—Jane

To all the children—our world's best hope; to those who have dedicated time and energy to understanding them and helping others understand them, too; and to Philip, who continues to teach me day by day the joys of being a mom, even though the preschool days are far behind both of us.

—Cheryl

To Vinnie; our children, Blue, Manus, Rose, and Bridget and their spouses; our grandchildren; and the Learning Tree Montessori Childcare—its parents, children, and staff—for sharing their lives with our family and from whom we learn more each day.

—Roslyn

CONTENTS

CONTENTS

POSITIVE DISCIPLINE

FOR PRESCHOOLERS

PROLOGUE

BY THE CHILDREN

"My name is Susan and I am three and a half years old. I talk a lot now. I get upset when people won't read me the same book over and over again, or when they try to leave out a part. My favorite question is 'Why?' I like to dress up and try on all kinds of different characters. I like to have stories told to me all the time. I like to have someone to play with me all the time, too. And I don't like to have my playtime interrupted."

"I am Jeffrey F. Fraser. The F stands for Frank, like my grandpa. I am friendly. I like talking. Yesterday I turned five years old. We can be friends and I will invite you to my birthday party. When I pick what I want to do, I pay attention really good. I have a little brother. He will do for a playmate if there's nobody better. I think this tooth is getting loose. Do you want to hear me count? I can sing a song for you. Do you want to play with me? Okay, you be the bad guy and I'll be the good guy. . . ."

"I'm four years old. I'm Cyndi. I have sparkly shoes. Do you know what kind of underwear I have on? They have the days on them. See how sparkly my shoes are when I twirl? I'm too big to be taking naps. If you read me a story, I'll be happier. I am really not tired. Do you *want to see my shoes? I am going to marry Chad. Do you know Chad? He has a Batman cape. Can you read me a story now?"*

"I'm Maria. My hair is long. I always wear dresses. I am four and three-quarters years old. Callie is my bestest friend. Sometimes Callie won't play with me. She is four and a half. I can play with Gina. I like to eat lunch with Callie and Gina. I want to sit next to them—not across the table from them. I like it when the teachers teach me things."

This is a book about us—the children. Each one of us is different. Not all three-year-olds or five-year-olds will be like us, but you will probably find a little bit of us in the children you know. This book will help you get to know us and find out what the world is like for us. It will give you lots of ideas about how to help us grow and how to encourage and teach us. We are alike and we are different. We want to be loved; this book is for the people who love us.

WHY POSITIVE DISCIPLINE?

Parenting classes are full of parents with preschoolers. Internet parenting forums echo with questions like "Why does my three-year-old bite?" or "How do I get my five-year-old to stay in bed at night?" Child development experts, preschool directors, and therapists all boast offices overflowing with parents whose offspring have reached the age of three or four or five and who are wondering what on earth has happened. Listen for a moment to these parents:

> "Our little boy was such a delight. We expected trouble when he turned two—after all, everyone had warned us about the 'terrible twos'—but nothing happened. Until he turned three, that is. Now we don't know what to do with him. If we say 'black,' he says 'white.' If we say it's bedtime, he's not tired . . . and getting him to let us brush his teeth turns into a full-fledged battle. We must be doing something wrong!"

"Sometimes I wonder if any sound comes out when I open my mouth. My five-year-old sure doesn't seem to hear anything I say to her. She won't listen to me at all. Is she always going to act like this?"

"We couldn't wait for our son to begin talking, but now we can't get him to stop. He has figured out that he can prolong any conversation by saying, 'Guess what?' He is our delight and despair, in almost equal measure."

As you will discover in the pages that follow (or as you may already realize), these years from ages three to six are busy, hectic ones for young children—and for their parents and caregivers. Preschoolers are physically active and energetic; researchers tell us that human beings have more physical energy at the age of three than at any other time in their life span—certainly more than their weary parents. Their inborn drive for emotional, cognitive, and physical development is urging them to explore the world around them; they're acquiring and practicing social skills and entering the world outside the protected haven of the family. And preschoolers have ideas—lots of them—about how that world should operate. Their ideas, along with their urges to experiment and explore, often do not mesh with their parents' and caregivers' expectations.

It's probably safe to say that what you will discover in the chapters ahead is a bit different from what you grew up with. You will discover concepts such as kindness *and* firmness at the same time and looking for solutions with your child. You will learn about the importance of teaching social and life skills. And you will learn how essential it is to view parenting as a long-term commitment, rather than a series of crises and questions. You may even wonder what happened to "good old-fashioned discipline." What would Dr. Benjamin Spock (or Grandma) think of all this?

ADLER AND DREIKURS: PIONEERS IN PARENTING

Positive Discipline is based on the work of Alfred Adler and his colleague Rudolf Dreikurs. Adler was a Viennese psychiatrist and a contemporary of Sigmund Freud—but he and Freud disagreed about almost everything. Adler believed that human behavior is motivated by a desire for belonging, significance, connection, and worth, which is influenced by our early decisions about ourselves, others, and the world around us. Interestingly, recent research tells us that children are "hardwired" from birth to seek connection with others, and that children who feel a sense of connection to their families, schools, and communities are less likely to misbehave. Adler believed that everyone has equal rights to dignity and respect (including children), ideas that found a warm reception in America, a land he adopted as his own after immigrating here.

Rudolf Dreikurs, a Viennese psychiatrist and student of Adler's who came to the United States in 1937, was a passionate advocate of the need for dignity and mutual respect in *all* relationships— including the family. He wrote books about teaching and parenting that are still widely read, including the classic *Children: The Challenge*.

As you will learn, much of what many people mislabel as "misbehavior" in preschoolers has more to do with emotional, physical, and cognitive development and age-appropriate behavior. Young children need teaching, guidance, and love (which is a good definition of Positive Discipline).

WHAT IS POSITIVE DISCIPLINE?

Positive Discipline is effective with preschoolers because it is different from conventional discipline. It has *nothing* to do with punishment (which many people think is synonymous with discipline) and everything to do with teaching valuable social and life skills. Discipline with young children involves deciding what *you* will do and then kindly and firmly following through, rather than expecting your *child* to "behave." As your child matures and becomes more skilled, you will be able to involve him in the process of focusing on solutions and participating in limit setting. In this way he can practice his thinking skills, feel more capable, and learn to use his power and autonomy in useful ways—to say nothing of feeling more motivated to follow solutions and limits he has helped create. The principles of Positive Discipline will help you build a relationship of love and respect with your child and will help you solve problems together for many years to come.

The building blocks of Positive Discipline include:

- **Mutual respect.** Parents model firmness by respecting themselves and the needs of the situation, and kindness by respecting the needs and humanity of the child.

- **Understanding the belief *behind* behavior.** All human behavior has a purpose. You will be far more effective at changing your child's behavior when you understand the motivation for it. (Children start creating the beliefs that form their personality from the day they are born.) Dealing with the belief is as important as (if not more important than) dealing with the behavior.

- **Effective communication.** Parents and children (even young ones) can learn to listen well and use respectful words to ask for what they need. Parents will learn that children "hear" better when they are invited to think and participate instead of being told what to think and do. And parents will learn how to model the listening they expect from their children.

- **Understanding a child's world.** Children go through different stages of development. By learning about the developmental tasks your child faces and taking into account other variables such as birth order, temperament, and the presence (or absence) of social and emotional skills, your child's behavior becomes easier to understand. When you understand your child's world, you can choose better responses to her behavior.

- **Discipline that teaches.** Effective discipline teaches valuable social and life skills and is neither permissive nor punitive.

- **Focusing on solutions instead of punishment.** Blame never solves problems. At first, you will decide how to approach challenges and problems. But as your child grows and develops, you will learn to work together to find respectful, helpful solutions to the challenges you face, from spilled Kool-Aid to bedtime woes.

- **Encouragement.** Encouragement celebrates effort and improvement, not just success, and helps children develop confidence in their own abilities.

- **Children *do* better when they *feel* better.** Where did parents get the crazy idea that in order to make children behave, parents should make them feel shame, humiliation, or even pain? Children are more motivated to cooperate, learn new skills, and offer affection and respect when they feel encouraged, connected, and loved.

MORE ABOUT DISCIPLINE

Do these parents' words sound familiar?

"I have tried everything when it comes to discipline, but I am getting absolutely nowhere! My three-year-old daughter is very demanding, selfish, and stubborn. What should I do?"

"What can I do when nothing works? I have tried time-out with my four-year-old, taking away a toy or television, and

spanking him—and none of it is helping. He is rude, disrespectful, and completely out of control. What should I try next?"

"I have a class of fifteen four-year-olds. Two of them fight all the time, but I can't get them to play with anyone else. I put them in time-out, threaten to take away recess if they play together, and this morning I started yelling when one of them tore up the other's drawing. I don't know where to turn—they won't listen to anything I say. How should I discipline them?"

When people talk about "discipline" they usually mean "punishment" because they believe the two are one and the same. Parents and teachers sometimes yell and lecture, spank and slap hands, take away toys and privileges, and plop children in a punitive time-out to "think about what you did." Unfortunately, no matter how effective punishment may seem at the moment, it does not create the long-term learning and social and life skills parents truly want for their children. Punishment only makes a challenging situation worse, inviting both adults and children to plunge headfirst into power struggles.

Positive Discipline is based on a different premise: that children (and adults) do better when they feel better. Positive Discipline is about teaching (the meaning of the word *discipline* is "to teach"), understanding, encouraging, and communicating—not about punishing.

Most of us absorbed our ideas about discipline from our own parents, our society, and years of tradition and assumptions. We often believe that children must suffer (at least a little) or they won't learn anything. But in the past few decades, our society and culture have changed rapidly and our understanding of how children grow and learn has changed, so the ways we teach children to be capable, responsible, confident people must change as well. Punishment may seem to work in the short term. But over time, it creates rebellion, resistance, or children who just don't believe in their own worth. There is a better way, and this book is devoted to helping parents discover it.

WHAT CHILDREN REALLY NEED

There is a difference between wants and needs, and your child's needs are simpler than you might think. All genuine needs should be met. But when you give in to all of your child's wants, you can create huge problems for your child and for yourself.

For example, your preschooler needs food, shelter, and care. He needs warmth and security. He does not need a pint-sized computer, a television in his bedroom, an iPod, or a miniature monster truck to drive. He may love staring at the television screen, but experts tell us that any kind of screen time at this age may hamper optimal brain development. (More about this later.) He may want to sleep in your bed, but he will feel a sense of self-reliance and capability by learning to fall asleep in his own bed. He may love french fries and sugary soda, but if you provide them you could be setting the stage for childhood (and adult) obesity. You get the idea.

From his earliest moments in your family, your young child has four basic needs:

1. A sense of belonging and significance
2. Perceptions of capability
3. Personal power and autonomy
4. Social and life skills

If you can provide your child with these needs, he will be well on his way to becoming a competent, resourceful, happy human being.

The Importance of Belonging and Significance

"Well, of course," you may be thinking, "everyone knows a child needs to belong." Most parents believe that what a child really needs is quite simple: he needs love. But love alone does not always create a sense of belonging or worth. In fact, love sometimes leads parents to pamper their children, to punish their children, or to make decisions that are not in their child's long-term best interest.

Everyone—adults and children alike—needs to belong somewhere.

We need to know that we are accepted unconditionally for who we are, rather than just our behavior or what we can do. For young children, the need to belong is even more crucial. After all, they're still learning about the world around them and their place in it. They need to know they are loved and wanted even when they have a tantrum, spill their cereal, break Dad's golf clubs, or make yet another mess in the kitchen.

Children who don't believe they belong become discouraged, and discouraged children often misbehave. Notice the word *believe*. You may know your child belongs and is significant. But if he doesn't believe it (sometimes for the darnedest reasons, such as the birth of another baby), he may try to find his sense of belonging and significance in mistaken ways. In fact, most young children's misbehavior is a sort of "code" designed to let you know that they don't feel a sense of belonging and need your attention, connection, time, and teaching.

When you can create a sense of belonging and significance for every member of your family, your home becomes a place of peace, respect, and safety.

Perceptions of Capability

Your preschooler will never learn to make decisions, learn new skills, or trust his own abilities if you don't make room for him to practice. Parenting in the preschool years involves a great deal of letting go.

You will learn more in the chapters ahead about encouraging perceptions of capability in your child, but for now, consider this: words alone are not powerful enough to build a sense of competence and confidence in children. Children feel capable when they experience capability and self-sufficiency—when they are able to successfully do something—and from developing solid skills.

Personal Power and Autonomy

As you will see, developing autonomy and initiative are among the earliest developmental tasks your child will face. And while parents may not exactly like it, even the youngest child has personal power—and quickly learns how to use it. If you doubt this, think about the last time you saw a four-year-old jut out his jaw, fold his arms, and say boldly, "No! I don't *want* to!"

Part of your job as a parent will be to help your child learn to channel his considerable power in positive directions—to help solve problems, to learn life skills, and to respect and cooperate with others. Punishment will not teach these vital lessons: effective and loving discipline will.

Social and Life Skills

Teaching your child skills—how to get along with other children and adults, how to feed and dress herself, how to learn responsibility—will occupy most of your parenting hours during the preschool years. But the need for social and practical life skills never goes away. In fact, true self-esteem does not come from being loved, praised, or showered with goodies—it comes from having *skills*.

When children are young, they love to imitate parents. Your child will want to hammer nails with you, squirt the bottle of detergent or prepare breakfast (with lots of supervision). As he grows more capable, you can use these everyday moments of life together to teach him how to become a competent, capable person. Working together to learn skills can occasionally be messy, but it's also an enjoyable and valuable part of raising your child.

WHY SOME PARENTS DON'T ACCEPT NONPUNITIVE METHODS

Because all children (and all parents) are unique individuals, there are usually several nonpunitive solutions to any problem. Some of the parents we meet at lectures and parenting classes don't immediately understand or accept these solutions; indeed, Positive Discipline requires a paradigm shift—a radically different way of thinking about discipline. Parents who are hooked on punishment often are asking the wrong questions. They usually want to know:

- How do I make my child mind?

- How do I make my child understand "no"?

- How do I get my child to listen to me?

- How do I make this problem go away?

Most frazzled parents want answers to these questions at one time or another, but they are based on short-term thinking. Parents will be eager for nonpunitive alternatives when they ask the right questions—and see the results this change in approach creates for them and their children. What are the right kinds of questions? Here's a good start.

- How do I help my child feel capable?

- How do I help my child feel a sense of belonging and significance?

- How do I help my child learn respect, cooperation, and problem-solving skills?

- How do I get into my child's world and understand his developmental process?

- How can I use problems as opportunities for learning—for my child and for me?

These questions address the big picture and are based on long-term thinking. We have found that when parents find answers to the long-term questions, the short-term questions take care of themselves. Children will "mind" and cooperate (at least, most of the time) when they feel a sense of belonging and significance, they will understand "no" when they are developmentally ready and are involved in solutions to problems, and they'll listen when parents listen to *them* and talk in ways that invite listening. Problems are solved more easily when children are involved in the process.

We have included Positive Discipline tips in every chapter of this book. In this chapter, we will tell you why punitive discipline methods should be avoided, and we will present suggestions for nonpunitive methods that will help your child develop into a capable and loving person.

DISCIPLINE METHODS TO AVOID

Most parents have done it at one time or another. But if you are screaming, yelling, or lecturing, stop. If you are spanking, stop. If you are trying to gain compliance through threats and warnings, stop. All of these methods are disrespectful and encourage doubt, shame, guilt, and/or rebellion—now and in the future. Ultimately, punishment creates more misbehavior. (There are many research studies that demonstrate the long-term negative effects of punishment. These studies are usually buried in academic journals where parents don't see them.)

"Wait just one minute," you may be thinking. "These methods worked for my parents. You're taking away every tool I have to manage my child's behavior. What am I supposed to do, let my child do anything she wants?" Of course not. Permissiveness is disrespectful and does not teach important life skills. You can never really control anyone's behavior but your own, and your attempts to control your child will usually create more problems and more power struggles. Later in this chapter, we offer several methods that invite cooperation (when applied with a kind and firm attitude) while encouraging your preschooler to develop character and valuable life skills.

Life with an active, challenging preschooler becomes much easier when you accept that positive learning does not take place in a threatening atmosphere. Children don't listen when they are feeling scared, hurt, or angry. Punishment derails the learning process.

Eight Methods for Implementing Positive Discipline

1. Get children involved:
   a. In the creation of routines
   b. Through the use of limited choices
   c. By providing opportunities to help
2. Teach respect by being respectful.
3. Use your sense of humor.
4. Get into your child's world.
5. Say what you mean, and then follow through with kindness and firmness.
6. Be patient.
7. Act, don't talk—and supervise carefully.
8. Accept and appreciate your child's uniqueness.

METHODS THAT INVITE COOPERATION

So, what tools and ideas will help your child learn all she needs to know? If punishment doesn't work, what does? Here are some suggestions. Remember, your child's individual development is critical in these years; remember, too, that nothing works all the time for all children. As your unique child grows and changes, you'll have to return to the drawing board many times, but these ideas will form the foundation for years of effective parenting.

Get Children Involved

Education comes from the Latin root *educare,* which means "to draw forth." This may explain why children so often tune you out when you try to "stuff in" through constant demands and lectures. Instead of telling children what to do, find ways to involve them in decisions and to draw out what they think and perceive. Curiosity questions (which often begin with "what" or "how") are one way to do this. Ask, "What do you think will happen if you push your tricycle over the curb?" or "What do you need to do to get ready for preschool?" Children who are involved in decision making experience a healthy sense of personal power and autonomy. For children who are not yet able to talk, say, "Next, we _____," while kindly and firmly showing them what to do.

There are several particularly effective ways of getting preschoolers involved in cooperation and problem solving. Here are three suggestions:

Create routines together. Young children learn best by repetition and consistency, so you can ease the transitions of family life by involving them in creating reliable routines. Routines can be created for every event that happens over and over: getting up, bedtime, dinner, shopping, and so on. Sit down with your child and invite her to help you make a routine chart. Ask her to tell you the tasks involved in the routine (such as bedtime). Let her help you decide on the order. Take pictures of her doing each task that can be pasted next to each item. Then let her illustrate the chart with markers and glitter. Hang it where she can see it, and let the routine chart become the boss. When your child gets distracted, you can ask, "What's next on your routine chart?" (Be sure not to confuse these with sticker or reward charts, which diminish your child's inner sense of capability because the focus is on the reward.)

Offer limited choices. Having choices gives children a sense of power: they have the power to choose one possibility or another. Choices also invite a child to use his thinking skills as he contemplates what to do. And, of course, young children often love it when choices include an opportunity to help. "What is the first thing you will do when we get home—help me put the groceries away or read a story? You decide." "Would you like to carry the blanket or the cracker box as we walk to the car? You decide." Adding "You decide" increases your child's sense of power. Be sure the choices are developmentally appropriate and that all of the choices are options you are comfortable with. When your child wants to do something else, you can say, "That wasn't one of the choices. You can decide between this and this."

Provide opportunities for your child to help you. Young children often resist a command to get in the car but respond cheerfully to a request like "I need your help. Will you carry the keys to the car for me?" Activities that might easily have become power struggles and battles can become opportunities for laughter and closeness if you use your instincts and your creativity. Allowing your child to help you (even when it's messy or inconvenient) also sets the stage for cooperation later on.

Teach Respect by Being Respectful

Parents usually believe children should *show* respect, not have it shown *to* them. But children learn respect by seeing what it looks like in action. Be respectful when you make requests. Don't expect a child to do something "right now" when you are interrupting something she is thoroughly engaged in. Give her some warning: "We need to leave in a minute. Do you want to swing one more time or go down the slide?" Carry a small timer around with you. Teach her to set it to one or two minutes. Then let her put the timer in her pocket so she can be ready to go when the timer goes off.

Remember, too, that making a child feel shame and humiliation—such as a child might feel if she was spanked in the middle of the park (or anywhere else, for that matter)—is disrespectful, and a child who is treated with disrespect is likely to return the favor. Kindness and firmness show respect for your child's dignity, your own dignity, and the needs of the situation.

Use Your Sense of Humor

No one ever said parenting had to be boring or unpleasant. Laughter is often the best way to approach a situation. Try saying, "Here comes the tickle monster to get children who don't pick up their toys." Learn to laugh together and to create games to get unpleasant jobs done quickly. Humor is one of the best—and most enjoyable—parenting tools.

> *Three-year-old Nathan had an unfortunate tendency to whine, and Beth was at her wits' end. She had tried talking, explaining, and ignoring, but nothing seemed to have any effect. One day Beth tried something that was probably more desperation than inspiration. As Nathan whined that he wanted some juice,*

Beth turned to him with a funny look on her face. "Nathan," she said, "something is wrong with Mommy's ears. When you whine, I can't hear you at all!"

Again Nathan whined for juice, but this time Beth only shook her head and tapped her ear, looking around as if a mosquito were buzzing near her head. Nathan tried once more, but again Beth shook her head. Then Beth heard something different. The little boy took a deep breath and said in a low, serious voice, "Mommy, can I have some juice?" When Beth turned to look at him, he added "Please?" for good measure.

Beth laughed and scooped Nathan up for a hug before heading to the kitchen. "I can hear you perfectly when you ask so nicely," she said. From that time on, all Beth had to do when Nathan began to whine was tap her ear and shake her head. Nathan would draw an exasperated breath—and begin again in a nicer tone of voice.

Not everything can be treated lightly, of course. But rules become less difficult to follow when children know that a spontaneous tickling match or pillow battle might erupt at any moment. Taking time to lighten up and to laugh together works where discipline is concerned, too, and makes life more pleasant for everyone.

Get into Your Child's World

Understanding your preschooler's developmental needs and limitations is critical to parenting during these important years. Do your best to be empathetic when your child becomes upset or has a temper tantrum out of frustration with his lack of abilities. Empathy does not mean rescuing. It means understanding. Give your child a hug and say, "You're really upset right now. I know you want to stay." Then hold your child and let him experience his feelings before you gently guide him to leave. If you rescue your child by letting him stay, he won't have the opportunity to learn from experience that he can survive disappointment.

Getting into your child's world also means seeing the world from his perspective and recognizing his abilities—and his limitations. Occasionally ask yourself how you might be feeling (and acting) if you were your child. It can be illuminating to view the world through a smaller person's eyes.

Say What You Mean, Then Follow Through with Kindness and Firmness

Children usually sense when you mean what you say and when you don't. It's usually best not to say anything unless you mean it and can say it respectfully—and can then follow through with dignity and respect. The fewer words you say, the better! This may mean redirecting or showing a child what she *can* do instead of punishing her for what she *can't* do. It also might mean wordlessly removing a child from the slide when it is time to go, rather than getting into an argument or a battle of wills. When this is done kindly, firmly, and without anger, it will be both respectful and effective.

Be Patient

Understand that you may need to teach your child many things over and over before she is developmentally ready to understand. For example, you can encourage your child to share, but don't expect her to understand the concept and do it on her own when she doesn't feel like it. When she refuses to share, rest assured that this doesn't mean she will be forever selfish. It will help to understand that she is acting age-appropriately. (More on social skills in Chapter 11.) Don't take your child's behavior personally and think your child is mad at you, bad, or defiant. Act like the adult (sometimes easier said than done) and do what is necessary without guilt and shame.

Act, Don't Talk—and Supervise Carefully

Minimize your words and maximize your actions. As Rudolf Dreikurs once said, "Shut your mouth and act." Quietly take your child by the hand and lead her to where she needs to go. Show her what she *can* do instead of what she can't do. And no matter how bright, cooperative, or quick to learn your child is, be sure to supervise her actions carefully. Preschoolers are often impulsive little people and your child will need your watchful attention for years to come.

Accept and Appreciate Your Child's Uniqueness
Children develop differently and have different strengths. Expecting from a child what he cannot give will only frustrate both of you. Your sister's children may be able to sit quietly in a restaurant for hours, while yours get twitchy after just a few minutes, no matter how diligently you prepare (refer to Chapters 3 and 6 on developmentally appropriate behavior and temperament for more on this subject). If you simply accept that, you can save yourself and your children a lot of grief by waiting to have that fancy meal when you can enjoy it in adult company—or when your children have matured enough for all of you to enjoy it together.

It may help to think of yourself as a coach, helping your child to succeed and learn how to do things. You're also an observer, learning who your child is as a unique human being. Never underestimate the ability of a young child. Watch carefully as you introduce new opportunities and activities; discover what your child is interested in, what your child can do by himself, and what he needs help learning from you.

WHAT ABOUT TIME-OUTS?

You may wonder where a common parenting tool, the time-out, fits in the Positive Discipline approach. Most parents use it (in one study, 91 percent of parents of three-year-old children admitted to doing so), but few really understand what it is or how best to use it with young children.

A *positive* time-out can be an extremely effective way of helping a child (and a parent) calm down enough to solve problems together. In fact, when we are upset or angry, we actually lose access to the part of the brain that allows us to think rationally and calmly, so a positive—

not punitive—time-out can help everyone a great deal. A punitive time-out is past-oriented, making children suffer for what they have done and not actually encouraging them to make good decisions about what to do in the future. A positive time-out allows for cooling off until both of you can access the rational part of the brain, and it is future-oriented because when children feel encouraged, they can learn to make positive decisions about self-control and responsibility.

It may be helpful to rename the time-out, taking away the implication of punishment or restriction. You can call a positive time-out a "cool-off" or even a "feel-good place." It is often effective to invite your child to help you create a positive time-out area, supplying this special spot with items that help your child soothe himself (soft toys, books, art supplies, a favorite blanket, etc.). Some parents and teachers believe that making a time-out area inviting and pleasant rewards children for misbehavior. Wise adults realize that all people have moments when they are too upset to get along, and a few moments in positive time-out (when it's not shaming or punishing) provides a cooling-off period. One child care center used the cooling-off image literally to help the children see it as a positive experience when they needed to calm down. The children helped to set up a corner of the classroom with pillows and cuddly toys and named it "Antarctica." Any child could choose to go to Antarctica to cool off when he needed to. The whimsy of this space really appealed to the children, taking away negative connotations and allowing cooling off to become a positive life skill. (Wouldn't it be great if adults had a handy Antarctica, too?) Make sure children know they're welcome to return from their cooling-off period when they are ready.

Here are several essential points to consider regarding time-out (or cool-off) for young children:

- *Time-outs should not be used with children under the age of three or four.* Until children reach the age of reason, which starts around age three (and is an ongoing process that even some adults have not fully mastered), supervision and distraction are the most effective parenting tools.

- *Children do better when they feel better.* Strong emotions can feel overwhelming to a young child. A positive time-out gives them an opportunity to calm down and catch their breath, so they are able to work with you to solve the problem. When your child is young, you can go with him to a positive time-out if it makes him feel better. Remember, the purpose is for both of you to feel better so you can choose better behavior—eventually.

- *Your attitude is the key.* Time-outs should not be used as a punishment, but rather as a way to give children time to calm down. When your child is feeling discouraged ("misbehaving"), you can ask, "Would it help you to go to your feel-good place?" If your child refuses, ask if she would like you to go with her. (Remember, the purpose is to help her feel better.) If she still refuses, go yourself to model a good way to calm down until you feel better. A positive time-out is most effective when it is offered as one of several choices: "Would it help you to go to the comfy area or to brainstorm for some solutions with me?" When children don't have a choice, even a positive time-out can turn into a power struggle, with an adult trying to make a resistant child stay in an area that feels like punishment to him—no matter what the adult calls it.

- *No parenting tool works all of the time.* Be sure to have more than just time-outs in your toolbox. There is never one tool—or three, or even ten—that is effective for every situation and for every child. Filling your parenting toolbox with healthy, nonpunitive alternatives will help you avoid the temptation to punish when your child challenges you—and he undoubtedly will.

- *Always remember your child's development and capabilities.* Understanding what is (and is not) age-appropriate behavior will help you not to expect things that are beyond the ability of your child.

Time-out can be an effective and appropriate parenting tool when it is used to teach, encourage, and soothe. (For more information about time-outs, see *Positive Time Out: And Over 50 Ways to Avoid Power Struggles in Homes and Classrooms* by Jane Nelsen, Ed.D., Three Rivers Press, 1999.)

WHEN YOUR CHILD "DOESN'T LISTEN"

One of the most common complaints parents have about young children is the mysterious hearing loss known as "my child won't listen." There are many reasons why children don't respond to adults' instructions—few of which have anything to do with their hearing.

Three-year-old Brianna is hitting her playmate and barely pauses when her teacher tells her to stop. Gregory's dad tells him it's time to leave the park and go home, then gets no response—until he raises his voice and grabs Gregory's elbow. Megan's mom tells her calmly and clearly before they enter the store that there will be no treats or toys today, and Megan nods when asked if she understands, but as they wait at the checkout stand, Megan howls loudly for candy anyway.

Sound familiar? The problem usually isn't that our children don't listen but that what we're asking of them runs counter to some more basic need. Brianna, for example, is very young and is still working on her social skills. She needs to be helped to "use her words" and, if she continues to hit, to be removed calmly to another place. Gregory is experimenting with his initiative and autonomy, which, unfortunately, don't match his dad's concept of what he should be doing. He can learn from limited choices and from kind, firm action. Megan is simply too young to remember instructions that were given an hour earlier—especially when they're contrary to what she wants now.

Since you can no more make your child listen than you can make him obey, what *can* you do? You can listen first, thus providing a model for listening. Understanding temperament and age-appropriate behavior will help; so will avoiding yelling, punishment, and nagging, which only invite power struggles. Also try inviting cooperation instead of insisting on obedience: "There are toys on the floor. Would you like to pick them up with me or can you do it all by yourself?" Children usually cooperate when they feel empowered to choose.

LET THE MESSAGE OF LOVE GET THROUGH

We often ask parents in workshops why they care about their children's behavior. After a few moments of head scratching and blank stares, they tell us that they love their children—as though that love ought to be obvious. But is it?

> ### Children Don't Listen Because:
>
> - Adults yell, lecture, or nag, which does not invite listening.
>
> - Adults don't *ask* a child what she should or should not be doing, but *tell* her.
>
> - Adults set up power struggles that make winning more important than cooperating.
>
> - The child is "programmed" by her instinct toward development to explore—and the adult doesn't want her to. The voice of a child's instinct is usually louder than the voice of an adult.
>
> - The child cannot comply with a request because it demands social skills or thinking skills that have not yet developed.
>
> - Children don't have the same priorities as adults.
>
> - Adults don't listen to children.

You know you love your child. Gaze down at her sleeping face or watch her grin at you through a mask of chocolate ice cream, and see if you can resist the urge to hug her. But does your child know that you offer discipline, skills, and teaching *because* you love her?

Even the most effective nonpunitive parenting tools must be used in an atmosphere of love, of unconditional acceptance and belonging. Be sure you take time for hugs and cuddles, for smiles and loving touches. Your child will do better when she feels better, and she will feel better when she lives in a world of love and belonging.

2

POSITIVE DISCIPLINE AND YOUR PRESCHOOLER

Preschoolers are engaging, charming little people. They can share ideas, show curiosity, exercise a budding sense of humor, build relationships of their own, and offer open arms of affection and playfulness to those around them. They can also be stubborn, defiant, confusing, and downright defeating.

Most parents worry about the world their children will inherit; they wonder how best to raise their children so that they can live successful, happy lives. And they watch the occasionally frustrating behavior of those same children and wonder what lies ahead—and what to do about it.

"WHERE HAS MY BABY GONE?"

Carlota watched three-year-old Manuel's progress across the playground—he was no longer toddling. She felt a jolt of surprise as Manuel climbed to the very top of the domed bars with surefooted skill. "Where has my baby gone?" she wondered out loud, with a bittersweet smile. "Who is this new little person?"

Dana automatically reached down to take her daughter's hand when the light at their corner turned green. Five-year-old Marta looked at her mother and made a face. Marta was willing to walk beside her mom, but she would not hold hands: that was for babies. Dana felt a bit silly. She realized Marta was careful and capable enough to cross the street without having her hand held, but at that moment Dana's own hand suddenly felt very empty.

Somewhere, somehow, during the second three years of life, the needy, helpless infant you used to marvel at and cuddle grows into a separate being, filled with plans, ideas, and opinions all his own. For most parents, this transformation happens so gradually that you feel a sense of shock when, at moments like those above, you see your child through new eyes. When was the wobbly toddler replaced by this sturdy youngster who can walk and even run (faster than you can) without a stumble? When did the wiry, endlessly distracted little explorer disappear, to be succeeded by the careful, capable, and more responsible young person standing beside you? When can you stop checking to see if she visited the potty, has a coat on, or remembered her lunch box? Some parents get so much in the habit of doing these things that they're still calling out instructions and warnings long after their children have become parents themselves!

LEARNING TO LET GO

At times it may seem to you that parenting is all about learning to let go. When your child is weaned from the breast or the bottle, you must let go of the special closeness nursing brings. When you can no longer measure how many ounces of juice your child drinks because he now uses a "big-people" glass, you must let go again. When you leave your child in someone else's care, even for as little as half an hour, you must let go in still another way.

Letting go is a process that begins the moment a baby separates from his mother's body, and it is essential to the healthy growth and development of each human being. Hanging on—which usually is done in the name of love—prevents healthy growth. Remember that you will have to let go again when your child grows past her teen years—the goal is to let her grow into a capable and happy adult. It often seems to watching parents that each step the child takes carries him farther from their arms: the more a child grows, the less he seems to need them. The challenge of parenting lies in finding the balance between nurturing, protecting, and guiding, on one hand, and allowing your child to explore, experiment, and become an independent, unique person, on the other. The truth is that your child will *always* need your guidance, encouragement, and love, but parenting does take different shapes as he grows and changes. At fourteen, he will need both love and limits, but he must make many life decisions on his own. In the same way, children at four years of age are far from self-sufficient, but they need some independence with which to learn and practice new skills. Providing a balance between guidance and independence requires that your role in his life adapt as he grows and acquires new skills to prepare him for successful living when he leaves your nest.

THE WORLD OUT THERE

Children are moving forward quickly during these years, and parents often find themselves scrambling to keep up. Preschoolers discover the many other people who share their world, and may no longer view Mom, Dad, or other immediate family members as the most important people in that world.

Children begin to make connections with other people; they discover the world of friends. Johnny figures out whether he is a boy or girl and that it is a permanent arrangement. He notices skin colors, body shapes, and lifestyles that differ from his own. He begins to make decisions about the world and how it works, what to expect from others, and what he must do to find love and belonging. In fact, as you will learn in Chapter 4, these decisions become part of the wiring of his growing brain. Every experience matters to your child as he develops his own unique approach to life.

Conflict may arise as parents struggle to make peace with the fact that their child has different needs than he used to. You must "let go of baby" and learn to see your child as capable and able to master new skills. Occasionally, he will make mistakes; you must learn to watch your precious child experience the discomfort some of those mistakes bring without rushing in to pamper or rescue him. Children will waver between fledgling independence and the need for Mom or Dad's sheltering arms.

During these years, your child will learn her first lessons about empathy, cooperation, and kindness. She doesn't realize it, but learning to build and maintain healthy relationships will take up most of her energy during these years. Teaching these skills (and helping smooth over the crises that are often part of the learning process) will keep her parents and caregivers busy indeed.

Raising an active preschooler is a big task and can feel overwhelming. No wonder parents find that they can hardly watch television or pick up a magazine without being offered the latest advice on discipline and development. Bookstore shelves bulge with volumes covering every aspect of parenting. In fact, most parents find that the problem isn't having enough information; it's knowing where to start and whom to trust. This book is based on principles of dignity and respect that help parents with differing views (and even the most loving parents occasionally disagree) find discipline methods that work for both of them.

ALL KINDS OF PARENTS

Parents come in many shapes and types, and each child has at least one of them—not to mention stepparents, grandparents, aunts, uncles, or housemates. Busy preschoolers have a gift for bringing out differences in parenting styles and opinions. Perhaps Dad believes that children should sit through a meal, waiting until everyone has finished eating. Mom thinks that children should be able to get up as soon as they have finished. In order to avoid endless dinnertime squabbles, these issues need to be discussed by the adults, and agreements reached and honored. It's critical to your family's well-being to work through your differences in opinion and remember to respect one another's parenting styles.

Knowing that differences are going to come up can help you face them with less worry. Adults need to develop the same skills for problem solving and achieving cooperation that they want their children to learn—after all, your children will imitate you. Consider your differences as opportunities to learn and grow (for everyone involved), as well as the means to exhibit valuable life skills.

Sometimes one adult will feel that a particular issue is important enough that he can let go of other issues and reach a compromise. If sitting through dinner matters so much to Dad, maybe he will permit a child to color quietly while she remains at the table. There are many possibilities. Learning to give and take, respect one another's ideas, and try out new ways of doing things will lead to true family cooperation.

ALL KINDS OF FAMILIES

Families are not all the same. They come in many different shapes, sizes, and configurations. Preschoolers may be raised in households with two parents, a single parent, adoptive parents, grandparents, or stepparents. Their parents may be of different genders or of the same gender. There may be several siblings or no other children nearby.

We believe that children can grow up with a healthy sense of respect and dignity in any sort of family. The decisions adults make about which values will be taught and reflected in their daily lives are what will shape a child's early life. Young children can grow up healthy and happy in any family as long as that family is built on love, respect, dignity, and belonging.

All families face pressure and stress, whether it's about finances, time, or relationships. If your family is not the traditional Norman Rockwell sort (and many these days are not), you may be wise to look for support and additional information; for example, check out *Positive Discipline for Single Parents,* Three Rivers Press, 1999, *Positive Discipline for Your Stepfamily,* Empowering People, an e-book available at www.focusingonsolutions.com, and *Positive Discipline for Parenting in Recovery,* Empowering People, an e-book available at www.focusingonsolutions.com.

With so many differing kinds of parents and families, can there really be one discipline philosophy that fits all? We think so.

WHY POSITIVE DISCIPLINE?

Positive Discipline (both the philosophy and the skills that go with it) will offer you effective, loving ways to guide your youngster through these busy, often challenging years. Whether you are a parent, a teacher, or a child care provider, you will find ideas in these pages that you can really use and that will help you give the children in your care the best start in life.

Does Positive Discipline work? Yes! In fact, the philosophy of Positive Discipline, which is built on mutual respect, encouragement, and teaching, meshes beautifully with our growing understanding of how the human brain develops and what best promotes healthy development. These principles have worked for us, our children, our preschool students, our clients, and hundreds of parents and teachers who have attended our classes and workshops. We share many success stories in this book: our own, as well as those of many parents, teachers, and care-givers who have expressed their gratitude for the success they and their children have experienced by using Positive Discipline concepts.

We've made many mistakes (where do you think we get many of the stories for our books?), but we truly believe that mistakes are opportu-nities to learn. We want to share what we have learned with you. As you read through the chapters ahead, you will add some valuable knowledge and skills to your Positive Discipline toolbox, tools such as understanding developmental appropriateness (Chapter 3), under-standing temperament (Chapter 6), social skill development (Chapter 11), and the mistaken goals of misbehavior (Chapters 8, 9, and 10). We will also explore the many ways of providing discipline—and pre-venting misbehavior—for preschoolers.

This is indeed a challenging world, and our children need all the confidence, wisdom, and problem-solving skills we can give them. They also need to believe in their own worth and dignity, to possess a healthy sense of self-esteem, and to know how to live, work, and play with those around them. It is the rare parent who doesn't occasionally feel overwhelmed and confused, who doesn't worry that his or her best just won't be good enough. The stakes are so high, and you love your child so much. Where should you begin?

Actually, the end is a good place to begin. By that we mean it is important to have a destination in mind so you can focus on parenting skills that help you achieve what you want for your child in the long term instead of focusing on short-term fixes that may not teach the life skills and character qualities you want your child to have.

THE IMPORTANCE OF LONG-TERM PARENTING

It is easy in the rush of daily life with a preschooler to focus on the cri-sis at hand. There's the morning to get through, with lunches to pack and jackets to grab and children who may or may not be willing to get dressed and put shoes on their feet. Parents must get to work, and children must go off to child care or preschool or must be supervised at home. Later on, dinner and household duties demand time and attention, and then there's bedtime at the end of the day. Just getting everyone fed, bathed, and to sleep can take your last remaining ounce of energy.

There's more that parents must do, however. You must think and dream and plan. You must learn to know your little one well, and you must decide what matters most to you in life. These last, most important tasks are often the ones parents never have time to do. But think for a moment: Wouldn't it be helpful, as you embark on the parenting journey, to know your final destination? How will you get there if you don't have a clear picture of where you want to go?

Perhaps one of the wisest things you can do right now is to take a moment to ask yourself a very important question. What do you want for your child? When your child has grown to be an adult, what qualities and characteristics do you want her to have? You may decide that you want your child to be confident, compassionate, and respectful. You may want her to be responsible, hardworking, and trustworthy. Most parents want their children to be happy, to have rewarding work, and healthy relationships. Whatever you want for your child, how will you bring it to pass? How will your child learn to have a contented, successful life? The good news is that the discipline methods you will learn in this book are designed to help your children develop the social and life skills that will help them achieve these goals.

KIND AND FIRM

Because it is so important, there is one Positive Discipline tool we want to mention at the outset: the ability to be both kind and firm at the same time. This is no small challenge. Any of us can be tempted to punish a child when a favorite crystal bowl is lying shattered on the kitchen floor. It is equally tempting to buy that candy bar at the checkout stand if it will avoid a public tantrum.

What Do You Want for Your Children?

Here is a typical list from parents and caregivers, gathered from many workshops and lectures:

Self-discipline	Self-reliance
Decision-making skills	Problem-solving skills
Self-motivation	Self-confidence
Cooperation/collaboration skills	Social skills
Creativity	The ability to see positives
Values	Resilience
Leadership skills	Foresight
Endurance	Accountability
Responsibility	Respect for self and others
Empathy/caring	Tolerance
Sense of humor	Determination
Thinking skills/judgment skills	Public-spiritedness/social interest
Honesty	Lifelong learning skills
Adaptability	Communication skills

The real question is: What kind of discipline works best to help children develop these skills? We believe that punitive methods do not work in the long run. Instead, Positive Discipline emphasizes nonpunitive discipline, intended to build skills and connection.

Being kind and firm in the face of these daily disasters gets easier (and the disasters fewer) when you realize that a little prevention can be incredibly valuable. Why was that tempting bowl left to sparkle on the table your preschooler uses? Was taking a tired and hungry child to the store setting both of you up for frustration? A bit of prevention will eliminate a lot of mischief—yours and theirs.

But prevention does not always work; even the sweetest preschooler will misbehave or make mistakes from time to time. In these moments, kind and firm parenting is called for. Kindness shows respect for the humanity of the child and emphasizes the teaching of valuable skills. Firmness backs up your words with necessary action, helping children learn that you mean what you say (which also means you must be careful of what you say).

Kindness in the face of that broken bowl would include commiserating with a child's dismay at what happened and helping him find a way to make amends of some sort. This could mean holding the dustpan while the broken pieces are swept into it or coming up with a list of small jobs to earn money toward its replacement. These choices should be based on a child's age and abilities. Kindness means not lecturing, shaming, or humiliating a child; firmness means being sure that the agreed-upon tasks are done.

In the grocery store, kindness may mean giving a hug and acknowledging that your child *really* wants that candy bar. Firmness means not buying it if you said you wouldn't, and kindly leading him out of the store without additional punishment or lectures if he loses his temper. Parents who don't practice firmness may become permissive, and permissive parenting does not benefit children or adults. Permissiveness leads children to believe that they can behave any way they wish without recognizing that choices have outcomes.

At the other parenting extreme is excessive control. Parents who insist upon inflexible control see punishment as their primary parenting tool; unfortunately, punishment does not teach children what parents think it does. Children are always making decisions about themselves, you, and the world around them. As we have learned and will show you, punishment most often results in more unpleasant behavior later on.

If you avoid both permissiveness and excessive control and you act in ways that are kind and firm, will your problems simply vanish?

Well, things will improve—but there are other factors at work. You will never be perfect, nor will your child. However, it helps to be aware of the many mistakes than can be made in the name of love so you can avoid them as often as possible—or at least correct your mistakes once they have been made.

IN THE NAME OF LOVE

It is a rare parent who does not love his or her child. Love, however, is sometimes not enough. Parents (and teachers) do many ineffective and even harmful things in the name of love. You may punish your child because you love him and think that's the only way to teach, or push her too hard to excel because you love her and want the very best for her. Parents also overprotect children, humiliate them, and scold them—all in the name of love.

Actually, love is the easy part. The real issue is whether you can show your love in ways that nurture accountability and self-esteem and that encourage your child to reach his full potential as a happy, contributing member of society. How much should you give your child? How much is too much? Is it harmful to let a child have her own way? Should you push your child or let her move at her own pace?

It is knowledge and skills that give legs to the love you feel. No one is born knowing how to raise an active preschooler; all parents learn from their own parents and experiences, and most do the best they can. And all parents make mistakes. Fortunately, parent education and training is gaining wide acceptance and credibility. Society has never questioned the need for training in occupational fields, but somewhere along the line the notion got planted that raising children should come "naturally" and that needing help was an admission of inadequacy.

The truth is that "good" parents take parenting classes, read books, and ask lots of questions. Congratulations to you for reading this book right now! Please, connect with other parents, too. We encourage you to get involved with a parenting group in your community or consider starting one yourself. Support groups exist for adoptive parents, grandparents who are raising their grandchildren, and just about every other imaginable form of family. It is not weakness to ask for help—it is wisdom.

Reading books and attending classes will not make you a perfect parent—there is no such thing. But you will have more awareness of what works and what doesn't work for the long-term benefit of your children. When you make mistakes, you will know how to correct them—and you will be able to teach your children that the crises and catastrophes of daily life shouldn't be embarrassing or shameful, but that they can actually be good for you.

MISTAKES ARE OPPORTUNITIES TO LEARN

The bad news: you will make lots and lots of mistakes, and your little one will make lots and lots of them, too. The good news is that mistakes are wonderful opportunities to learn and grow. As long as you are willing to hug, forgive, and figure out a better way, you can grow closer. You and your child can learn valuable skills. In fact, your relationship with your child may even improve when you can acknowledge a mistake and learn how you both can work to prevent it next time.

When you truly understand that mistakes are opportunities to learn, you can create a sense of fun and wonder around mistakes and what you can learn from them and, thus, instill a healthy attitude about mistakes in your children. This will help you both relax and enjoy life—and to trust your heart.

TRUST YOUR HEART

Parenting is rarely a simple matter; there is so much in our crowded lives that must be juggled and balanced. No one can challenge and stretch a parent or teacher like a young child (or a classroom full of them) who is just learning to explore his world. For now, remember that it is always the *relationship* between parent and child that matters most. It is often the quiet, everyday moments—the cuddle before bed, the tears after a quarrel, working and laughing side by side—where the best sort of parenting takes place. If your relationship is based on unconditional love and trust, if your children know that you love them *no matter what,* you will probably do just fine.

CELEBRATE YOUR GROWING, CHANGING CHILD

Babies do grow up, and parents change right along with them. As she grows, your preschooler will need you in different ways than she used to. You must learn to let go and support her as she masters new skills, offer encouragement when she stumbles, and provide connection to familiar places and faces as she moves away from the safety of your arms. Your baby is gone. But oh, what a terrific child came along to replace her! Be sure you spend lots of time getting to know this new person and building a strong, loving connection with her. Remember, your relationship is always more important than even the most effective tools and skills.

    Whether you are a parent, a teacher, or a child care provider, you will find ideas in these pages that will help you give the children in your life the best start in life. These are wonderful years, and the experiences, memories, and moments you share during them will resonate throughout all the years ahead.

3

UNDERSTANDING DEVELOPMENTAL APPROPRIATENESS

Each human being is a work of art. Look at the variety we see in appearance alone: skin color, hair color and texture, shape of the nose, color of the eyes, height, weight, shape—each one of us is unique. And physical characteristics are only the beginning of our uniqueness.

Temperament is as individual as a fingerprint. So is the rate at which we develop and grow. Understanding developmental appropriateness means taking into account things children are generally able to do, think, and accomplish at different ages—as well as individual variations of each child's development within the broader context of her family, culture, and life circumstances. That is a lot to consider.

UNDERSTANDING AGE-APPROPRIATENESS: HOW TO TEACH AND EMPOWER

Around the age of one to two, children enter the "me do it" stage. This is when they develop a sense of autonomy (as discussed in *Positive Discipline: The First Three Years,* second edition, by Jane Nelsen, Cheryl Erwin, and Roslyn Duffy, Three Rivers Press, 2007). The ages of two through six herald the development of a sense of initiative, meaning that it is a child's developmental job to explore and experiment. Can you imagine how confusing it is to a child to be punished for what he is developmentally programmed to do? He is faced with a real dilemma (at a subconscious level): "Do I obey my parents, or do I follow my biological drive to develop autonomy and initiative by exploring and experimenting in my world?" Punishment—a typical adult reaction to new and challenging behavior—leads to a sense of guilt and shame.

These stages of development do not mean children should be allowed to do anything they want. They do explain why your efforts to gain your child's cooperation should be kind and firm instead of controlling and/or punitive. Your child's brain is forming connections that will influence her personality and approach to life, and you most likely want her to decide, "I am competent. I can try, make mistakes, and learn. I am loved. I am a good person." If you are tempted to "teach" your child by guilt, shame, or punishment, you will be creating discouraging beliefs that are difficult to reverse in adulthood.

One way to use developmentally appropriate parenting tools is to build on a child's strengths—what she can already do—and challenge her to learn a bit more with a small nudge in a new direction. The child who can count to three can begin counting out three spoons to use at breakfast, select three crayons for coloring, or stir the pancake batter three times. A child masters these new skills with an adult's help, then with an adult counting aloud nearby, and finally on her own. You will use this process over and over for many kinds of learning throughout these years, as your child grows from the helpless baby you cradled in your arms to the wonderful and capable child you will soon accompany to her first elementary school classroom.

AGE AND WINDOWS OF OPPORTUNITY

Children are, in many ways, similar. Juan and Mary, for instance, both learned to walk in the first thirteen months of life. Children are different, too. Mary doggedly pulled herself along the furniture and took her first steps at ten months of age, while Juan was still contentedly crawling at eleven months.

Picture a window in your mind. Although the window is framed on all sides, there is a great deal of space in the middle. There are age windows for some functions of physical, intellectual, and emotional development, but each child has his or her own individual schedule within those windows, neither exactly like nor completely unlike anyone else's. Other abilities, such as social skills, continue to develop into adulthood.

Because our focus is discipline, let's take a look at some of the factors that influence a child's perceptions and behavior.

PROCESS VERSUS PRODUCT

The way children see the world changes a lot between the ages of three and six. It isn't until the end of these years—around age five—that children begin to do things with a specific goal in mind. Until that time they are far more interested in the doing itself, or "process," than the product or goal of what they do.

Imagine that it's a busy Friday evening and you're off on a quick trip to the grocery store with your preschooler. You have a definite goal in mind—to grab the necessary ingredients for dinner in time to get home, prepare and eat it, and still be on time for your older son's soccer game. For your young child, however, the product just isn't the point. A trip to the store is all about the process—the smells, the colors, the feelings, and the experience. Being sandwiched into a busy schedule just doesn't allow time to enjoy the process!

Children may not share our goal-oriented expectations. But it isn't always possible to go along with a child's relaxed approach, either— sometimes we really do need to run in, grab the chicken, and run home again. Being aware of your child's tendency to focus on process rather than product can help you provide a balance. There may be times when you can take a leisurely browse through the store, enjoying the smell of flowers in the floral department, the colors of the fruits and vegetables, and the brightly colored magazines in the rack. When you must hurry, take a moment to explain to your child why you must shop quickly this time. You can explain that you want him to hold your hand and that you will have to walk past the toys and other interesting things. You can offer to let him help you find the chicken and carry it to the checkout stand. Then you will walk back to the car and drive home. Helping a child understand what is expected and what will happen makes it easier for him to cooperate with you.

> Patsy arrived at the child care center one afternoon just in time to see Laura and her son leaving with a huge, colorful painting. Patsy looked around eagerly to see what her son, Paul, had painted, but none of the pictures had his name on them. Baffled, Patsy cornered the teacher and asked why Paul hadn't had a chance to paint that day. "Paul was very interested in the paint," the teacher said, "but not in putting it on the paper. He stirred the colors and experimented with the feeling of the paint on his fingers, then decided he'd really rather build with blocks."

Paul's mom will feel reassured when she understands this process-oriented aspect of Paul's development.

POINT OF VIEW

What does the world look like when you are less than three feet tall? How might your choices, needs, and behavior be influenced by this particular point of view? Well, get down on your knees and take a look around.

What does the painting six feet up the wall look like from this angle? How inviting is a conversation with adult knees? What kind of challenge does hand washing present when the sink begins a foot above where you end? Understanding a young child's physical perspective and limitations can help parents and teachers fit the environment to a child's abilities. Whenever you take the time to think about such factors and make appropriate adjustments, you will increase your child's feeling of competence and decrease his frustration—which may make both misbehavior and the need for discipline less likely.

"FOR REAL?": FANTASY AND REALITY

Young children often have difficulty understanding the difference between what is real and what is imaginary.

Three-year-old Philip's parents were excited to take him to see the Disney classic Snow White. *They first explained that the movie was fun but did have some scary parts. "It isn't real," Karen told her small son. "You don't need to be afraid." Philip grinned and bounced up and down, too excited about seeing his first movie to pay much attention to his mother's warning.*

Everything went well until the scene where the wicked queen drinks the potion that will turn her into a withered old hag. Suddenly, with a shriek like a teakettle boiling over, Philip leaped from his own seat into his mother's lap, where he huddled shaking for the rest of the movie.

"Hey, kiddo, didn't we tell you the movie wasn't real?" Bill

asked his small son on the way out to the car. Philip looked up at his dad in amazement. "But Dad," he said slowly, "it was real. I saw it!"

Philip's parents learned that the best lectures in the world don't change the fact that a child's definition of reality is far broader than an adult's.

By age five, the difference between fantasy and reality becomes clearer, but a child's interpretation of what he perceives is still limited by his development. During the 9/11 attacks on New York City, news programs agreed to stop rebroadcasting images of the planes flying into buildings because young children thought that this was happening anew each time—over and over again. Young children do make sense of the world, but not in the same way adults do.

Parents sometimes reprimand children for what is simply part of their development, or interpret this behavior as lying. If you can accept your child's fear and listen to his feelings, your child will feel safe sharing his world with you.

"TELL ME THE TRUTH!": YOUNG CHILDREN AND LYING

Q. How do I deal with my four-year-old's lies? She lies about even little things. I can't let her get away with such behavior. Please offer some advice on how I should handle this delicate situation.

A. Children can "lie" for all sorts of reasons. Sometimes they are confused about what is real and what is not. They may lie because they are anxious for approval and don't want to admit doing something they shouldn't have done. Sometimes they want to avoid the consequences of their actions. (Adults may lie for exactly the same reasons.)

Your statement about letting her "get away with it" gives a clue about your attitude. At four, most children can understand that their behavior has consequences, but they don't have maturity and judgment. They still need far more *teaching* than they do discipline. If your daughter suspects that wrong choices and mistakes will earn her punishments or lectures, she will not want to tell you the truth.

Children are not born understanding the difference between truth and lies, and they will not automatically value honesty. Parents should plan to do some teaching on why trust and telling the truth are important, but don't expect young children to understand until they are more mature. It is also true that children are more likely to value honesty when they see the adults around them practicing it. (In other words, your children will not learn to be truthful if they hear you calling in sick to work because you would rather go skiing.)

Most children (and most adults) lie from time to time. Remember that mistakes are inevitable—especially when you're four—and if they're viewed as opportunities to learn rather than sins or failures, they're not as scary. If you want your child to be truthful, you must be willing to listen, to refrain from shaming or punishing, and to work with her to develop her skills and understanding as problems arise. When a child does not tell the truth and is spanked, sent to time-out, or shamed, she learns unintended lessons. Punishment only *appears* to work; it usually produces children who are fearful or who may try to wriggle out of taking responsibility for their actions.

Listen to one father's experience with his son's "lying":

Colin is not thrilled to find a broken egg on the kitchen floor. "Hey," he calls with exasperation in his voice, "who broke this egg?" Four-year-old Sam replies calmly, "An alligator did it."

Colin knows there aren't any alligators in Kansas. He wants to find a way to handle the situation that both solves the egg problem and teaches Sam the importance of telling the truth. "An alligator!" he exclaims. "Was it orange? I think I just saw it in the driveway." Sam grins and agrees that it was an orange alligator.

Colin smiles, too, and then says, "You know, I'm just pretending that there was an alligator. I know we don't have alligators around here." He then suggests that they clean up the broken egg together, knowing there will be opportunities to talk as they work.

"Sam, were you afraid I would yell at you about the egg?" Sam drops his eyes and nods slowly. Colin makes his voice warm and gentle as he says, "I know it's tempting to blame things on an alligator or to make up something that didn't really happen. But it's important for you to know that you can tell me the truth, even when you feel scared. Do you know why it's important to tell the truth?" Sam shakes his head. Colin ruffles his son's hair. "I want to be able to trust what you tell me, buddy. I love you very much, and I want to know that when you tell me something, it's what really happened."

Sam looks up and says slowly, "I love you, too, Daddy. I was just pretending."

Colin says, "Yes, I know we were pretending. And it's fun to pretend sometimes. It's important to know that we can tell the truth, though. We're pretending when we make up a story together. We're lying when we use a story to avoid admitting we've made a mistake."

Sam will probably have to learn this lesson more than once. Few adults can claim to be completely truthful all of the time, and Sam may still err before mastering this new concept.

Colin could also simply have asked Sam if he felt scared. Or he could have asked the original question in a less threatening way, saying, "Sam, this broken egg made a mess. How can we solve this problem? Can you clean it up by yourself, or would you like me to help?"

Removing the sense of fear and getting the message of love through to our children (or even participating in a bit of nonsense with them) can help them learn to tell the truth.

CHILDREN AND STEALING

Ownership is another example of a child's differing thought processes. Young children don't make the same assumptions about property rights that adults do. (In fact, the development of morals and ethics continues well into adolescence.) Because children learn by watching adults, they sometimes make surprising decisions about what they've seen.

Jason goes into the supermarket with his mom. He watches Mom pick up a copy of the free local paper and place it in her purse. Further down the aisle a woman is offering samples of cookies. Mom takes one for her and offers one to Jason, who munches on it happily as they complete their shopping.

When they arrive at the car, Mom lifts Jason into his car seat and discovers a bulge in her son's pocket. Further examination reveals a candy bar.

"You stole this," Mom exclaims, shocked.

"What's 'stealing'?" Jason wonders.

It's not really surprising that Jason is confused; what difference is there between the paper, the cookies, and the candy bar? If Mom is paying attention, she may realize that the problem is not one of stealing or dishonesty but of differing perceptions. Now her task is to help her little boy understand why he can take some things out of the supermarket but not others.

Ways to Respond to Lying

Here are some suggestions to consider using when your child tells a "lie."

- Join in, pretending with the child by exaggerating the story and making it funny and absurd.

- Focus on solutions rather than on blame. Instead of asking who made the mess, ask if the child needs help cleaning it up, or ask if the child has ideas about how to solve the problem.

- When you suspect a lie, state it: "That sounds like a story to me. I wonder what the truth is."

- Empathize with a child. Ask if he feels scared to admit to making a mess. Assure him we all feel scared at times.

- Explain the need to accept responsibility for his actions: "We all make mistakes, but blaming others, even imaginary people, does not take away responsibility for what we did."

- Talk about the meaning of trust. Help a child see the connection between telling the truth and having others trust what he says.

If Mom lectures Jason, shames him, and makes him feel guilty and afraid, he may be more likely to believe that right and wrong are a matter of getting caught. He may also be less able to apply what he has learned to a future situation. Discipline is meant to teach, and mistakes are opportunities to learn. We really can't say it often enough!

"WHO AM I?"

How we define ourselves in relation to the rest of the world changes so much in these late preschool years.

> *Alice walks into the preschool shaking her head. She prides herself on being a no-frills sort of person: she wears no makeup, pulls her hair back simply, and usually dresses in jeans and T-shirts. Right behind Mom is her daughter, Sally—and four-year-old Sally is a sight to behold. She is wearing a lacy pink dress, ribbons in her hair, her best shiny shoes, and a jangly assortment of bracelets on her arms. Sally, it seems, is all girl. Not only was she born a girl, but she will remain one for the rest of her life (despite her earlier declaration that she would become a boy after her next birthday). Sally may not always insist on ruffles and bracelets, but for now she is busy exploring all the aspects of her perception of what it means to be a girl.*

This sex role identification takes place even when parents are careful to minimize gender stereotypes. On playgrounds everywhere games emerge during the preschool years that focus on gender. "No boys allowed," say the girls. "Girls, ick," reply the boys with equal fervor. Although this is a natural phase, parents can still teach young children to respect all people.

Children naturally learn that they are either male or female, but this learning process needn't involve gender-based limitations. Girls can play army and boys can play with dolls and all can learn to develop their own special abilities, regardless of sex. Limiting children to sex-typed roles, expecting play to fall into male or female compartments, or discouraging abilities on the grounds that they are "too feminine," not "masculine" enough, or not "ladylike" may cause children to stifle their unique skills and interests. Their tastes in clothing and play will change as they grow, as will their desire to have same- or opposite-sex friends.

Children also begin to notice their physical differences during the preschool years. In these days of explicit television and advertising, questions related to sexuality may come earlier than ever before (another excellent reason for staying tuned in to what your child is watching on the tube). A little boy may want to touch Dad in the shower. Watching Mom nurse a baby brother or sister may lead to all sorts of interesting questions. Both boys and girls may stuff teddy bears under their shirts and announce, "I'm having a baby!" as they simulate the growing belly of a pregnant teacher, parent, or relative.

As much as possible, try to remain calm, relaxed, and "askable." Use accurate terms such as *penis, breast,* or *vagina.* Children don't need a great deal of detailed information about sexuality (in fact, their eyes will probably glaze over if you try), but most experts agree that it is wise to answer questions or offer explanations in simple, accurate terms, such as "Auntie has a baby growing inside her" or "Boys have penises but girls have vaginas."

Children won't always get the details right.

Chelsea is four and a half. One evening, as she enjoys her bath, she carefully drapes her private parts with a washcloth. Giggling, she explains to her mother that she has to "cover her peanuts."

Make every effort to enjoy all stages of your child's development. Being open to topics involving sexuality will establish an atmosphere of comfort and trust and will enable your children to seek further information later on, when they really need it.

RACE AND OTHER DIFFERENCES

Just as children learn to sort objects by color, size, and shape, they notice that the people around them look and act differently, too.

Randy's mother is black and his father is white. When Randy was three, the black couple next door announced that they were expecting their first child. With the innocence of childhood, three-year-old Randy wondered aloud whether the baby would be black or white. To him, anything was possible. By

Gender and Development

Research on how the brain develops has led to some interesting information about the way gender influences development. For reasons that are not clearly understood, girls gain access to the left hemisphere of their brains sooner than boys do. Each child is unique (and most of these differences disappear around the time children enter school), but you may notice some of the following as you raise your preschooler.

- Girls often learn language and emotional skills sooner than boys do.

- Boys may be more emotionally sensitive than girls early in life and may have a harder time calming themselves down when they become upset.

- Boys often are more physically active, more impulsive, more aggressive, and more competitive than girls.

Of course, you may find it helpful to pay attention to your child's unique qualities, rather than expecting certain behaviors based on gender.

the time Randy was four and a half, he had noticed that his skin looked different from some of his playmates. What decisions will Randy make about this fact?

Juanita and her classmates were excited when Khadima joined their class. They loved pushing his wheelchair through the halls. To them, his disability was simply part of who he was; the most important fact was that he was their friend.

Delia invited her best friend, Nora, to the dance program her Greek school was putting on. Delia was proud of the Greek songs she had learned and was excited to share her special culture with her friend.

Wouldn't life be boring if we were all the same? People are different, and the conclusions children draw about these differences will depend upon what you teach and model. Parents and teachers have the opportunity to teach children to value differences instead of condemning or fearing them, and that everyone is worthy of respect—even those different than themselves. Prejudice, whether it concerns race, culture, or attitudes toward different physical abilities, is learned. Even young children can learn to respect differences in race, gender, or religious beliefs. And because children of this age are learning so much about themselves, it is vital that they learn about others in ways that are respectful and positive.

CULTURE, SOCIETY, AND ANTI-BIAS

Your child's development is also influenced by the culture and society within which she lives. Wise parents and teachers recognize the role of culture and respect the influence society's expectations have on children without bias or judgments.

A professor visiting the United States from her home in Singapore saw a picture of an American toddler feeding herself.

The child's happy face shone with dripping blobs of yogurt, and more yogurt had been spread on the high chair tray. Shaking her head, the professor said, "Only in America." What an eye-opening statement that was for both the visiting professor and her Western colleagues. What did she mean?

Asian children are often fed by adults until they are three, four, or even five years old, for two reasons. The first is that food is never to be wasted. The second reason has deep cultural roots: in Asian cultures the highest value is often placed on relationships. Time spent feeding a child gives the child and adult opportunities to savor and strengthen their relationship, binding them closer together. In contrast, the American attitude of encouraging independence far exceeded either of these concerns for the Western educators present. For them, supporting a child's growing autonomy and helping her experience her own capability far outweigh messiness or concerns over lost food. (Because this book is written from a Western perspective, the ideas presented are in line with this second model.)

The skills that are expected or more valued may differ by culture. Western culture prizes individualism, while many other cultures see collective needs as more important. This may influence the age at which a child is expected to dress or feed herself and what kinds of tasks or choices she will be given. Parents and teachers would be wise to recognize the influence of culture on development and parenting.

BIRTH ORDER

The preschool years are a time when children are making many of the decisions about themselves and others that will influence the rest of their lives. They are asking themselves, "What must I do to find belonging and significance in this family—and with my friends? Am I good enough or must I keep trying harder—or should I just give up?" Preschoolers will carry the answers to those questions with them into the world around them, and they will practice what they are learning and deciding as they explore social relationships.

Beyond the influence of development and culture, each child's experiences are shaped by the family position into which she is born. It has been said that every child is born into a different family, because the arrival of a new child causes each member of the family to shift to make room for the new member. Those first-time parents who hovered over their firstborn, worrying about every burp, are not the same people who bring home baby number two or three. By the time additional children are born, these same parents know how to change diapers, aren't surprised by a midnight ear infection, and are much less impressed by the newcomer's tantrums. Each child will experience this changed family in a different way, and will most likely begin to display the traits of the birth order position she identifies with.

Keep in mind that birth order is much more than a matter of numbers; there will be many exceptions to the behaviors associated with each birth order position. Sometimes the oldest boy and the oldest girl will each experience firstborn status because they are the oldest of their gender, and sometimes siblings are born so far apart that each feels like an only child. Overall, though, although the numerical order of a child's birth position is not the determinant of which birth order perspective he will adopt, the longer a position is maintained, the stronger its hold.

Each birth order position has a common set of traits that are usually associated with it. Because these are only likely traits, birth order should not be used as a label or given any mythic power. And remember, there are no advantageous or disadvantageous birth order positions. (According to Jane Griffith, "every vantage point has both ad-vantages and dis-advantages.") Birth order refers to the world that we are born into and how life looks from that particular vantage point. It is simply another means of getting into a child's world, providing additional guidelines for sorting out what might be motivating a child's behavior and life decisions.

Understanding birth order can give you tips for which experiences a child may need strengthened or which ones are less helpful or could cause difficulties.

BIRTH ORDER CHART

Vantage Point	Motto	Likely Attitudes (Advantages)	Challenges (Disadvantages)	Tips
Only/First	Me, myself, and I	Independent Self-reliant Responsible	Sometimes lonely May have trouble relating to peers Overly alarmed by conflict	Provide time with peers Engage in group activities Model/practice problem solving
First	Me first!	Responsible High achiever Take-charge, leader	Perfectionist Fear of mistakes Too-early adult role	Reduce expectations and pressure Model acceptance of imperfection (yours and theirs) Limit responsibilities
Second	Me too!	Team player Innovative Good observer	Seldom feels "good enough" Constant comparisons Follower/dependent on firstborn	Treat each child as unique (and take photos!) Avoid comparisons Encourage leadership roles
Middle	What about me?	Successful social skills Empathetic Champions of justice May be a rebel with or without a cause or may be very easygoing	Feels lacking (from comparisons) Vulnerable to undue peer influence Proves worth through competition	Recognize individual traits Foster family involvement/contribution Channel competitiveness into team sports
Baby	Take care of me!	Charming Fun and/or funny Easygoing	Manipulative Defers decision making to others Does not feel taken seriously	Raise expectations Offer leadership opportunities Ask for his ideas/opinions
Youngest (not baby)	Make way for me!	Energetic Focused High achiever	Daredevil Ignores others' needs Driven	Set boundaries Encourage teamwork Model stress management

Firstborn Children

The firstborn must shoulder the responsibilities of trailblazer. Her view of the world is summed up in her motto, "Me first!" with all its attendant benefits and burdens. Firstborn children are often treated as a revelation, for theirs is a transformative role: changing a couple into parents, siblings into aunts and uncles, and parents into grandparents. Born into a world populated by adults, firstborns may acquire language early, often becoming quite articulate (with no one around to either interrupt or interpret for them). Firstborn status may bring extra privileges—but more will be expected of them, too. Firstborns lead the way in family firsts: from the first birthday party to the first lost tooth to the first midnight fever and ear infection, or the first to graduate, the first to learn to swim, and the first to bring home an award of any kind. All of this responsibility leads to seeing oneself as responsible. It is easy for firstborn children to become perfectionists, often seeking to do things "right." Some succeed in their quest for excellence and become high achievers, while others feel so pressured to live up to expectations that they give up or quit trying if they can't be best.

Second-Born

A second child arriving with a bigger, more skilled and developmentally advanced sibling already ahead of him wants to get in on the action. It is no surprise that one of his favorite toddler phrases will be the same as his life's motto: "Me too!" A second-born child's birth position may be temporary (she may become a middle child) or lifelong (she may turn out to be the youngest), or if several children follow, her second-born position may persist. For a second-born, "who I am" is often a process of elimination—choosing roles and interests that the others have not. If the firstborn is a sports star, the second-born may long for trophies as well, but will pursue them in a different arena—music, dancing, horse riding, and so on. Second-born and middle children share similar experiences, often feeling overshadowed by the siblings at either end of their family spectrum. It is speculated that second-born and middle children may have the fewest photographs taken of them.

Middle Children

If a second child is thrust into the middle position by another newcomer, he may change his motto to "What about me?" The middle can be an uncomfortable spot, with pressure from above and behind. Middle children don't have the privileges of the oldest and have lost the fleeting benefits of being the baby (if they ever had time to savor them). With pressure from an older, more advanced sibling ahead and a cute and demanding one from behind, middle children sometimes feel unfairly cheated out of their fair share of time, attention, or material goods. Because they may sometimes feel lost in the larger family's dynamics, middle children often seek out peers or siblings for support and encouragement, the benefit of which is that they can develop outstanding social skills. They also have the unique perspective of learning to see in both directions, a built-in invitation to see both sides of a situation.

The Baby

When that final family member arrives, hovered over by a houseful of older, more competent family members, he can simply coo, kick back, and live out his motto: "Take care of me!" This child may well find that the rules have relaxed for him. His parents know he is their last child and are reluctant to let go of their baby. He can be a fun and delightful companion with wonderful social skills. He knows how to fit into a group—because he has been doing it all his life. When a child is babied he will have little expected from him. It is no wonder that such an experience of the world can lead to an attitude of "take care of me," inviting a serious disadvantage. A person who is cute, adorable, and engaging (all very lovely attributes) can also learn to apply those attributes to get others to do his bidding, that is, manipulation. When the baby cries, everyone comes running—not always a good idea for the runners . . . or the baby.

Sometimes, though, a youngest child may tire of being last in line and choose to reject the baby role. Such a child becomes determined to find the quickest route to the top, galloping past his siblings while waving his motto, "Make way for me!" He may become the family's high achiever.

Only Children

If no other children come into the family and the firstborn remains the unchallenged only child, growing up in an adult-centered environment will teach her to march to her own drumbeat. Her banner, "Me, myself, and I," will flap overhead as she marshals her own parade, an experience that can be both exhilarating and lonely. Only children are the recipients of their parents' undivided love and attention, with no need to share or be flexible. On the other hand, having no one with whom to share can be very lonely—a feeling common to the only child's vantage point. They also may be more comfortable than other children with "alone time" and identify with adults more than with their peers.

Some Words of Caution Regarding Birth Order

Any child, in any birth order position, can be spoiled. You may even admit to spoiling your child with a self-indulgent chuckle. But spoiling is not really funny. The reason is inherent in the word itself. Jane Griffith articulates this for us: "When we say an orange or piece of meat is spoiled, aren't we saying it is ruined? Do we want to ruin a child? Spoiling *ruins* a child." A spoiled child is given a set of expectations that the world will seldom be able to equal. Excessive pampering and overindulgence are recipes for lifelong discouragement.

Whatever a person's birth order, remember that one's decisions about these early experiences are made on a subconscious level. Each child will choose his life attitudes based upon his unique vantage point. Each birth order will bring with it certain strengths (advantages), as well as traits that will be less developed or need strengthening (disadvantages). By taking a child's birth order into account, you can find ways to broaden the way each child experiences his world.

Teema, the youngest in her family, had three older siblings. Francie, Teema's mother, got a surprising glimpse into Teema's view of the world when she took her to feed the ducks at a nearby lake, followed by a stop for hot chocolate and cookies.

At the time, Teema was just under three. Throughout the entire outing, Teema talked about throwing bread to the ducks for her absent sister, Angie (age five); pointed to the ducks she thought Sophie (age eight) would like best; or declared that brother Jonas (age ten) could "swim like duckies!" She even insisted on wrapping a half-eaten cookie in a napkin to bring back for Angie. Teema was so used to seeing herself as one among many that she did not have any experience to guide her in being the only child sharing time with Mom. Francie simply had not realized how seldom Teema got to do things without at least one of her siblings along. Francie determined to give Teema more such experiences to expand her perspective of both the world and her unique role in it.

Birth order does not determine who a child will be, but it may give valuable insights about the decisions she is making—and why she does or does not behave in certain ways. Birth order provides a first window to the world around us.

ADOPTION: "SHOULD WE TELL OUR CHILD?"

One special type of family is that created when a child is adopted. Adoption is a wonderful thing, providing many children with safe and loving homes that they might not have had otherwise. Still, most adoptive parents will have questions: How much should children be told about their birth parents? Will your adopted child truly feel like a part of your family? When should you tell your child that he is adopted?

Adoption research does not give a clear answer to the question of when a child should be told about his or her adoption. Some research says that too much information before age six or seven only confuses a child. Other researchers believe that the older a child is when told, the more upsetting the news may be. Much of human behavior relates to our feelings of belonging. As children put together the unique puzzle of who they are, questions about adoption ("Where did I come from?" "Why did my parents give me away?") should be expected.

An adopted child who looks racially different from his adoptive parents will begin to notice this difference by the age of four or so. Knowing that a child is becoming aware of race may help parents decide when to tell him that he is adopted.

There are important cultural considerations as well. Children adopted from different cultures often enjoy participating in special cultural classes during their preschool years. For example, Tory, Sarah, and Anna were all born in Korea and adopted into American families. Each summer the three girls attended a special Korean cultural camp where they could learn about Korean clothing, food, art, and language. Their parents wanted them to enjoy the richness of their birth culture. These girls knew of their adoption from their earliest years and were proud to wear their Korean outfits to preschool.

Another family would bring treats to their daughter's preschool to help her celebrate her "adoption day," much as birthdays are enjoyed. Her parents explained the idea of adoption to all of the children in her class. Her classmates benefited from learning about the different ways families come into being.

Attitudes toward adoption vary widely. These families treated the issue of adoption as another version of their definition of a "normal" family. This attitude encourages children to feel safe, trusting, and comfortable with adoption. If your family includes both adopted and natural children, be aware that eventually everyone will have questions. Behaving as if there is anything disturbing, secretive, or mysterious about adoption invites distrust, fear, and anxiety. If you treat all of your children with respect and teach them to treat each other (and themselves) that way, then the inevitable questions will not feel threatening.

All children need to feel that they truly belong; we encourage families with adopted children to focus on giving children many opportunities to experience belonging and to know that they have worth and significance.

ALL THE WORLD'S A STAGE

Parents constantly hear the words "It's just a stage." There's a great deal of truth in the concept; children are usually in one phase or another. It is also true that no two children grow and develop exactly alike. Understanding your own child's development will enable you to deal more effectively with his behavior, with his successes, and with his occasional mistakes. You can help your child learn that the world is a place where he can love, be loved, and learn about himself and the others he meets.

THE MIRACULOUS BRAIN

Learning and Development

Robbie is five years old. His older sister goes to school with the other "big kids," and Robbie can hardly wait until he's old enough to join them on the big yellow bus. He loves his books, knows his letters and numbers, and can write his own name and that of his dog, Comet. Robbie is eager for the next important part of his life. Robbie's mom, though, has mixed emotions. She knows it will be hard to let her baby go. And while Robbie enjoys learning and displays an avid curiosity about the world around him, he is also shy and sometimes has trouble getting along with other children his age. He clings to his mom in public places. And sometimes he draws the few letters he knows backward. Robbie's mom worries that he isn't really ready for school.

"What should I do?" she asks her next-door neighbor, whose three children all attend the nearby elementary school.

"Should I enroll him in a prekindergarten program to get him ready? Maybe I should get some flash cards and teach him to read. Or maybe I should keep him back for a year. I don't want Robbie to fail—but I don't want him to be disappointed or discouraged, either." Robbie's mom shakes her head in confusion and concern.

THE HOW, WHEN, AND WHY OF LEARNING

The late preschool years are an unnerving time for many parents—and for their children. As preschoolers approach the age of five or six, the prospect of school and formal learning looms on the horizon. The world broadens beyond the home and family to include friends and teachers, all of whom will take on greater significance in a child's life as the years go by. It isn't always an easy transition for parents or for children.

Most parents realize that ours has become a highly competitive world. Most have read the newspaper stories detailing the decline in academic performance of American children. And because parents love their children and want them to succeed, they have many questions. What should we be teaching them, and when should we start? How much should children know about reading, writing, and arithmetic before they enter school? How well developed should their social skills be? And how do children learn, anyway? What happens in their growing brains that enables them to absorb and use knowledge and skills? Why are some children better at it than others?

Over the past few years, our understanding of how the human brain grows and develops has changed dramatically. We now understand that the early years of a child's life are critically important in the formation of thinking and reasoning skills—and in the actual "wiring" of the brain itself. The brain continues to grow and learn throughout childhood and adolescence; in fact, the prefrontal cortex of the brain, which is responsible for emotional regulation, impulse control, and more "adult" forms of reasoning, does not develop fully until at least the age of twenty-five. The way parents and caregivers interact with children during their preschool years is crucial to brain development and learning.

HOW THE BRAIN BEGINS

Not too many years ago, we believed that babies were born with brains that were more or less developed; all that remained was to fill their waiting brains with the necessary information. Nowadays, however, we know better. Sophisticated imaging techniques have allowed researchers to peer inside a child's living brain, to observe its structure and to discover how it uses energy, blood flow, and special substances called neurotransmitters to think, to perceive, and to learn. What those researchers have discovered is extraordinary.

The human brain begins life as a small cluster of cells in the fetus. By the fourth week of pregnancy, these cells have begun to sort themselves out according to the function they will one day perform and to "migrate" to the part of the brain they are destined to occupy. Nature provides the fetus with more cells than it will need; some do not survive the migration, but others join together in a network of connections called synapses. The human brain is "under construction" for the first three years of life, and what a child learns and decides about himself and the world around him becomes part of the wiring of his brain.

Stimulation from the outside world, as experienced through a child's senses (hearing, seeing, smelling, and touching), enables the brain to create or change connections and primes it to learn. While the brain is amazingly flexible and is able to adapt to change or injury, there are windows early in a child's life during which important learning (like vision and language development) takes place. If those windows are missed, it may become more difficult for a child to acquire those abilities. By about the age of ten, a child's brain begins to prune away the synapses that haven't been used enough. By adolescence, half have been discarded. So, for some functions, brain development is a "use it or lose it" proposition. (For others, such as social skills development, learning continues well into early adulthood.) What is used (and kept) depends in large part on the adults who shape a child's world.

NATURE OR NURTURE?

Perhaps you are wondering where your child gets his or her particular, unique combination of traits and qualities—and why, if you have more than one child, they can be so amazingly different!

Researchers now believe that genes may have an even stronger influence on temperament and personality than we previously thought; many researchers believe that genes influence such qualities as optimism, depression, aggression, and whether or not a person is a thrill-seeker—which may come as no surprise to parents whose preschoolers thrive on gymnastics, hurl themselves at the ball in soccer, and climb trees faster than their harried parents can say abracadabra! (We will discuss temperament further in Chapter 6.) Parents may find themselves wondering just how much influence they have on their growing child. If genes are so powerful, does it really matter how you parent your child?

The answer is that it matters a great deal. While a child inherits certain traits and tendencies through her genes, the story of how those traits develop hasn't been written yet. Your child may have arrived on the planet with her own unique temperament, but how you and her other caregivers interact with her will shape the person she becomes. (Brain researchers call these early decisions and reactions "adaptations"; they are part of an intricate dance between a child's inborn qualities and the world she inhabits.) As educational psychologist Jane M. Healy puts it in her book *Endangered Minds: Why Children Don't Think and What We Can Do About It* (Touchstone, 1990), "Brains shape behavior, and behavior shapes brains."

Parents and caregivers, fragile and imperfect as they may be, bear the responsibility for shaping a child's environment, and therefore her development. The human brain never stops growing and never loses the ability to form new synapses and connections. Change may become more difficult as we age, but change—in attitudes, behavior, and relationships—is always possible.

COLLEGE FOR KIDS?

Occasionally a newspaper will carry the story of a precocious child who finishes grade school early and is ready for higher learning. Then there are children like Robbie, whose parents worry that, for a variety of reasons, their child may not be ready to learn when other children are.

Should parents begin teaching academics at an early age? If brains are growing, shouldn't we be putting in as much information as we can? The truth is that children learn in different ways, many of which are still not fully understood. Some researchers believe that it may even be harmful to force children to learn too quickly or to absorb concepts that their brains are not yet mature enough to handle. If the brain isn't ready to learn abstract concepts (math, for instance), it may patch together a pathway of connections that is less effective than the one that would have been used later on—and the less effective pathway becomes "wired" in place.

Forcing children to learn before they are ready may also have psychological effects. Children are always making decisions about themselves and the world around them. When children have difficulty mastering a concept forced upon them by loving (and well-intentioned) parents, they may make the decision "I'm not good enough," when in truth their brains just are not ready to absorb certain concepts. That can stick with them, and they may feel too intimidated to ever learn the concept.

There are few absolutes: each human brain is unique and special, and it is impossible to generalize about what is right or wrong for an individual child, but some scholars, like Jane Healy, believe that our fast-paced modern culture (and some of our "educational" television shows) may be affecting children's ability to pay attention, to listen, and to learn later on in life. Some early childhood educators report that preschoolers these days seem to have more difficulty sitting still and paying attention to class lessons or stories. At the same time, many of these children appear to be sophisticated beyond their years because they have acquired a large (and sometimes disturbingly adult) vocabulary from television. Perhaps all learning isn't "good"; parents need to pay close attention to what their young children are exposed to and make sure that character and values are taught along with vocabulary and skills.

Young children learn best in the context of *relationships,* and what they most need to learn in their preschool years isn't found on flash cards (or on television). Children learn best through active involvement that engages their senses: sight, smell, hearing, taste, and touch. They also need opportunities to connect what they already know to new information as they construct their understanding of the world. Isn't it interesting that play meets all of these requirements? Play is vital in the preschool years. Remember, a child at play is actually working hard to develop a healthy brain.

HARDWIRED TO CONNECT: WHAT YOUR CHILD *REALLY* NEEDS

Preschoolers are undoubtedly such busy little people because they have so much to learn. As we've mentioned, young children learn best in the context of relationships. Brain development is all about connection, and your child's brain is wired to seek connection from the moment of birth. How you and your child's other caregivers relate to her—how you talk and play and nurture—is by far the most important factor in her development. (You will learn more about emotional development in Chapter 7.)

According to Ross A. Thompson, a professor of psychology at the University of California at Davis and a founding member of the

National Scientific Council on the Developing Child (www.developingchild.net), young children learn best when they are unstressed and when they live in a reasonably stimulating environment. Thompson believes that special stimulation, such as videos and other academic learning tools, is unnecessary; in fact, what children really need to grow and develop is unhurried time with caring adults, people who will focus on the child and follow his cues without distraction or expectations. (Both parents and child care providers can provide this sort of child-centered interaction.) It is important to note that this does *not* mean allowing children to rule the home. (More about that in the chapters to come.)

A WORD ABOUT ATTACHMENT

When you connect well with your child—when you recognize and respond to his signals, offer love and belonging, and allow him to develop a sense of trust and security—you help him develop what is called a *secure attachment*. Securely attached children can connect well with themselves and with others and have the best opportunity to develop healthy, balanced relationships. Interestingly enough, researchers such as Mary Main have discovered that the best predictor of a child's

Miraculous Mirror Neurons

Have you ever wondered how your child learns to clap his hands, push the vacuum cleaner, or "gimme five"? Researchers recently discovered the presence in the human brain of *mirror neurons*, which perceive physical action, facial expression, and emotion and prepare the brain to duplicate what it "sees." Mirror neurons help your child figure out how to imitate you. In the same way, when you are angry, excited, or anxious, his mirror neurons will "catch" your emotion and create that same feeling within your child. Mirror neurons help explain why we weep, laugh, or get angry with each other so easily. It also explains why what you *do* (the behavior you model) as a parent is so much more powerful than your words in teaching your child.

sense of attachment is his *parent's* level of attachment to his or her own family growing up. (Erik Erikson also found that an infant's development of a sense of trust in the first year of life is directly related to a mother's sense of trust in herself.) How you understand and make sense of your own history and experiences has a direct effect on your growing child. Understanding and resolving your own struggles, challenges, and emotional issues may be one of the greatest gifts you ever give your child. (To learn more about attachment, brain development, and parenting, see *Parenting from the Inside Out: How a Deeper Self-Understanding Can Help You Raise Children Who Thrive,* by Daniel J. Siegel, M.D., and Mary Hartzell, M.Ed., Tarcher/Putnam, 2003.)

ENCOURAGING HEALTHY GROWTH AND LEARNING

Remember Robbie? His mother wanted to know what she could do to help him succeed in school. Actually, parents can begin setting the stage for learning from the day a baby is born—not by using mobiles, flash cards, or "superbaby" programs but by responding to their child in ways that foster healthy brain growth, build trust and loving relationships, teach skills, and encourage a love of learning.

Demonstrate Affection, Interest, and Acceptance
A child never outgrows the need to feel a sense of belonging and significance. It is not enough just to love your child; that love must be demonstrated daily in healthy ways. Keep in mind that rescuing, overprotecting, and overindulging are not healthy ways to demonstrate love.

Research has shown that children who receive warm, consistent, loving care produce less of the stress hormone cortisol, and when they do become upset, they are able to "turn off" their stress reaction more rapidly. On the other hand, children who suffer abuse or neglect early in life are likely to feel more stress more often—and with less provocation.

Hugs, smiles, and laughter are wonderful parenting tools and will mean more to your child in the long run than the most marvelous toys and activities. Spending special time with a child, showing curiosity about his activities and thoughts, and learning to listen well will show your child on a daily basis that he is accepted and loved, and will shape and strengthen the development of his brain.

Practice the Art of Conversation

Contrary to popular belief, children do not learn language from even the most educational television shows; television is passive and requires no response from its audience. Children develop language by having the opportunity to speak and be spoken to by real humans. By age four, children who are exposed to healthy doses of language will have a vocabulary of as many as six thousand words and can construct sentences of five or six words. By age five their vocabulary may increase to around eight thousand words, a leap of as many as five words a day, every single day for a year. Awesome, isn't it?

Conversation with any preschooler is truly an art, requiring both humor and patience. Most young children pass through the phase when every other utterance is "Why?" or "How come?" We heard from one weary mom who, bombarded by questions from her curious four-year-old son, told him she was tired of answering questions for one day and suggested that he keep quiet for a while. The boy looked

> ### How to Grow a Healthy Brain
>
> - Demonstrate affection, interest, and acceptance.
> - Practice the art of conversation.
> - Read, read, read!
> - Encourage curiosity, safe exploration, and hands-on learning.
> - Limit television time.
> - Use discipline to teach, not to shame or humiliate.
> - Recognize and accept your child's uniqueness.
> - Provide learning experiences that use the senses.
> - Provide time for your child's learning through play.
> - Select child care carefully—and stay involved.
> - Take care of yourself.

at his mom with puzzlement and informed her, "But Mom, that's how little boys learn!" And he is absolutely right.

Adults sometimes speak to young children in ways that do not allow for much response. Much adult "conversation" is merely directive: "Put on your jammies," "Eat your potatoes," and "Do it right now, young man!" don't invite conversation. Questions like "How was preschool today?" or "Did you win your tee-ball game?" can be answered with a single syllable or even with a grunt. One effective way to invite conversation with a preschooler (and to develop language skills in the process) is to ask curiosity questions (which often begin with the words *what* or *how*). "What did you like about school today?" or "How do you think you might solve that problem?" invite a more thoughtful response and give a child the opportunity to practice vital reasoning and language skills. Of course, they also call for focused and attentive listening from parents, something that demands a surprising amount of energy and patience. Just remember, relationship and connection support brain development.

Read, Read, Read!
There is no substitute for reading when it comes to preparing for formal learning, and it's never too soon (or too late) to start. Books open new worlds to children. And because the setting and characters must be created inside a child's mind, books also stimulate thinking and learning.

Be sure to select books that are age-appropriate and that appeal to your child's special interests—your local librarian or bookseller can recommend age-appropriate books and series. Studies have shown that boys sometimes are not inclined to read because the books they are offered do not interest them. If you have a preschool boy, check out www.guysread.com for titles and suggestions about developing a love of reading in your young son.

When you read, make the story come alive—change your voice to play different characters, and stop to talk about the story or the pictures. Adults usually tire of favorite books and stories long before children do, but be patient: preschoolers learn by repetition. They often memorize favorite books and want to "read" to you themselves, turning the pages at all the right spots. Children who grow up with books often develop a love of reading and learning that lasts a lifetime and sets the stage for success in school. Many families find that reading time is also time for snuggling and connection; it remains a favorite shared activity well into the elementary school years, long after children learn to read well themselves.

Incidentally, storytelling also is a wonderful way to stimulate learning. Sharing stories from your family's history or experiences you had when you were your child's age builds closeness and trust as well as encouraging listening and learning skills. Retelling a shared memory can also help a child to expand his memory of an event.

Encourage Curiosity, Safe Exploration, and Hands-On Learning
Parents and caregivers can provide lots of safe opportunities to run, climb, jump, and explore. Honor your child's interests: young children rarely appreciate (or learn from) being forced into activities they do not like or that actually frighten them. It is not necessary to sign up children for organized activities; they can learn to paint, play baseball, sing, or plant a garden by working alongside welcoming adults.

Preschoolers usually want to *do* rather than just watch, so be prepared for a few messes along the way. Remember, too, that some children demonstrate curiosity and talents at this age that are very real and that will be important for the rest of their lives.

Not all preschool interests reveal lifelong talents. Still, providing reasonable opportunities for children to experiment with a variety of activities will give them ways to build a sense of self-esteem and self-confidence and to develop into healthy, active people.

Limit Television Time

Walk into many living rooms today and you will notice that one item has the place of honor. Centrally located in the entertainment center, supported by satellite or cable and sophisticated remote controls, the television has become the center of family life in many, many homes. "Family time" is often illuminated by the flickering blue light of the screen—and the bigger the screen, the better!

Unfortunately, there is much we do not fully understand about the way television affects growing brains, and what we do know is not encouraging. Most young children spend a phenomenal amount of time in front of the TV, watching favorite shows and videos—or whatever the adults are watching. How does this affect their brains, their capacity to learn, and their ability to pay attention?

Researchers and educational psychologists like Jane Healy believe that excessive television may actually be changing the way the brain functions. Watching TV and videos is essentially a passive activity; there is little or no critical thinking going on in the mind of a young child propped in front of the tube. Even so-called educational shows such as *Sesame Street* may not be helpful; the flashy, frantic format does not encourage sustained attention, and some studies indicate that children begin school expecting entertainment and special effects like those they've seen on TV and are bored by classroom teaching. Many teachers report that attention spans, comprehension, and written language skills have declined significantly over the past decade or so. We will explore the influence of the culture, computers, and other electronic media in greater depth in Chapter 17. For now, be aware that it is best to limit the time your child spends sitting in front of a screen.

Use Discipline to Teach, Not to Shame or Humiliate

Remember, the synapses your child will keep are the ones that are used most often, and shame, punishment, and humiliation can shape the way a young child's brain is wired. This is just one of the many reasons we keep emphasizing that the best sort of discipline is *teaching*. Children respond well to loving, effective discipline and will be healthier for having it. Isn't it good to know that your Positive Discipline skills are also encouraging healthy brain development?

Recognize and Accept Your Child's Uniqueness
Young children learn about themselves and the world around them by watching and listening; what they decide about themselves (and about you) depends in large part on the messages they receive from parents and caregivers. Learning to accept your child for exactly who she is not only builds her sense of self-worth, but also supports healthy brain development and encourages her to value her own special qualities and abilities and to have the courage to try new things—the best insurance policy there is against the challenges and pressures she will face as she grows into adolescence and adulthood.

Provide Learning Experiences That Use the Senses
Young children experience the world through their senses, and those experiences help shape their developing brains. Offer your child lots of opportunities to see, hear, smell, touch, and taste his world—with your careful supervision, of course. Your child's senses will enrich his experience and increase his ability to learn.

Provide Time for Your Child's Learning Through Play
For a preschooler, play is more than mere amusement. Play is the laboratory in which a child experiences his world, experiments with new roles and ideas, and learns to feel comfortable in the world of movement and sensation. It is often more convenient for parents to schedule a child's playtime, but children need unstructured time in which to exercise their imaginations and their bodies. Provide the raw materials, then turn your child loose to play and learn.

Select Child Care Carefully—and Stay Involved
Child care is critically important. Many, many children spend all or part of each day in the care of someone other than their parents. It is

crucial that child care providers and teachers also know how young brains grow and that they do their best to foster health and learning. Leaving your child in another's care may be difficult, but it helps to recognize that high-quality care can support a child's development. It also underscores how important it is to be sure that the care your child receives when he is away from you truly is *quality* care. (Chapter 15 will explain what constitutes quality care and how to find it.)

Take Care of Yourself

You may wonder what taking care of yourself has to do with your child's brain. But think for just a moment: nurturing and guiding an energetic, curious preschooler is hard work—and a full-time job. Parents and caregivers need every ounce of energy and wisdom they possess, and all too often the well runs dry just when the crisis occurs.

You will do your best work as a parent when you are rested and reasonably content. Yes, weariness and stress seem to be an everyday part of life with young children, particularly if you also have a partner or job to deal with. Still, caring for your own needs must be a priority. Exercise, eat healthy foods, and do your best to get enough sleep. Take time on a regular basis (no, once a year isn't enough) to do things you enjoy. Spend time with your partner, have a cup of coffee with a friend, sing in a choir, take a class, read a book—anything you do to refill the well will benefit your children. They will learn respect for you (and for themselves) when they see you treating yourself with respect. And they will find a calm, rested, happy adult much easier to respond to than an exhausted, grumpy, resentful one. Keeping yourself healthy isn't selfish; it's wisdom.

OFF TO SCHOOL: "IS MY CHILD REALLY READY?"

Kate had sworn she wouldn't cry. She was going to celebrate with Nicole on the first day of kindergarten, and then go get the shopping done without any interruptions. Somehow, though, the morning didn't work out the way she'd planned.

Oh, Nicole was fine. A bit nervous, maybe, but excited and happy. She had dressed herself with care in her new outfit, combed her hair neatly, and packed a few articles into the brand-new backpack that marked her new status as a "big kid." Kate and Nicole had visited the classroom the week before school began, explored the playground, and met the teacher, an energetic, friendly young woman who remembered everyone's name.

Everything was fine—until Kate watched Nicole, looking suddenly very small, filing into the classroom with the other children. As she turned to walk back to her car, she discovered that some sort of fog seemed to have descended on the neighborhood—she couldn't see a thing. She realized with a shock that she was crying. A dad walking nearby grinned at her. "Gets to you, doesn't it?" he said.

"It certainly does," Kate replied, shaking her head. "It certainly does."

A child's first day of "real" school is a landmark event. The world will never again consist just of a small circle of family and friends; it has suddenly expanded to include other adults and children who may spend more time each day with your youngster than you do. Many parents wonder how they will know if their children are ready—intellectually and emotionally—for the wider world of school.

It is important to recognize that all children (and all schools) are different. By the time a child is ready for school, parents have had years to get into that child's world and understand the way he thinks, feels, and sees the world. Most school systems group children by chronological age, but age is not a true indicator of a child's development. Many children are eager for school to begin and enter the world of academic learning with hardly a backward glance. Others hover at the fringes or seem to struggle with even the simplest tasks. Assessing learning disabilities or psychological problems is beyond the scope of this book, but there are things parents can consider that will help them feel comfortable sending their children to school. (More on this in Chapter 18.)

KNOW YOUR CHILD

No one knows a child as well as an attentive, loving parent, especially one who has made the effort to understand development and acquire effective parenting skills. Most school districts offer readiness interviews to help parents and teachers decide if a child is ready to begin kindergarten or would benefit from waiting a year.

Remember Robbie? His mother eventually decided it was best for him to wait a year, until his emotional development caught up with his intellectual development. School success involves more than just academic skills; children also must be able to tolerate time away from parents, respond to a teacher, and make friends with other children. There is no disgrace in waiting to begin school; in fact, children do better with academic learning when they are emotionally and socially ready to be away from home. It is less upsetting for everyone to delay the start of school rather than to be held back later on. Considering a few simple questions may help you assess your child's readiness.

- Does your child enjoy learning? Is he curious about the world around him?

- Does your child tolerate separation from you reasonably well?

- Is she eager to make friends and open to peer relationships?

- Is he able to pay attention to a task for an age-appropriate length of time?

- Does she express interest in school or does she seem very fearful?

Taking time to visit the school and meet the teacher usually resolves most of a child's anxieties. It is also helpful to talk about feelings (more about feelings and active listening skills in Chapter 7) and to share with your child that most people are nervous when they do something new. The more tuned in you are, both to your child and to the teacher, the happier the school experience will be. You and your child may feel more comfortable if you have time to volunteer in the classroom and attend school events and parent-teacher conferences. School will be part of your lives for years to come; getting off to a good start is worth the effort it takes.

LEARNING TAKES A LIFETIME

It has been said that "learners inherit the earth" and "the truly educated never graduate." There is always something new and wonderful to learn, for you and for your child. The outside world isn't always kind or welcoming; as your child moves away from your side she will experience hurts and difficulties and you will not always be there to smooth the way. There are many important lessons that you will teach your child in her preschool years, however. You can teach her that you are always on her side, that you will always listen, and that you believe in her ability to learn, to grow, and to thrive. Regardless of the new people and experiences she encounters as she grows up, your child can trust that you will always have faith in her and will always welcome her home.

5

"I CAN DO IT!"

The Joys (and Challenges) of Initiative

Raising three-year-olds would be an easy task if they didn't have so many ideas of their own—and so much energy with which to implement them! Take this little fellow, for example:

Q. My son doesn't walk anywhere—he gallops. He chases the birds at the beach, leaps into the wading pool for his swim lesson, and this morning I found him trying to saddle the dog with a blanket because he wanted to ride him. I had to explain that dogs are not strong enough to carry people on their backs. He gave up the riding plan, but I know he will come up with something else any moment. He seems so fearless, and I worry that he will get hurt. I'm worn out trying to keep track of him. Should I allow him to do these things?

A. You sound exhausted by the effort of supervising and guiding your active young child! Never fear; most parents have had moments when they wondered why three-year-olds have so much more energy and creativity than their parents. Think for just a moment, though: your son is demonstrating a number of wonderful qualities. He is courageous and not afraid to try new things. He is able to connect ideas and actions, and he hurtles through life with excitement and curiosity. The same traits that exhaust you today may be just the traits that will make him a successful, capable adult later on.

Erik Erikson, a pioneer in understanding human development, tells us that from about the ages of two to six, children experience a crucial stage in their development that he called "initiative versus guilt" (Erik H. Erikson, *Childhood and Society,* Norton, 1963). Children need this initiative—those who are not able to nurture and develop the sense of initiative that the youngster described above is so ably demonstrating can turn into adults who struggle with life's challenges, who have a lingering sense of guilt, and who may believe that nothing they do is good enough.

When we say that a child needs a healthy sense of initiative, we do not mean that he should be allowed to carry out every idea that pops into his head. We do mean that he needs secure boundaries and limits within which he can explore, experiment, and learn to develop his belief in his own competence and capability. Creating a balance between safety (and appropriate behavior) and creativity and courage is the essence of parenting three- to six-year-olds. Parents can create this balance and avoid instilling a sense of guilt by enforcing boundaries with kindness and firmness rather than humiliation or punishment. It is kind and firm to say, "Climbing on the bookcase is dangerous. Where is it safe for you to climb?" It is humiliating to say, "I can't believe you would be so careless. Don't you know you could hurt yourself?"

These are the years when parents are apt to hear a great deal of the phrase "I can do it!" Your children are trying to let you know that they are more capable than you think they are. Children in the early preschool years want to try everything: they want to push the vacuum, wash the dishes, and dig holes in the garden. All too often, parents stifle their would-be helpers by telling them, "No, you're too little. Wait until you're bigger. It is easier and faster for me to do it." It usually *is* easier (and less messy) for adults to do these tasks, but denying a child the opportunity to learn and practice new skills may plant the seeds of guilt instead of initiative. And years later, those same adults may find themselves wondering why their child "just won't do *anything*!" The drive to develop initiative versus guilt and shame continues throughout the preschool years. Again, we are talking about *a sense of* initiative—not actual ability. Parents, preschool teachers, and caregivers who understand this important developmental stage can create an environment that enhances initiative instead of guilt, discouragement, or manipulation.

INITIATIVE IN ACTION

Michael's mom took him to a nearby park for an outing. Michael, who had just turned three, was eager to play on the jungle gym. He scrambled up the lower rungs easily enough, but then he looked down—and his stomach did a flip-flop. Michael whimpered for Mom to rescue him and lift him down, but Mom just smiled and placed an encouraging hand on Michael's back. She spoke reassuringly to her frightened son, helping him find his way back down. When he was on the ground his mother gave him a big hug and congratulated him on getting down "by himself." Michael beamed a proud smile. Mom and Michael returned to the same park regularly, and by the end of the second week Michael was scampering up and down the jungle gym with ease.

Margaret's mother faced the same dilemma but responded much differently. When Margaret, also three, cried out from the top of the same playground equipment, her mother ran up and gathered Margaret into her arms. She cuddled her and told her firmly how dangerous it could be to climb up so high. Margaret cried a little, then went over to play in the sandbox. Even though they visited the park often, two months later Margaret still avoided the jungle gym, clinging to her mother's leg whenever anyone invited her to climb it.

Preschoolers see the world as an exciting and fascinating place, especially as they develop more initiative and a greater physical and intellectual capacity to explore. When adults get in the way of this, children may feel frustrated and withdraw, adopting a sense of guilt about their inabilities, while others give up and allow their anxious parents to overly protect them, keeping them from experiencing the frustration or bruises they need in order to grow. In either case, their developing sense of initiative and capability may be thwarted. Margaret's mother wanted to protect her daughter from injury but ended up convincing her to avoid climbing at all. Later in life, Margaret may still find it difficult to take risks—even those that could benefit and enrich her life.

Adults can choose to encourage children as they face challenges, just as Michael's mom did. Michael's mom showed faith in his ability to master a new skill, and his experience told him "I am capable" in a way his mother's words never could. When Michael and Margaret face challenges and new responsibilities as they grow, how will they respond? What will they believe about their own abilities?

The need to develop initiative is inborn, whether parents and caregivers find it convenient or not. Even when they are frustrated, some children (the spunky, determined ones) keep fighting to develop initiative. Adults usually call this behavior "defiance" and work to control, coddle, or overprotect the child. Yes, children must be kept safe and must be taught to behave appropriately—but this task is easier to accomplish when adults are also providing opportunities for preschoolers to experience initiative.

INITIATIVE—OR MANIPULATION?

A child who is discouraged from developing initiative sometimes responds by developing manipulation skills instead. This is the child who withdraws into helplessness and insists that you do everything for her. Instead of developing the attitude "I can do it," she seeks belonging and significance through an attitude of "I can't." She "can't" walk to the car, she "can't" put on her socks, and she "can't" pick up her toys. Whenever your child misbehaves, you might ask yourself, "Could this behavior be founded in discouragement and mistaken ideas about how to belong?" Consider the dilemmas these two parents face:

Q. My three-year-old daughter screams and cries when I say no. She never eats what we give her: she asks for bread with peanut butter and licks off the peanut butter, refusing to eat the bread. Then she will insist on putting more peanut butter on the bread. If I don't do as she says, she will start whining or crying. She's at child care during the day and is very well behaved there.

Q. I believe that "no" means no, but my daughter doesn't realize that yet. I used to put her in a corner where she couldn't see us until she stopped crying, but it only worked for a while. Now my husband puts her in our small bathroom with the light off. I believe that this will make her claustrophobic. She does sleep in her own bed, but she wets almost every night. Bedtime is a hassle, as she won't stay in bed. I have to pat her on the back until she falls asleep. I hate the constant battle with my child, but she won't do what I say.

A. Situations like these are heartbreakingly common. So many of these battles could be eliminated if adults understood developmental and age-appropriateness, the mistaken goals of misbehavior (see Chapters 8, 9, and 10), and nonpunitive methods of discipline that set limits while inviting cooperation.

There is a way to avoid manipulations like these. The mother in the first example could choose appropriate moments to give in (such as letting her daughter spread the peanut butter on the bread and teaching her to clean up afterward). Involving this child in meal preparation will increase her drive for initiative, will help her feel more capable by teaching her a life skill, and will motivate her to eat what she helps prepare.

As you learned in Chapter 2, there is never any need for a punitive time-out; it is not helpful to put a child in a corner or in a room without a light. These punitive time-out experiences create doubt, shame, and guilt. Instead, the mother and father can say no and then allow their child to have her feelings. When she cries, they can empathize: "I know this is disappointing and that you are upset." If the parents can't stand the crying, they can leave, saying, "It is okay to feel sad as long as you want to. Come find me when you are done."

Preschoolers need to know that you mean what you say and will follow through with kind and firm action (instead of lectures). Children "listen" to kind, firm, and consistent action more than they listen to words.

HOW TO ENCOURAGE INITIATIVE AND DISCOURAGE MANIPULATION

Encouraging the development of initiative is a tricky task precisely because parents and caregivers find it so challenging and inconvenient. Still, adults at home and school can help develop preschoolers' confidence and initiative by providing a range of opportunities, time for training, and encouragement for the many things children *can* do. When supported in this way, children learn to trust themselves and to feel capable.

Does this sound time-consuming? Actually, providing opportunities for children to develop their sense of initiative is less time-consuming than dealing with the misbehavior of discouraged children. Who said parenting was easy and shouldn't take much time? Too many parents want confident, respectful, resourceful, responsible children but don't want to invest time in methods that teach these characteristics. There are many ways to help children develop initiative rather than manipulation and misbehavior. One of the best ways to help children develop initiative is through family meetings or preschool class meetings, as discussed in Chapter 16. Other ways include playing Let's Pretend, stating clear expectations, offering limited choices, and following through, along with other Positive Discipline methods discussed in this book. These methods can be used to help children learn to behave appropriately at home and out in public, while encouraging their developing sense of initiative.

Play Let's Pretend

Children love to play, so Let's Pretend (what adults sometimes call role playing) can be a fun way to teach them skills and help them understand the difference between effective (respectful) and ineffective (disrespectful) behavior. Preschoolers are not too young to understand Let's Pretend when you make it simple.

One way to set up Let's Pretend is to say to your child something like this: "You be the daddy, and I'll be the little boy. We are at the pancake house. How should I behave? Should I cry and run around and throw my food like this?" Then demonstrate crying and running around. "Or should I sit quietly in the seat and eat, or perhaps color quietly while I wait?" Then demonstrate by pretending you are sitting in the restaurant and have your child supervise your behavior. Reverse roles and let the child portray being both disrespectful and respectful. Be sure to engage your child in a conversation so he can learn the benefits of respectful behavior.

State Clear Expectations

One of the oldest bits of parenting advice is still one of the best: say what you mean, and mean what you say. How should you establish clear, appropriate expectations for young preschoolers? Let's listen in as Cody's father gives it a try:

Even though he is only four, Cody loves baseball. He's been collecting baseball cards since he was tiny, loves to play Wiffle ball in the backyard with his dad, and knows the entire starting lineup of the San Francisco Giants. Tim, Cody's father, is planning to take his small son to his first real baseball game. Previous experience has taught him that in order to enjoy the day with his curious, active preschooler, some preparation and groundwork will be necessary.

First, Tim decides to take Cody to the local park for a Little League game. As they sit in the bleachers together, Tim asks Cody how he thinks they should act at the "big stadium." Cody considers this question thoughtfully, furrowing his small brow in concentration.

"We should sit still?" he offers tentatively, knowing this is a tough rule for him to follow.

"Well," his dad says with a smile, "we can stand up sometimes. And we can walk together to get a cold drink or a hot dog."

"We can do seventh-inning stretch!" Cody shouts excitedly, and begins to sing "Take Me Out to the Ball Game."

Together, father and son explore the guidelines for the big day. Tim makes it clear that lots of people will be at the game, so Cody will have to hold his hand when they walk anywhere. Tim and Cody agree that Cody can have a hot dog, a cold drink, a snack, and one souvenir of his choice—as long as it costs ten dollars or less. And they agree that if Cody runs away or climbs on the seats, they will have to return to the car.

Tim knows his son well; when Cody's curiosity gets the better of him, a firm hand on his shoulder (without scolding or a lecture) draws him back to Dad's side. And when Cody decides he wants to climb down a row (and over three people) to see better, Tim only has to ask him what their agreement was for Cody to plop quickly back into his seat.

Because Cody is four, his dad knows that the day will not be perfect. He also knows that Cody may not be able to follow the guidelines for nine full innings. He knows they may even have to go sit in the car for a while until Cody is ready to try again. But by setting clear expectations (in advance) and following through on these simple limits, Cody's first baseball game will be an occasion father and son will enjoy remembering for years to come.

Offer Limited Choices and Follow Through

Parents sometimes believe that giving children what they want and not burdening them with rules will show them that they are loved. We want to stress that permissiveness is not the way to help children develop initiative—or any other valuable social or life skill. One alternative to permissiveness is offering limited choices with kind and firm follow-through. Limited choices are effective when they are related, respectful, and reasonable.

Elena's family went to the zoo with another family from their neighborhood. Elena asked for cotton candy, snow cones, and everything she saw other children enjoying. Her father told Elena she could have either a snow cone or popcorn. Elena chose popcorn. Her father purchased the popcorn and then told Elena that if she continued to ask for other treats she would need to return to the car with him, where they would wait until the others finished viewing the exhibits.

Partway through eating the popcorn, Elena saw a child with a snow cone and began to ask for one. Elena was determined: she emphasized her demand by flinging the remaining popcorn down, spilling it all over the walkway. Her father calmly asked Elena if she wanted to hold his hand on the way to the car or be carried. (He decided to ignore the spilled popcorn, since the pigeons were already taking care of that problem.) When she refused to move, her father picked her up and left for the car. He did not scold, spank, or remind her why they were leaving. He treated her respectfully, and when she began to wail that she wanted to see the monkeys, he assured her that he was confident that next time they came to the zoo, Elena would make better choices—and would be able to visit the monkeys.

Giving a child a chance to try again is reasonable and encouraging. It is not reasonable to say, "I'm never taking you there again—or anywhere else, for that matter!" Most parents do not follow through on such threats—which only teaches children that they can safely disregard both the rules and their parents.

Yes, it would be inconvenient for you to miss your family outing while using kind and firm follow-through. You also have a choice. Which is more important, a family outing or the self-esteem, initiative, and confidence your child will develop by learning appropriate social skills? When you follow through with kindness and firmness, you won't have to miss many outings before your child learns that you say what you mean and will follow through. Of course, follow-through requires that adults think before they speak. If you can't do it, don't say it!

POSITIVE DISCIPLINE IN ACTION

Myrna and Lamar decided they would teach their son, Mark, to dress himself when he was three years old (excellent training for budding initiative). They purchased clothes that were easy for a small child to manage, such as pants with elastic waistbands, wide-neck T-shirts, and sneakers with Velcro fasteners. Mark was a willing student and soon mastered the art of dressing himself (even though he put his shoes on the wrong feet about half of the time).

Mark attended preschool, and his morning routine included getting himself dressed in the morning, helping with breakfast, and being ready to leave by 7:30, when his dad would drive him to school on the way to work. Mark and his dad had created a special morning routine chart with a picture of him doing each task—which Mark followed enthusiastically for several days. Myrna and Lamar knew that Mark might use his initiative to "test" the routine. In preparation, they worked out a plan with Mark in advance that included a limited choice and follow-through. Together they decided that anytime Mark was not dressed in time to go, they would put Mark's clothes in a paper bag so he could finish dressing at school. They weren't sure how much Mark really understood about their discussion of choices and follow-through, but they had faith that he would learn if they ever had to carry out their plan.

Sure enough, after several weeks of smooth mornings, the day arrived when Myrna noticed Mark wasn't following his routine. When it was time for Lamar to leave for work, Mark was still in his pajamas. Myrna had prepared the sack of clothes, so Lamar kindly and firmly picked Mark up under one arm, took the sack of clothes in his other hand, and walked to the car through pouring rain—just as a neighbor was out picking up his newspaper.

Lamar sighed and reminded himself, "Well, taking time for training with Mark is more important than what the neighbors think."

Mark cried and complained that he was cold while they were driving to school. Lamar pointed to Mark's coat lying beside his car seat and suggested he would be warmer if he put it on. Lamar also reminded Mark that he could get dressed as soon as they got to school. Mark continued to complain. When they arrived at the school, Joyce, the preschool director (who understood these moments well), smiled as the pair approached.

"Oh, hi, Mark!" she said warmly. "I see you didn't get dressed this morning. That's okay. You can take your bag of clothes into my office and come out as soon as you are dressed." Mark got himself dressed.

A month later, Mark decided further research was in order and tested the routine again. Lamar responded matter-of-factly, *carrying the clothes bag to the car. When they arrived, Mark's teacher invited him to get dressed, reminding him that he would need to be dressed for outside playtime. He refused and began to play with the blocks, nattily attired in Mickey Mouse pajamas. Mark played happily until it was time to head outside. Mark's teacher assured him that as soon as he was fully dressed he could join his classmates in the play yard. After a moment of reflection, Mark decided that proving his point was not worth missing recess, and he scrambled into his clothes.*

Mark's parents and teacher did not nag, lecture, or remind Mark about getting dressed. They simply did what they said they would do—carry his clothes to the car for him, limit his ability to play outdoors until properly dressed, and allow him to dress himself at school. (It's important to note that this plan would not be appropriate for an older child who might feel humiliated by arriving at school in pajamas. Adult actions that cause shame or embarrassment are unlikely to encourage respect or cooperation.)

Lamar could have made this experience humiliating to Mark by piggybacking, which means adding blaming or shaming lectures to his kind and firm actions. Lamar did not say, "It serves you right! Maybe next time you'll hurry up. The other kids will laugh at you for not getting dressed." Instead, Myrna, Lamar, and Joyce treated Mark kindly and firmly, which helped him learn the benefits of using his skills to help himself and cooperate with others.

"OOPS, I MADE A MISTAKE!"

By now you might be thinking that you have to be a perfect parent and raise a perfect child. There are no such things. Isn't that wonderful? It doesn't matter how much we learn or how much we know; we never stop making mistakes. All human beings sometimes forget what they know and get hooked into emotional reactions—or they just plain goof up. Once you understand this, you can see mistakes as the important life processes they are: interesting opportunities to learn. Instead of feeling discouraged when you make a mistake, you can say, "Terrific! I've just been given another opportunity to learn!"

Wouldn't it be wonderful if you could also instill this attitude in your children so they wouldn't be burdened with all the baggage you carry about mistakes? How many adults developed a greater sense of guilt than of initiative because they were shamed and punished when they made honest mistakes? Mistakes aren't the same as failures, although people often behave as though they are. And even so-called failures can provide opportunities to learn and grow. The process of nurturing initiative is less painful when adults can make a slight attitude adjustment. Of course, preschoolers will not do things perfectly. But which is more important: perfection or helping your children develop healthy self-esteem and strong life skills?

ASKING CURIOSITY QUESTIONS

Children do not develop a strong sense of initiative when parents and teachers spend too much time lecturing: telling children what happened, what caused it to happen, how they should feel about it, and what they should do about it. Telling may keep children from seeing mistakes as opportunities to learn. Telling instills guilt or rebellion because it sends the message that children aren't living up to adult expectations. Perhaps most important, telling children what, how, and why teaches them *what* to think, not *how* to think.

Children will develop thinking skills, judgment skills, problem-solving abilities, and initiative when adults ask them curiosity questions: "What happened? What were you trying to do? Why do you think this happened? How do you feel about it? How could you fix it? What else could you do if you don't want this to happen again?"

When Mark, who wouldn't get dressed in the morning, complained about being cold in the car, his dad might have used it as an opportunity for asking questions: "Why do you think you are cold? What might you do to feel warmer?" These questions would have helped

Mark make the connections between clothing and warmth. He might also have discovered why pajamas aren't a good choice when it is cold outside. Perhaps Mark does not truly understand this connection and would have answered, "Because I didn't eat all my toast." This would have given his dad an opportunity to help Mark learn the effect clothes have on whether we feel warm or not. Believe it or not, children do not always understand the reasoning that seems so obvious to adults. That is why it is so important to understand child development and age-appropriateness—and encouragement.

IT'S ALL ABOUT ENCOURAGEMENT

Rudolf Dreikurs said over and over, "A child needs encouragement as much as a flower needs water." So what is encouragement?

The word *encouragement* comes from a French root that means "to give heart to." Encouragement helps children develop courage: the courage to learn and grow, the courage to learn from mistakes without blame and shame, the courage to develop social and life skills. How do they do this? They develop courage when their parents and other adults in their lives create a safe place where they can practice their developing autonomy and initiative and make mistakes without experiencing doubt, shame, or guilt.

Remember that remorse is not the same as guilt. Children will feel remorse when they make a mistake and when they hurt others. (Remorse is appropriate sometimes, and is the beginning of valuable qualities such as compassion. Remember, though, that you cannot force a child to feel genuine remorse.) Adults offer encouragement when, through curiosity questions, they help children explore the consequences of their choices instead of imposing consequences on them. Curiosity questions also help children understand what they feel, why they feel that way, and how they can make amends. In this way, children will feel encouraged to learn from their mistakes.

As Dreikurs said, "A misbehaving child is a discouraged child." This is why adults need to understand the long-term effects of what they do. We believe that parents and teachers mean to encourage. They just don't realize that they are often more discouraging than encouraging.

VAGUE PRAISE IS NOT ENCOURAGING

Vague "attaboys" aren't the best way to encourage young children— keep your encouragement specific. For instance, if a three-year-old at the child care center brings you his latest drawing and you tell him, "Oh, it's the most gorgeous picture I've ever seen—I'm going to frame it and hang it on the wall," you may not be helping him as much as you think. You may have taught him that the most important thing he can do is to please people, which can be a dangerous creed to live by. Telling that same child, "I see you really like red and yellow. Can you tell me about these shapes?" opens the door for talking and learning together.

Another way to determine if something is true encouragement is that it can be said only to that person at that time, whereas praise is more general. You could say "That's a great project" to most anyone, anytime. You could only say, "You built a very tall block tower. Look how high you had to reach to place those top blocks on it—it's taller than you are!" to a particular child in a specific situation. This child will feel you noticed what she did and that you were speaking uniquely to her.

The chart on the next page will make these distinctions clearer.

HELPING CHILDREN REACH THEIR FULL POTENTIAL

Joyce, the director of the preschool Mark attends, believes in the importance of using encouragement and the other concepts in this chapter to give children opportunities to develop initiative. Her staff looks for every opportunity to let children experience how capable they are by taking time for training and

DIFFERENCES BETWEEN PRAISE AND ENCOURAGEMENT*

	Praise	Encouragement
Dictionary definition	1. To express favorable judgment of 2. To glorify, especially by attribution of perfection 3. An expression of approval	1. To inspire with courage 2. To spur on: stimulate
Addresses	The doer: "Good girl"	The deed: "Good job"
Recognizes	Only complete, perfect product: "You did it right"	Effort and improvement: "You gave it your best" or "How do you feel about what you learned?"
Attitude	Patronizing, manipulative: "I like the way Suzie is sitting"	Respectful, appreciative: "Who can show me how we should be sitting now?"
"I" message	Judgmental: "I like the way you did that"	Self-directing: "I appreciate your cooperation"
Used most often with	Children: "You're such a good girl"	Adults: "Thanks for helping"
Examples	"I'm proud of you for getting an A" (robs person of ownership of own achievement)	"That A reflects your hard work" (recognizes ownership and responsibility for effort)
Invites	Children to change for others: approval junkies	Children to change for themselves: inner direction
Locus of control	External: "What do others think?"	Internal: "What do I think?"
Teaches	What to think; dependence on the evaluation of others	How to think; self-evaluation
Goal	Conformity: "You did it right"	Understanding: "What did you think/learn/feel?"
Effect on sense of worth	Feel worthwhile when others approve	Feel worthwhile without the approval of others
Long-term effect	Dependence on others	Self-confidence, self-reliance

* From *Positive Discipline*, by Jane Nelsen (Ballantine, 2006).

then letting the children do many things that are usually done for them by adults.

For example, when Joyce goes shopping for groceries, she lets the children take turns going with her to help her put items in the grocery cart. When she returns to the child care center, she backs the van into the play yard and calls the children to help take the groceries to the kitchen one item at a time. The cook helps the children remember where to put the items.

During lunchtime, the children dish up their own food. One little fellow named Matt would consistently take too much food. After about a week, his teacher helped him explore what was happening by asking, "What happens when you take too much food?"

Matt responded, "I can't eat it all and I have to throw some away."

The teacher continued: "What would happen if you took smaller helpings of food?"

Matt looked like he had made a great discovery as he said, "I could eat it all."

The teacher said, "I'm sure you could." Then she asked, "If you took less food, ate it all, and were still hungry, what could you do then?"

Matt beamed as he said, "I could take some more?"

The teacher asked, "When will you start doing that?"

Matt looked like he could hardly wait as he crowed, "Tomorrow!"

After lunch, each child scrapes his own food into a plastic dishpan, rinses his own plate in another dishpan, and then puts the dish in the dishwasher. This routine is definitely more time-consuming than having an adult clean up after lunch. But Joyce and her staff of teachers are more interested in helping children develop their full potential than in getting chores done quickly. They also love the children, enjoy them, and feel privileged to be part of their growth and development.

There it is again: love and joy. The more you know about what is developmentally appropriate, how to enhance the environment in which children grow, learn the skills that will encourage them to reach their full potential, and forgive yourself when you make mistakes, the more you can relax and just enjoy watching your children grow, knowing that they're learning to trust their own abilities, to believe in the support of the adults in their lives, and to experience the wonder of life all around them.

6

ACCEPTING THE CHILD
YOU HAVE

Understanding Temperament

Most parents know it's not wise to compare children. Still, most parents occasionally compare their children to those around them, privately if not publicly: the other girls and boys at the preschool, the neighbors' kids, nieces and nephews. And comparisons usually lead to judgments: Bobby is "such a good boy"; Miranda is "a little monster."

You have already learned that preschoolers are passing through some interesting developmental stages; you know that experimenting with autonomy and initiative can lead them to behave in ways that adults perceive as "bad." Is there such a creature as a perfect child? Would you really want one?

THE MYTH OF THE PERFECT CHILD

A perfect child is often pictured as the one who quietly obeys his parents, doesn't fight with his brothers or sisters, does his chores without complaining, saves his money, does homework without being reminded—and who gets good grades, is athletic, and is popular. Does this mean that a child who doesn't fit this description is imperfect?

Frankly, we worry about the child who fits this fantasy description. This is usually the child who does not feel secure enough to test power boundaries and find out who she is apart from her parents and teachers, who is afraid to make mistakes or risk disapproval. We say usually, because a few children do fit the fantasy description yet still feel secure and aren't afraid to make mistakes.

As discussed in Chapters 4 and 6, brain researchers believe that temperament traits are inborn, part of each child's "wiring." How your child interacts with you and her other caregivers appears to have a strong effect on how these inborn tendencies actually develop. It's a complex process, one that we don't yet fully understand. While attitudes, behavior, and decisions may change with time and experience, temperament appears to be part of us for life. Understanding your child's unique temperament will help you accept the child she truly is and work *with* her to learn, to grow, and to thrive. You will understand the source of your occasional frustrations with your child, the best ways to nurture your child, and how to build a stronger relationship by working on your goodness of fit.

GOODNESS OF FIT

Stella Chess and Alexander Thomas emphasize the importance of "goodness of fit," which is the depth of understanding parents and teachers have of a child's temperament and their willingness to work with that child to encourage healthy development. (See Stella Chase and Alexander Thomas, *Goodness of Fit,* Brunner/Mazel, 1999.) Children experience enough stress in life as they struggle for a sense of competency and belonging. It does not help to compound that stress by expecting a child to be someone he is not.

Understanding a child's temperament doesn't mean shrugging and saying, "Oh, well, that's just the way this child is." It is an invitation to help a child develop acceptable behavior and skills. For instance, a child with a short attention span will still need to learn to accept some structure and stay focused. Offering limited choices is one way to be respectful of the child's needs and of the needs of the situation (meaning the behavior appropriate for the present environment).

Working out a match between parents and children that meets the needs of both is critical to goodness of fit. If your child has difficulty adapting to new situations while you are the life of the party, you have a poor fit. The good news is that, with understanding, you can find balance and create a good fit. Your child may not make friends quickly, but she can learn social skills that will help her find one or two good friends. She may feel discouraged if you push her to be like you but will find it encouraging if you gently teach her that it is okay to take her time while being open to the friendly overtures of other children. Finding the balance between your needs and those of your child can take some time and practice, but learning to accept and work with the individual, special temperament of your child will benefit you both as the years go by. Now that you know why understanding temperament is so important, let's learn more about it.

THE BERKELEY STUDIES

Each child is born with a unique style of processing sensory information and responding to the world around her. Drs. Stella Chess and Alexander Thomas investigated the miracle of personality in their longitudinal study of the nine major temperaments in the late sixties and seventies. The Berkeley Studies were a longitudinal study of two basic temperaments, active and passive. This study revealed that these two temperaments are lifelong characteristics; in other words, passive infants grow up to be passive adults, while active infants grow up to be active adults. In fact, activity levels can be measured in the womb.

The nine temperaments found by Chess and Thomas—the qualities and characteristics that contribute to individual personalities—serve to describe three types of children: the "easy" child, the "difficult" child, and the "slow to warm up" child. All are good; some are just more challenging than others. We will discuss these nine temperaments, but for more information we highly recommend *Know Your Child,* Jason Aronson, 1996, and *Temperament: Theory and Practice,* Psychology Press, 1996, both by Stella Chess and Alexander Thomas.

THE NINE TEMPERAMENTS

All children possess varying degrees of each of the nine characteristics studied by Chess and Thomas. The following sections will describe what they look like in real life. (You may want to think about children you know as we examine these aspects of temperament.)

Activity Level
Activity level refers to a child's level of motor activity and the proportion of active and inactive periods. A high-activity preschooler might delight in energetic running games, while a low-activity child chooses something quiet, like drawing or looking at a book.

Q. My three-year-old son doesn't know what the words "Wait, please!" mean. He never slows down. I am worn out. My sister's child seems so much calmer. Am I doing something wrong?

A. Have you ever noticed how often parents and teachers of preschoolers use the phrase "worn out"? Most preschoolers have a high level of physical energy—after all, there's so much they have to do and learn each day—but some youngsters seem to have far more than their share. If you have one of these highly active little ones in your home, rest assured there is nothing wrong with you or your child. All people are born with different temperaments. An active child is not "bad"; he does not jet around out of a desire to wear you out. He simply is busy being who he is. The key to living peacefully with your active preschooler is to find a way to meet his needs without abandoning your own. Here are some suggestions:

The following nine temperaments shape a child's personality and approach to life:

1. Activity level
2. Rhythmicity
3. Initial response (approach or withdrawal)
4. Adaptability
5. Sensory threshold
6. Quality of mood
7. Intensity of reactions
8. Distractibility
9. Persistence and attention span

- **Plan ahead with your child's needs in mind.** Provide him with space, challenging activities, and opportunities to run off excess energy. Take him to parks, enroll him in swim classes or gymnastics, or provide plenty of time for energetic play. It may also be wise to skip, for now, the ballet class, the music recitals and plays, and the four-course restaurant meals. Set yourselves up for success. Remember to match your expectations to your child's abilities.

- **Schedule time for yourself.** Get a sitter, enroll your child in preschool or other classes to give yourself a break, or ask a friend or partner to spend time with your child on a regular basis. This is not selfishness; it's common sense. You need lots of energy to deal calmly and effectively with an active preschooler, and you need time to rest and refresh yourself.

- **Learn to love your child for who he is.** He did not choose his temperament. Rejoice in his strengths. There is much he can accomplish later in life with his abundant energy.

Monica has learned to plan her days with her twins' different temperaments and activity levels in mind. One Saturday after-

noon at the community swimming pool, three-year-old Ned and Stacy keep Mom company while their older sister takes swimming lessons. As the hour progresses, Ned plays happily with the bag of plastic animals that his mother has brought along. The entire hour passes with Ned happily absorbed in his play.

Twin sister Stacy is a different story. She begins coloring in the book her mother has brought along, but within ten minutes has marked up all of the pages and wants her mom to read to her. Halfway through the story, Stacy decides she is thirsty, so Monica takes her to the drinking fountain. Then Stacy begins to climb on the bleachers. Before half an hour has passed, Stacy has colored, heard a story, gotten a drink, and explored the bleachers. Monica knows her daughter well and is already expecting to take a walk to the swings—and she knows they'd better be ready to leave the minute lessons are over.

Ned has a low activity level, while Stacy's is high. Monica used to feel frustrated by the differences between her twins, especially since she thought she treated them the same way. Information about temperaments helped her understand them better. She decided she might as well relax and simply enjoy (and plan for) the uniqueness of each child.

Rhythmicity

Rhythmicity refers to the predictability (or unpredictability) of biological functions, such as hunger, sleeping, and bowel movements.

The Silvertons could set their clocks by the routine of their younger son, three-year-old Martin. He woke up at 6:30 every morning, he wanted the same lunch every day, always chose to play with the same toys, and went to bed every night at the same time.

Martin provided a needed rest for the Silvertons after their experience with his five-year-old brother, Stanley, who was as unpredictable as his younger brother was predictable. They wondered what they did "wrong" with Stanley and what they did "right" with Martin, until they learned about temperament and realized they couldn't take credit or blame for their children's individual wiring. However, they could learn to be more patient with Stanley and avoid showing preference for Martin's style. They got both boys involved in planning morning and bedtime routines (even though Martin didn't need one). Stanley found it helpful to follow routines that he had helped create.

Understanding rhythmicity can help parents and caregivers plan a child's schedule in ways that ease conflict and stress for everyone.

Fred knows that his four-year-old daughter still gets weary and welcomes a nap precisely at 1:30 each afternoon. He makes sure that her weekday caregiver understands this, and he leaves space in his weekend schedule to help her get her rest. Fred has discovered that respecting his daughter's temperament and need for regular naps helps prevent those endless afternoons with a cranky, tired child.

Initial Response

This temperament describes the way a child reacts to a new situation or stimulus, such as a new food, toy, person, or place. Approach responses are often displayed by mood expression (smiling, speech, facial expression) or motor activity (swallowing a new food, reaching for a new toy, joining a new playmate). Withdrawal responses look more negative and are expressed by mood (crying, speech, facial expression) or motor activity (running away, spitting food out, or throwing a new toy). Learning to parent your unique child means recognizing these cues and responding in encouraging, nurturing ways.

Older preschoolers reveal this temperament in the way they cope with new experiences, either running to join a new group or hovering on the sidelines awhile to check things out.

> *Amanda came to her new child care center when she was four years old. Whenever the children gathered for a group activity, Amanda would hang back and refuse to join in. Because her teacher was sensitive to her temperament, she did not insist that Amanda join the group, although she made sure that Amanda knew she was welcome. For two weeks, Amanda held back, watching what happened and gradually moving closer. By the third week, she was happily playing with the others. Amanda's initial response was withdrawal, and her teacher wisely honored this aspect of her temperament.*

Again, temperament is inborn, and research indicates that these deeply ingrained personality traits are not easily changed by anxious parents.

> *Bonny worried about her five-year-old son, Jeremy: she feared that his shyness would keep him from ever having happy relationships or enjoying the activities that she and his father had always loved. Bonny found that when she pushed him forward, urged him to speak to or play with someone new, or signed him up for a sport or activity, he only retreated further, hiding behind her leg and burying his head against her side.*
>
> *When Bonny realized that Jeremy might always be wary of new situations, she decided to accept her son for who he was—and to find ways to help him feel more comfortable and confident. She learned to provide opportunities for Jeremy to watch other children playing tee-ball before signing him up. She learned not to push him to speak to new acquaintances but to carry on a friendly conversation herself, keeping a gentle hand on her son's shoulder as reassurance.*

Bonny made time to stay awhile with Jeremy in new situations, accepting that he felt comfortable more quickly when she was with him. Most important, she offered him acceptance and encouragement without requiring that he "get over" his shyness. Jeremy may always be slow to warm up to new people and circumstances, but his mother's patience and loving encouragement will help him to believe in—and accept—himself.

Adaptability

Adaptability describes how a child reacts to a new situation over time—her ability to adjust and change. Some children initially spit out a new food but accept it after a few trial tastes. Others accept a new food, a new article of clothing, or a new preschool far more slowly, if at all.

When three-and-a-half-year-old Maria's parents decided to file for divorce, her dad found an apartment a few blocks away. Any child finds divorce painful, but Maria's "slow to warm up" temperament increased the stress associated with such a major change. Although both parents agreed to share parenting duties, with Maria spending several nights each week with her dad, they decided to take a gradual approach at first.

When Maria's dad moved out, he invited her to help him carry things to his new apartment. Over the next few weeks he took Maria to his apartment several times, increasing the length of these visits. After three weeks, Maria was spending full days with Dad and eating dinner at his new apartment but returning to her familiar bedroom at the family home to sleep.

Gradually, Maria and her dad set up a bedroom for her at his new home, picked out some furniture, and selected clothes she could move to her new room. A month had passed before Maria and her parents felt comfortable with overnight visits at Dad's apartment.

It would not have been appropriate for Dad to immediately ask Maria if she wanted to spend the night at his house. This would have placed too great an emotional burden on a young child who was already experiencing a sense of upheaval and divided loyalties. Maria's parents put her needs first and gave her time to adjust to this change. (For more information on divorce and single parenting, see *Positive Discipline for Single Parents* by Jane Nelsen, Cheryl Erwin, and Carol Delzer, Three Rivers Press, 1999.)

Many children would benefit from this gentle, gradual approach. If your little one struggles with rapid transition and change, then recognizing and allowing for her temperament may save you both discomfort and unhappiness.

Sensory Threshold

Some children wake up from a nap every time a door opens, no matter how softly, while others can sleep through a thunderstorm. Some children complain about tight clothes or rough sheets, while others scrape their knees or thump their heads without even slowing down. The level of sensitivity to sensory input varies from one child to the next and affects how they behave and view the world.

Amber was celebrating her fourth birthday. She opened a present containing a beautiful flowered dress and smiled in delight. The smile changed to dismay, however, when she noticed that the puffy skirt was held in place by a layer of stiff nylon net. "Do I have to wear this part?" she asked in alarm. "It'll scratch my legs."

Such minor details didn't faze Andy. He loved to walk barefoot and took off his shoes at every opportunity. His parents would point with concern to the gravel playground or exclaim about the hot pavement, but textures and temperatures didn't bother Andy. His little feet padded along undaunted, while their owner enjoyed the feeling of each toe wiggling freely.

Sensory Integration Dysfunction

Some children are deeply influenced by sensory input; in fact, in some cases, a child's brain may have difficulty integrating sensory information. A child may find his socks "painful" or his shirt "too tight"; he may insist on the same foods and routines because others are uncomfortable or "bad." Other children do not respond strongly to any stimulation; they may rock, spin, or bang their heads in an effort to generate sensory input, which they find comforting. Such children may have sensory integration dysfunction and can benefit from a variety of therapies that will help them make sense of sensory information and feel more comfortable.

If you suspect that your child reacts differently to sensory input than other children the same age, it may be wise to ask your pediatrician for an evaluation. (For more information, see Carol Stock Kranowitz's excellent book, *The Out-of-Sync Child*, revised edition, Perigee, 2006.)

Time and experience will teach you about your own child's sensitivity to physical sensation and stimulation. Does your child like noise and music, or does he become irritable? Does he gaze at bright or flashing lights, or does he turn his face away? Will he eat new foods, or does he spit out unusual tastes or textures? Does he like to be touched and hugged, or does he wriggle away from too much contact?

If your child is more sensitive to stimulation, you will need to go slowly when introducing new toys, new experiences, and new people. Soft light and gentle music may help him calm down and he may become nervous or irritable in noisy, crowded places (such as birthday parties, amusement parks, or busy malls). A less sensitive child may be more willing to try new experiences. Discover what engages his attention, then create opportunities for him to explore and experiment.

Quality of Mood

Have you ever noticed how some children (and adults) react to life with pleasure and acceptance while others can find fault with everything and everybody? One child might favor her family with sunny smiles, while another feels compelled to pout or scowl, just "because."

Parents of less sunny children can take heart. If your child wears a "frowny face" more often than you would like, remember that those scowls are not in response to you or your parenting skills. Be sensitive to his mood, but take time to hug your sober little fellow and share your own sunshine with him. It can be discouraging for parents and teachers to deal with a child who always looks on the dark side, but there are ways to both accept this temperament and help a child to face life more positively.

> *Stephen came home from his parenting class with a new idea: he would ask his five-year-old son, Carl, about the happiest and saddest moments of his day. Stephen looked forward to making this a part of their bedtime routine and having a chance to get into his son's world. When Stephen asked Carl about his saddest moments, he often had a long list of troubles to relate, but when asked about his happy moments, he couldn't think of any. Stephen began to feel real dismay that Carl was so miserable.*
>
> *When Stephen learned about temperament, he was able to stop getting hooked by Carl's negative mood. He would listen to his son's list of troubles, then share some of his own sad moments. Then he would share his happy moments. As Stephen continued to show Carl that it was okay to see both negatives and positives, Carl started sharing happy times, too. He still sees lots of negatives, but he is learning to see the positive things as well.*

Carl simply has a negative mood temperament and sees the world from that perspective. By accepting his temperament, Stephen learned more about his child and how to help him feel better, and they will both benefit.

Intensity of Reaction
Children respond to events around them in different ways. Some smile quietly or merely take a look, then go back to what they were doing;

others react with action and emotion. For instance, the tantrums of your high-intensity child can be heard throughout the apartment complex, while your neighbor's son retreats into quiet when faced with disappointment.

> *Mrs. Peters was getting ready for art time with her class. While the children played quietly, Mrs. Peters set out paper, markers, pastels, and scissors. She was carrying the box containing the trays of watercolors and brushes when she tripped over a forgotten block and the box of painting supplies crashed to the floor.*
>
> *The group of children reacted in a number of interesting ways. Some looked up, startled, then returned to playing. Little Steffi and Adam began to cry loudly. Matt got up to poke through the debris with his toe, while Amy ran around the room giggling.*

The children responded differently to the same situation because their intensity levels were different. Understanding that children react to stimuli with varying degrees of intensity can help both parents and teachers deal with behavior more calmly.

Distractibility

"If my daughter decides she wants to go out and play but it's lunchtime," one mom says, "she'll fuss and fuss and won't get involved in anything else." Another says, "My little guy knows when he's hungry, and he follows me around the kitchen until I have his lunch ready." They may not realize it, but these parents are actually talking about their children's distractibility, the way in which an outside stimulus interferes with a child's present behavior and his willingness (or unwillingness) to be diverted.

> *It is nap time at the child care center when Melissa makes the unfortunate discovery that her special teddy bear has been left*

at home. The teacher holds her, talks with her, and offers one of the center's toys as a substitute, but nothing helps. Melissa spends the entire nap time sitting on her mat whimpering for her teddy.

Melissa has low distractibility, which will be a real asset someday when she's hired to be an air traffic controller. But for now, Melissa is not a child who should be brought to child care without her precious teddy. In fact, it might be wise to have two teddy bears, one for home and another for school, so this sort of crisis can be avoided.

Aaron, on the other hand, is perfectly happy to curl up with whatever toy is available. Today he has forgotten his stuffed dinosaur, but when his teacher offers a blue rabbit, Aaron smiles and contentedly drifts off to sleep.

Later on in life, Aaron may prove to be an easygoing person who can do many things at once, an invaluable asset to a busy corporate office. It is encouraging to adults and children when parents and teachers remember to focus on the assets of a child's temperament.

Persistence and Attention Span

Persistence refers to a child's willingness to pursue an activity in the face of obstacles or difficulties; attention span describes the length of time he will pursue an activity without interruption. The two characteristics are usually related. The child who is content to tear up an old magazine for half an hour at a time has a fairly long attention span, while another who plays with ten different toys in ten minutes has a short one. A child who is threading beads on a string might give up if a bead doesn't go on immediately; another will try again and again until she succeeds. These children are demonstrating different levels of persistence. Again, no temperament is necessarily better than another; they're simply different and present different challenges in parenting and teaching.

*Five-year-old Mitchell has been tracing a map from his chil-
dren's atlas every morning for a week. He has carefully continued his work, adding details and humming contentedly to
himself as he draws. Mitchell's best friend, Erica, comes over to
play, and she sits down to help him—for a while. Within half
an hour, Erica has three hastily completed drawings and turns
her attention to Mitchell's new Play-Doh. Someday Erica may
be discovering new strains of bacteria and new medications
with her ability to detect and investigate new things, while
most of us would be very comfortable with the future Dr.
Mitchell performing our six-hour open-heart surgery.*

It is important to understand that a child with a short attention span
and little persistence does not necessarily have the condition known as
attention deficit disorder (ADD). ADD is a very real neurological condition that should be diagnosed by a pediatric neurologist or a pediatrician
trained to recognize its special symptoms. It is not usually wise to act on
a "diagnosis" offered by another parent or a caregiver—although such
suggestions may be worth investigating with your child's physician.

Most physicians are reluctant to diagnose ADD until a child is at
least five or six years old; before that time, impulsive behavior, high
activity levels, and short attention spans may be due to temperament
or developmental differences. If you're concerned, check with your
child's pediatrician or a child therapist trained to evaluate young children. Medication is an option, but one that should be exercised carefully (more about special needs in Chapter 18). In either case,
understanding development and temperament, being both firm and
kind, and using Positive Discipline skills will help both you and your
child experience success at home and at school.

TEMPERAMENT: CHALLENGE OR OPPORTUNITY?

If asked, most parents and teachers would probably prefer children
with a long attention span and high persistence; they're much easier to

teach and entertain. However, few children fit this ideal description. In fact, most families include children of different temperaments, and teachers can find themselves working with a large assortment.

Teachers may find it helpful to provide information about temperament to parents, too. An understanding of temperament can help both parents and teachers encourage acceptance instead of unrealistic expectations. Each child—and every temperament—possesses both assets and liabilities, strengths and weaknesses. None is "good" or "bad," and as we've already seen, comparison and judgments can lead to discouragement and disappointment. Effective parenting and teaching will help each unique child build on her strengths and manage her weaknesses, providing opportunities to learn skills that will last a lifetime.

All parents must eventually recognize and accept the ways in which their children's dreams and temperaments are different from their own.

Evan's parents are artistic people who design beautiful wall hangings and nontraditional clothing. They became concerned that Evan wasn't being given ample opportunity for artistic expression at his preschool, as Evan never came home with paint on his clothes or clay under his fingernails. In fact, Evan had many opportunities to explore the world of art. He just wasn't interested. Evan was a precise, orderly youngster who preferred to work quietly putting together puzzles or building with blocks. His sensory threshold made the slippery feel of paint on his hands or the gooey mess of clay distasteful. Evan's parents were viewing their son in light of their own temperaments, not his. When Evan's teacher explained the facets of his temperament, his parents were grateful. Now they could begin to accept Evan for the unique person he is and encourage him to follow his own dreams, not theirs.

NEEDS OF THE SITUATION

We want to emphasize again that an awareness of temperament in children will help you understand why different methods are more effective with some children than with others. There are some universal principles, such as everyone's right to dignity and respect, but this doesn't mean you can *demand* that your children treat you with dignity and respect—or that children will automatically know how to do so.

In school, for example, the needs of the situation are that learning must take place and children should respect themselves and one another. Giving a child a limited choice of more than one way to learn or do an activity would fit the needs of the situation, take the child's temperament into account, and still be respectful to everyone concerned. A child with a long attention span may need encouragement to expand her horizons to include a variety of interests and activities.

Each individual must learn to take personal responsibility for his own dignity and respect. You cannot demand that your child treat you with respect, but you can treat yourself with respect. If your child is behaving disrespectfully, you can choose to leave the room or find another Positive Discipline method to deal with the behavior. It is neither effective nor respectful to withdraw love or acceptance from a child because her behavior needs work.

> *Marty did nothing in half measures. His mother described her four-year-old son as "passionate," an admirable trait—in the right circumstances. One afternoon, Marty's mom told him it was time to put away his crayons. Marty did not want to stop coloring. His face scrunched up in anger, his jaw jutted out, and in a burst of anger he launched his crayons at his mother. Marty's mom recognized that his frustration was understandable, but his feelings and his intense temperament did not give him permission to mistreat others. Marty's mother took a calming breath to control her own anger, then proceeded to leave the room without any comment.*
>
> *Marty yelled. His mother remained calm, going to her own room. A few minutes passed, and Marty began to realize that tantrums feel pretty silly when there is no one around to witness them. Marty wandered off in search of his mother.*

When he found Mom in her room, Marty climbed onto the bed with her and snuggled wordlessly against her side. Mom realized she had a choice: she could lecture Marty about his unacceptable behavior and march him into the next room to pick up the crayons, or she could respond to his desire to be close. Marty's mom chose to give her small son a hug.

After they had established a good connection, Mom told Marty that it was okay to feel angry sometimes, but it was not okay to throw things at her or anyone else. He snuggled closer to her and nodded to indicate that he knew he shouldn't throw things. After a few quiet moments, Mom asked whether he wanted help picking up the crayons that he had thrown or if he could do it on his own. Marty bounced off the bed and with one more hug dashed off to gather his crayons.

Did Marty "get away with" misbehavior by throwing crayons at his mother? Actually, Marty's mother chose to deal with the situation in a manner that allowed for both her own temperament and her son's. Had she yelled, demanded immediate compliance, or punished Marty, the situation would likely have grown passionate on both sides. Instead, she respected her needs by removing herself as a target, modeling self-control, and taking her own cool-off moment. She let Marty know that he was still loved by returning his hug, then invited him to correct the situation by picking up the crayons when he had calmed down.

Both Marty and his mom learned powerful lessons about how to deal with their own intense temperaments. Temperament and strong emotions are not an excuse for inappropriate actions. Taking into account a person's natural tendencies simply provides perspective, guides your responses, and reminds you that your child always needs your love, especially as he struggles to improve his life skills.

POSITIVE DISCIPLINE SKILLS FOR PARENTS AND TEACHERS

Many of the Positive Discipline skills we suggest are appropriate for children of all temperaments, because they invite children to learn cooperation, responsibility, and life skills. However, an understanding of temperament helps us understand why different methods may be more effective, depending on the temperament and needs of an individual child.

For example, a positive time-out, when properly used, can be an encouraging way to help children who need time to calm down and cool off (see Chapter 1). Family meetings and class meetings are essential to help all children learn problem-solving skills and cooperation (see Chapter 16). Asking curiosity questions encourages children to focus on personal accountability as they explore what happened, what caused it to happen, how they feel about it, and what they might choose to do differently next time. Parents and teachers can help children develop into the best people they can be when they understand and respect differences, individuality, and the creativity of each child.

Parents who understand their child's temperament can be knowledgeable consultants to teachers and other people who may be working with that child. For example, if your child is slow to adapt, ask for a conference and explain to the teacher that your child adapts slowly but responds to patience and kind firmness. If your child has a short attention span, find a teacher who appreciates creativity and provides a variety of experiences during the day. Avoid authoritarian teachers who require children to spend a great deal of time sitting still and who punish children who do not conform to expectations. Be sure that it is your child's temperament and not your own that motivates you. You should always be your child's best advocate and supporter.

INDIVIDUALITY AND CREATIVITY

Parents and teachers may not be aware of how they squelch individuality and creativity when they buy in (often subconsciously) to the myth of the perfect child. It is tempting for adults to prefer the "easy" child or to want children to conform to the norms of society. Parental egos often get involved; we worry about what others think and fear that our competency may be questioned if our child isn't "good" in the eyes of others.

One of the primary motivators for Chess and Thomas' study of temperament was the desire to stop society's tendency to blame mothers for the characteristics of their children. Chess and Thomas state, "A child's temperament can actively influence the attitudes and behavior of her parents, other family members, playmates, and teachers, and in turn help to shape their effect on her behavioral development." In this way, the relationship between child and parents is a two-way street, each continuously influencing the other.

An awareness of temperament and of the immense value of individuality and diversity can help parents avoid the criticism and rejection that come from a lack of information and understanding.

LOVING THE CHILD YOU HAVE

Most parents have dreams for their children. You undoubtedly want your child to be healthy and happy, but more than that, you want her to fulfill all the potential you see in her. You may cherish visions of your child as a star athlete or musician, a Nobel Prize–winning scientist, or even (yes, it's true) president of the United States.

Will had dreamed of the day his son would be born. He proudly carried his newborn into a room decorated with pennants and some of Dad's own trophies, and he placed a tiny blue football in the infant's crib. As little Kevin grew, he was signed up for every sport. His dad was never too busy to toss the football or to take some batting practice. Kevin played tee-ball with the other five-year-olds and soccer with the youngsters' league. He had a miniature basketball hoop and a perfectly oiled baseball glove. His dad never missed a practice or a game.

There was only one problem: Kevin hated sports. He did his best, but he had little natural ability and he loathed competition. Alone in his room, he dreamed of being an actor or a comedian, of standing on a stage before smiling, applauding people. He lined up his stuffed animals and told his favorite stories and jokes, hearing in his mind the enthusiastic responses. He regaled his neighborhood buddies with tall tales.

As Will talked eagerly to his son about "the majors," Kevin only sighed. Shattering his dad's dreams would take more courage than he possessed; he was afraid of losing his father's love and approval. So he played on, growing just a little more discouraged with every game, feeling disappointed that he would never be the son his father really wanted.

Does Will love his son? Undoubtedly. But one of the most beautiful ways of expressing love for a child is learning to love *that* child—not the child you wish you had. All parents have dreams for their children, and dreaming is not a bad thing. If we are to encourage our children, though, and build their sense of self-esteem and belonging, we must take time to teach and encourage their dreams—not our own.

WORK FOR IMPROVEMENT, NOT PERFECTION

Even with understanding and the best intentions, most parents struggle occasionally with their children's temperaments and behavior, especially when they lose patience, focus on their own ego, or get hooked into reacting to behavior instead of acting thoughtfully. You and your children are all too human: you will have good days and days when you're just cranky. Awareness and understanding do not mean you become perfect; mistakes are inevitable. However, once you have had time to cool off after you make a mistake, you need to resolve it with your child. Children are usually more than willing to hug and offer forgiveness, especially when they know you'll do the same for them. It is important to help your child work for improvement, not perfection; you can give this gift to yourself as well.

KINDNESS AND FIRMNESS

Rudolf Dreikurs believed it was most effective for parents and teachers to use kindness and firmness with children. An understanding of temperament shows just how important this is. Kindness shows respect for the child and his uniqueness; firmness shows respect for the needs of the situation. By understanding and respecting your child's temperament, you will be able to help him reach his full potential as a capable, confident, contented person. And there's a bonus: you will probably get a lot more rest, laugh more, and learn a great deal about yourself and your child in the process.

7

"DON'T TALK TO ME IN THAT TONE OF VOICE"

Emotions and the Art of Communication

Feelings can be such bewildering things, and a preschooler's world is a riot of feelings. Take a moment sometime and watch your child try to deal with frustration or anger. She may throw a toy across the room, stamp her foot, make demands, fall over backward in a tantrum, or collapse in a flood of tears. In fact, she may do all of the above within the span of a few minutes.

It is difficult enough for adults to cope with emotions, but for young children there is an added wrinkle: they haven't yet learned exactly what emotions are or how to identify and talk about them, let alone how to cope with them effectively. And of course, it doesn't help when adults tell children they shouldn't feel the way they feel. "Quit acting like that" is easily interpreted as "Don't feel like that."

Understanding and communicating with your child means deciphering her nonverbal clues, understanding what she is feeling, and helping her to understand it as well. It means teaching her that what she *feels* is always okay, but what she *does* may not be okay. In other words, it is okay to be angry at her baby brother, but it is not okay to hit him. Learning to recognize and deal with your child's feelings is a vitally important step in understanding her behavior and beliefs about her world.

WHAT ARE EMOTIONS?

Researchers who study the human brain have discovered an interesting truth: emotions are far more than just unruly impulses that flood children and adults from time to time. Emotions are generated by the limbic system and are actually the energy that fuels the human brain. Feelings are your barometer, a way of knowing whether you are safe and comfortable or need some sort of help or support. Feelings are intended to give you valuable information; in fact, some of them, like fear, protect you from foolish actions. Paying attention to your feelings can help you decide what to do or let you know that you need to make changes. Human beings access vitally important information when they learn to tune in to the deeper message feelings convey, instead of suppressing them.

Young children have the same emotions their parents and teachers do. There is one significant difference, however. As you learned in Chapter 4, the prefrontal cortex (which is responsible for emotional regulation) does not fully develop until the age of twenty-five. Learning to identify and manage feelings is a process that will take your child many years; as in so many other areas of parenting, she will need your patience, understanding, and kind, firm teaching.

Just as they learn other things in life, children learn to cope with their feelings by watching adults. (Remember, you and your child both have mirror neurons, which makes it easy for you to "catch" each other's feelings.) All too often, parents deal with difficult feelings either through emotional displays or by squelching them entirely. You may believe you have hidden the feelings you refuse to express, but they still affect you and those around you, and the results usually are more damaging than if the feelings had been appropriately expressed early on.

Actually, feelings themselves don't cause problems. Certain *actions* (or a failure to act at all) may cause problems. Some people put feelings in the same category as emotional displays. A temper tantrum is an emotional display; acting depressed may be an emotional display. A feeling, though, is simply a feeling. And everyone, whatever his or her age, has feelings.

TEACHING CHILDREN THE DIFFERENCE BETWEEN FEELINGS AND ACTIONS

It's important to help children identify their feelings and express them appropriately. Children (and adults) need to learn that feelings are different from actions. Many adults struggle with acknowledging and expressing their feelings. It often seems easier (or more polite) to simply repress feelings, although those feelings often leak out in the form of anger or depression. This mistaken pattern of denying feelings often is passed on to children. Consider this familiar exchange: An angry child says, "I hate my brother!" An adult responds, "No, you don't. You know you love your brother." It would be more helpful to say to the child, "I can see how angry and hurt you feel right now. I can't let you kick your brother, but maybe we can find a way to help you express your feelings in a way that doesn't hurt anyone."

Young children often choose inappropriate ways to express their feelings, not because they're "bad" or malicious but because they don't know what to do with those tidal waves of emotion that wash over them. Let's look at how you can teach your child to accept and understand her feelings and to express emotions in ways that not only will help her feel better but will help her find solutions to the problems she encounters in life.

LEARNING TO FEEL

Feelings are the language of energy. The very word *emotion* has as its base the word *motion;* our feelings and emotions do move us, mentally, verbally, or physically. The energy of emotions can be positive or negative. You can't see energy or hear it (even though you can feel it), and for this reason some people try to ignore it (and teach their children to ignore it). This is unwise, because the energy of feelings can give you valuable information when you learn to trust it. Adults and children express emotional energy on their faces, in their voices, and in the way they move or stand. (In this sense, you can see it.) Because preschoolers are still developing their language skills, they trust the message of this nonverbal communication far more than they do mere words.

Three-year-old Kyle scampers into the kitchen where Linda, his mother, late for a meeting, is preparing dinner.

"Look, Mommy, look—I drew an airplane!" Kyle bubbles, waving his paper excitedly.

"That's great, sweetie. You're quite an artist," his harried mother replies without glancing up.

Linda undoubtedly means well, and there is certainly nothing wrong with her words, but Kyle notices that her hands never stop grating cheese for the casserole and her eyes never quite look at his airplane. What message has Kyle really received?

Five-year-old Wendy is helping her dad make lunch. Wendy's little brother is cranky, and Dad is trying to watch the football game on television while he makes the grilled cheese sandwiches. Wendy is valiantly pouring milk when the heavy carton slips from her grasp, sending a half gallon of foamy liquid across the kitchen floor.

Wendy looks up timidly into her father's face. "I'm sorry, Daddy," she says. "Are you mad?"

Dad's eyebrows lower ominously, his jaw tightens, and when he speaks his voice is thin and tense. "No, I'm not mad," he says. When Wendy bursts into tears, he wonders why.

Ms. Santos is reading a nap-time story to her class of four-year-olds. She hasn't had a break because her replacement didn't show up and no substitute teacher is available. Little Allie looks at her teacher and asks, "Don't you like this story?"

Ms. Santos looks at Allie in surprise and answers, "Of course I do. Why?"

Allie answers, "Because your face is all scrunched up."

THE POWER OF NONVERBAL COMMUNICATION

As your child grows and develops, you need to be constantly aware of the messages you are sending him—and whether your words and your actions agree. Children notice what we do, even more than what we say. For instance, saying "I love you" may not be the most effective way to communicate that message to your child. Saying the words often (and meaning them) is important, but words alone won't communicate this vital message to your young child.

Eye Contact

Try an experiment sometime. Stand back to back with someone and try to tell him or her about something that happened to you or explain how you're feeling. If you're like most people, you'll find yourself wanting to crane your neck and turn around to look your partner in the eye.

In Western cultures, eye contact signals attention. A good public speaker will catch the gaze of audience members and by doing so will involve them in what he or she is saying. In the same way, making eye contact with your child signals to him that he is important, captures his attention, and increases the effectiveness of your message.

Unfortunately, parents often reserve eye contact primarily for certain occasions. Can you guess what those are? Adults tend to make direct eye contact with children most often when they are angry or lecturing them, saving their most powerful communication for their most negative messages. Toni Morrison once asked a poignant question on an *Oprah* show: do your eyes light up when your child walks into the room?

It is important to recognize that in some cultures, making direct eye contact is regarded as a sign of disrespect. One teacher thought a child was being "sneaky" by avoiding eye contact but changed her mind once she understood the respect this young child's lack of eye contact conveyed in his native culture. Her attitude shifted and she communicated far more effectively with this child and his family when she understood the message his lack of eye contact conveyed.

Posture and Position

Making eye contact with your child may not be as simple as it sounds. Without help, your child will tend to look you right in the knees! If you want to communicate, get down on his level. Kneel next to him, sit beside him on the sofa, or (as long as you hold on to him) set him on a counter where his eyes can meet yours comfortably. Now, not only can you maintain eye contact while you speak to him, but you've eliminated the sometimes overpowering difference in size and height. Also, watch out for the signals your posture sends: crossed arms or legs, for example, can indicate resistance or hostility. Your child will be quick to notice.

> *Susan was trying to coax her daughter, Michele, into sharing what was upsetting her.*
>
> *"Come on, honey," Susan said gently, "I really want to help."*
>
> *Michele hesitated, then said, "But you might get mad at me."*
>
> *Susan smiled encouragingly and replied, "Michele, I promise I won't get mad. I care about you, and I want you to be able to tell me anything."*

Michele thought for a moment, then looked up into her mother's face. "I'll tell you if you promise not to look at me with your lips all tight."

Poor Susan—she was trying hard to be unconditionally accepting and loving. Her daughter, however, was able to read the body language that betrayed her true feelings. When Susan's words and her expression match consistently, Michele will feel more comfortable talking openly with her mother.

Tone of Voice

Your tone of voice may be the most powerful nonverbal tool of all. Try saying a simple sentence, such as "I can't help you," emphasizing a different word each time. How does the meaning change? Even inoffensive phrases like "Have a nice day" can become poisonous if you choose a particularly cold tone of voice. It is often the way you say something, rather than the words you use, that carries the message. Remember, children are especially sensitive to the nuances of nonverbal communications.

Facial Expressions and Touch

When you're feeling particularly blue, does it help when a friend smiles and gives you a pat on the shoulder or a friendly hug? The way you look at your child and the way you use your hands can communicate very effectively without a single word being spoken.

Tommy is curled up on the couch under a blanket, suffering from a bad case of the flu. Dad walks by, adjusts the blanket, and gently ruffles Tommy's hair.

Has anything been communicated? Chances are Tommy knows without words that his dad cares about him, wants to help, and hopes he'll soon feel better.

Let's go back to where we started. How might you say "I love you" to your child now? Imagine how powerful it will feel if you kneel in

The Elements of Nonverbal Communication

- Eye contact
- Posture and position
- Tone of voice
- Facial expression and touch

front of him, look him directly in the eye, smile, and in your warmest tone of voice say, "I love you." Now the words and nonverbal cues match up—and a big hug may be on the way! Nonverbal communication teaches children about connection, feelings, and, eventually, the words that go with them.

THE ART OF ACTIVE LISTENING

Active (or reflective) listening is another effective tool of communication, one that will serve you well as you parent your child and (sooner than you may think) the adolescent that child will become. Active listening is the art of observing and listening to feelings, then reflecting them back. Active listening does not require that you *agree* with your child's feelings, but it allows your child to feel connected and understood—something all people need—and provides an opportunity to explore and clarify those mysterious impulses known as emotions.

Four-year-old Chrissy ran through the front door, slamming it so forcefully that the pictures rattled on the wall, and promptly burst into tears. "Tammy took my ball," she wailed. "I hate her!" Then Chrissy threw herself onto the sofa in a storm of sobs.

Her mom, Diane, looked up from the bills she was paying. Resisting the impulse to scold Chrissy for slamming the door, she said quietly, "You seem pretty angry, kiddo."

Chrissy pondered for a moment. "Mom," she said plaintively, sniffling a little, "Tammy is bigger than me. It isn't fair for her to take away my stuff."

"It must be pretty frustrating to be picked on by a big girl," Diane said, still focusing on reflecting her daughter's feelings.

"Yeah. I'm mad," the little girl said firmly. "I don't want to

play with her anymore." She sat quietly for a moment, watching as Diane put stamps on envelopes. "Mom, can I go play out in the backyard?"

Diane gave her daughter a hug—and a great deal more.

By simply reflecting back her daughter's underlying feelings (active listening), Diane refrained from lecturing, rescuing, or discounting her daughter's feelings. She allowed Chrissy the opportunity to explore what was going on for her, and in the process, Chrissy discovered a solution to her own problem. Some other time, Diane might be able to talk with Chrissy about avoiding future problems—and perhaps ask her what she could do to express her anger instead of slam the door.

Diane also showed respect for her daughter's feelings. Parents often do not agree with (or completely understand) their children's emotions, but active listening does not require you to agree or completely understand. It invites children to feel heard and lets them know it's okay to feel whatever they feel. Validating a child's feelings with love and understanding opens the door for real connection and problem solving and works toward building a lifelong relationship of love and trust.

Pretend these statements are made by a child. How would you respond?

- "No! I won't take a nap!"

- "I want a bottle like the baby has."

- "I hate going to the doctor."

- "Nobody will let me play with them."

Parents sometimes respond with "adultisms" like these: "How come you never . . . ?" "When will you ever . . . ?" or "How many times do I have to tell you . . . ?" Parents often try to argue a child out of her feelings in hopes of changing her mind or helping her feel better. These attempts may sound like this:

- "Of course you need your nap—you've been up since six. When will you learn that you need to rest?"

- "Don't be silly. Only babies use bottles. You're a big boy now."

- "I keep telling you, you have to go to the doctor to feel better."

- "Why sweetie, you know you have lots of friends. What about . . ."

Each of these examples may leave the child feeling misunderstood and defensive—with the likely result of an argument and frustration for both of you.

Active listening might sound like this:

- "You look disappointed that you have to stop playing with your toys. You were having a lot of fun."

- "Sounds like you're feeling left out in all the fuss over your new baby sister. Is there more you can tell me?"

- "Sometimes I feel a little afraid of going to the doctor, too."

- "You seem pretty sad about being ignored by the older kids."

These responses make no judgments and open the door for children to go further in exploring their feelings. Asking "Is there more?" indicates a willingness to listen and may help a child discover deeper, buried feelings.

Like most adults, sometimes all children really need is for someone to listen and understand. Active listening will help your child learn about his own feelings (and appropriate ways to express them) and will help you focus on what's really important.

WHAT ABOUT ANGER? DEALING WITH DIFFICULT FEELINGS

Like adults, children feel angry and frustrated from time to time. After all, there is so much that a young child cannot understand or do.

Unfortunately, young children do not yet have the skills or maturity to express anger and frustration in ways that are acceptable to adults—which is why angry children are usually viewed as misbehaving children. Adults and children alike need to find acceptable, positive ways of dealing with feelings, even the difficult ones.

When you become angry or extremely emotional, an interesting thing happens in your brain. The prefrontal cortex—the part responsible for emotional regulation, impulse control, and good judgment—essentially "disconnects," leaving you with physical sensations and feelings. (This is commonly known as "losing it," something all parents experience eventually!) Remember, mirror neurons make it easy to catch strong emotions; when you lose it your child is likely to do the same—and vice versa. It is impossible to solve problems effectively without your prefrontal cortex, which is why it is so important to take a positive time-out to cool off *before* attempting to deal with problems.

When a child becomes angry, adults usually call it a "tantrum." Offering a hug or a positive time-out (and understanding that a young child simply can't deal with strong emotions in a mature manner yet) is a helpful first step. Sometimes it is most helpful to simply allow a child

The Importance of Emotional Literacy

Michael Thompson, Dan Kindlon, William Pollock, and other researchers have discovered that while no child is born with an "emotional vocabulary," it may be especially important for parents to use words that describe emotions with their sons. Boys often develop emotional skills more slowly than do girls; in addition, Western culture often labels feelings such as fear, sadness, or loneliness as "weak" and encourages boys to suppress them. Using simple, accurate language to reflect and describe emotions teaches your child to identify what he feels and enables him—with time and practice—to use words rather than behavior to express them.

to feel angry (without rescuing or trying to "fix" her feelings) until the anger dissipates. Later you can follow up with curiosity questions to help your child understand her feelings and figure out solutions.

There is more parents and caregivers can do to respond to a child's anger than simply responding to tantrums. After she has calmed down, you can teach your child to notice why she becomes angry. You can also help her recognize that anger is a deeply physical emotion and help her develop ways to cope with it.

HOW TO HELP YOUR CHILD RECOGNIZE AND MANAGE FEELINGS

Here are some ways you might help a young child explore and express strong emotions.

- Invite the child to draw a picture of how the emotion feels. Does it have a color? A sound?

- Ask the child to talk through rather than act out what she is feeling. Because most children are not consciously aware of their feelings and may lack words to describe them accurately, you might try asking simple yes-or-no questions about the feelings: "Sounds like you might be feeling hurt and want to get even." "Are you having a hard time holding your anger inside?" "When you don't get what you want, does it make you so angry you can hardly stand it?" When you are correct in guessing her feelings, your child will feel validated and relieved at being understood.

- Ask the child what she notices happening in her body when she gets really angry. Because anger triggers physical reactions (adrenaline is released, heart rate and respiration increase, blood vessels expand, and so on), most people actually feel anger *physically*. If your child reports that her fists clench, or she feels a knot in her stomach, or her face feels hot (all common responses), you can work together to help her recognize when she's getting really angry and provide ways to cool off before anger gets out of control. (Adults, too, can benefit from paying attention to their body's cues.)

- Keep a feelings faces chart handy and refer to it with your child, asking, "Does one of these faces show how you feel?"

- Provide an acceptable way to deal with anger. You may help your child express her feelings physically by running around the yard, punching a "bop bag," or even pretending to be a ferocious dinosaur. (Stay nearby to talk through those strong feelings as your child expresses them.) Some preschools have an "anger box," a knee-high cardboard box where an angry child can go to stand, jump, or yell when upset. Sometimes the teachers use it, too! Screaming into a pillow or playing with Play-Doh can also help vent emotions and restore calm.

- Teach a slow-breathing technique. One of the handiest tools of all is that of slow, focused breathing, something a child (or adult) can do anytime and anywhere. Practice breathing in and out while counting slowly to four each time you inhale and exhale. Do this for several breaths. An older child can learn to take his pulse and discover how slow breathing actually slows his heartbeat, too. What an exciting and empowering discovery!

- Ask the child if it will help her to take a positive time-out to cool off before acting on her strong emotions. (This is effective only if the child understands the concept of a positive time-out, as explained in Chapter 1.) You can go to time-out with your child or on your own, as an extra display of support or because you need it, too.

- Use books and pictures to initiate discussions about anger and other emotions. Two excellent books on anger and emotions are *Bombaloo* by Rachel Vail, Scholastic, 2002, and *The Way I Feel* by Janan Cain, Parenting Press, 2000. Pictures of other people displaying different feelings is helpful because it teaches children to recognize facial and body language cues—which help in the development of empathy—as well as to name those feelings. It also helps children to identify their own emotions and accompanying body signals. (This technique is best when you and your child are calm and can talk together about what you learn.)

- Help your child create an anger wheel of choice. Then he can choose something from the wheel that he feels would help him express his anger in a nondestructive manner. Use any of the ideas listed below or add your own.

- Let your child have the last word. It isn't helpful to try to talk a child out of her feelings or to try to fix things for her. Have faith in your child; let her feelings run their course and, when she is calm, focus on teaching skills so she can look for solutions to her problems.

Anger isn't the only difficult emotion young children must learn to deal with. By practicing active listening, taking time to understand, and using some of the ideas above, adults can also help children deal honestly with jealousy, fear, sadness, and all of the other emotions that are a part of human existence.

Conflicts have a way of escalating quickly when many small children are involved. Teachers may find it helpful to practice ways of defusing anger or to allow groups of children to play Let's Pretend about what happens when they feel angry. Talking in advance about emotions and actively teaching skills to manage them can give everyone, children and teachers alike, a plan to follow when strong feelings erupt. A classroom anger wheel of choice is a helpful tool to model and discuss appropriate behaviors and to provide ideas for coping with this strong emotion.

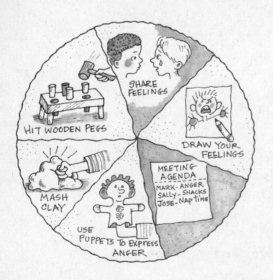

PRACTICING EMOTIONAL HONESTY

Parents (and teachers) often wonder how much of their own feelings they should share with children. As with so many things in life, children learn best by watching their adult role models. The way you manage (or fail to manage) your own emotions sends a strong message to your child. If you deal with anger by yelling, you shouldn't be surprised if the young ones in your life do, too. If, on the other hand, you can find helpful ways of expressing your own feelings, you will reduce the chance of conflict and provide children with a wonderful example of how to deal appropriately with emotions.

As you have probably discovered, sharing your world with a young child can stimulate all sorts of interesting emotions in you. In the course of a single day, a parent or teacher can feel love, warmth, frustration, anger, irritation, weariness, hope, and despair. Children are amazingly sensitive to the emotional state of those around them; their mirror neurons and ability to read nonverbal cues often let them know what you're feeling even when you think you're acting "normal." So, how should adults explain and express their feelings to children?

Emotional honesty is often the best policy. It is not only okay but may also be real wisdom to tell a child, calmly and respectfully, "I'm feeling really angry right now." Notice the word *you* is missing from this statement. This is very different from saying "You make me so angry." Blaming or shaming statements aren't necessary; simply explaining to your child what you're feeling and why can help you deal with your own feelings and teach your child about possible results of his own behavior. Remember, too, that young children are egocentric at this age and often assume that whatever you're feeling is about them. Explaining your feelings and the reasons for them may save you and your child a great deal of misunderstanding and confusion.

One helpful way of expressing feelings is by using "I statements." An "I statement" in a simple formula such as "I feel _____ about _____ because _____, and therefore _____" (Formulas come in handy when you're too emotional to think straight.) allows you to explain what you're feeling and why.

An "I statement" might look something like this:

- "I feel worried when blocks are thrown in the playroom, because one of the other children might get hurt. Would it help you to take some time out until you have calmed down, or do you have another solution to this problem?"

- "I feel angry when cereal is dumped on the floor, because I'm tired and I don't want to clean up the mess. If cereal is dumped on the floor again, I'll know you've decided not to eat and you can either put away your bowl or I will do so for you."

- "I feel upset and frustrated because the car has a flat tire, and now I'm going to be late to work."

- "I'm so angry right now that I need some time out until I can calm down, so I don't do or say something I'll regret later."

Parents and teachers also can practice separating a child from his sometimes inappropriate behavior. You can reassure your child about his place in your affections and encourage his efforts to understand his world, while still teaching him that certain behaviors or actions are not acceptable. For example:

- "I love you, and I can't allow you to kick me when you're angry."

- "I'm glad you want to learn about the kitchen, and you can't melt your crayons on the stove."

- "I appreciate your help, and you're not quite old enough to fix the vacuum cleaner."

(Remember, action is a more effective teaching tool with young children than words. If your child is at risk of injury or harm, act first—with kindness and firmness—then talk later.)

"SHOULD I PROTECT MY CHILD FROM SADNESS OR WORRY?"

Adults sometimes feel the need to shield children from sadness, loss, and the other unpleasant realities of life, but it is usually best to be as honest with your child as you reasonably can be. As we've mentioned, children usually know when something in the family is amiss, and without enough information, they may assume they have done something wrong. Because of their egocentricity, children are quite ready to believe that they cause bad things to happen. Children shouldn't be asked to shoulder burdens too heavy for them or to take responsibility for their parents' problems, but they can be given an opportunity to understand and share in whatever is going on. This draws children into the family circle and helps build in them a sense of belonging and connection.

If a family member or loved pet has died, it is best to provide a child with information that will help him make sense of what has happened. It is tempting to tell a young child that Grandpa is "sleeping" or has "gone away," but that may lead a child to fear going to bed or to wonder whether Mom or Dad will also "go away" unexpectedly. Death can be explained in simple but honest terms and children can be helped to grieve and to heal. (Yes, children grieve, although their grief sometimes resembles irritability rather than sadness.) It isn't necessary to tell children more than they can comprehend. You may want to explain that many adults also have difficulty understanding death, and many people have different beliefs about what it means and what happens afterward. Including children in the rituals surrounding death, such as funerals, may actually be less frightening for them than being left out. Death is part of the cycle of life; treating it as such will make coping with death easier for parents and children alike.

In the same way, if the family is undergoing financial strain or other stresses, parents can give children simple facts to help them understand and then use active listening to explore and deal with their feelings. Be aware that children will have strong feelings and reactions to traumatic events in the family, such as divorce, and it is unwise to simply assume that they'll be "fine." Take time to explain, without blaming or judging, what has happened and how it will affect your child. Be sure she knows that it wasn't her fault and that she is loved and cherished. And stay tuned in; use active listening to check your child's perceptions and allow her to express her fears and feelings openly. (For more information on helping children cope with death or divorce, see *Positive Discipline for Single Parents* by Jane Nelsen, Cheryl Erwin, and Carol Delzer, Three Rivers Press, 1999; *Positive Discipline A–Z*, Three Rivers Press, 2006; and "A Time to Laugh, a Time to Cry: The Grieving Process" in *Top Ten Preschool Parenting Problems* by Roslyn Ann Duffy, Exchange Press, 2007.)

By including young children in the life of the family, parents help them learn about feelings and what it means to be human. By exploring and respecting your children's feelings and by being honest about your own feelings, you will build a relationship of trust and connection, along with problem-solving skills that will last a lifetime.

THE TIME YOU SPEND

Another way in which parents communicate love and caring is by how they spend their time. Your child needs to know that you consider her important enough to spend time on—and it doesn't take large doses of time to do this. Spending regular, focused one-on-one time with a child, something we call "special time," is one of the most important things you can do for your child. Few things say "I love you" as well as time spent alone and involved.

Because "special time" is so powerful, we really can't emphasize the need for it enough. No one—adult or child—ever outgrows the need to spend time with those they love.

IT'S NEVER TOO SOON TO BEGIN

"My parents just don't understand me."

"I want to talk to my kid about sex and drugs, but I don't know how."

"I worry that my teenagers are getting into trouble, but they don't seem to trust me . . . I just don't get it."

"I would never tell my parents what my friends and I do—they'd only lose it. We just never talk at all."

Many teenagers—and many parents of teenagers—wish things could be different; they wish they could understand and trust each other enough to talk openly about the choices and issues that face them. All too often, regardless of how much they may love one another, they simply can't. They can't trust each other; they don't understand each other. While it's never too late to change, it certainly is harder the longer you wait.

If you're fortunate enough to be the parent of a young child, you have a golden opportunity. The best time to begin building a relationship of trust and openness isn't after your child has become an adolescent and you suddenly realize how serious the issues are; the time is *now,* while he's young. Time spent talking to your child, listening to his daydreams and thoughts and feelings, teaching him about life, and simply being human together is an investment in the future you will never regret.

If you are a preschool teacher, remember that the time your young students spend with you shapes the way they view their world—you truly do touch the future when you teach young children. For parents and teachers alike, taking the time to understand emotions and to express them in positive ways will help you build relationships where love and trust can flourish.

8

"WHY DOES MY CHILD DO THAT?"

The Messages of Misbehavior

Understanding your preschooler's development and filling your toolbox with Positive Discipline parenting tools will go a long way toward resolving conflicts with your young child. It also helps to know that temperament, birth order, brain development, physical and intellectual abilities, and skill acquisition underlie much of your child's behavior in these early years. Still, even the most delightful preschooler isn't perfect, and misbehavior can be frustrating. Why *do* children misbehave? And what should parents do about it?

Carly is playing happily on the floor while her mom pays the bills. The phone rings, Carly's mom answers—and suddenly Carly is glued to her mother's leg, whining for juice. No amount of whispered urging will make Carly return to her play. Why?

Alberto knows that brushing his teeth is part of his bedtime routine. He also knows that this procedure is extremely important to his father. When Alberto's dad approaches with a loaded brush, Alberto folds his arms, furrows his brow, and clamps his mouth tightly shut. Alberto's dad threatens, pleads, and brushes Alberto's lips, but Alberto keeps his mouth tightly closed. Why?

Are these children misbehaving? Well, it certainly seems so. Most parents have experienced moments like these and have struggled to find a solution. As you will learn, before you can help your child choose different behavior, you must understand why your child is behaving this way, and what he is trying to accomplish with his behavior.

Behavior actually is a coded message that reveals a child's underlying beliefs about himself and about life. When your child misbehaves, he is telling you in the only way he knows that (at least for the moment) he is feeling discouraged, or that he doesn't belong. As you learn to decipher the code, you will find that your responses (and eventually, your child's behavior) will change.

There is a parable that urges us to walk a mile in someone else's shoes before we condemn or criticize his actions. When you can get into your child's world (and walk in his small shoes), his behavior may begin to make sense.

WHAT IS MISBEHAVIOR?

Parents sometimes view any atypical behavior as misbehavior. For just a moment, put yourself in your child's place; make an effort to get into his world.

Four-year-old Richard was at home with his mom, recuperating from the chicken pox. Mom had had to take a few days off from work and needed to spend some time on the phone keeping up with business. One afternoon, after a particularly long phone call, she walked into Richard's room and found him absorbed in using the permanent marking pens. The imaginative little boy had looked at his chicken pox spots and been reminded of his dot-to-dot coloring book. Richard had removed his clothes and was busily drawing lines from one spot to the next with the marking pens. He was covered with brightly colored lines connecting his red spots.

Richard's mom was wise enough to realize that this was not misbehavior. He was not trying to get attention or make a mess; he was being wonderfully creative. Richard had discovered that his body looked like a large dot-to-dot drawing, so he had simply connected the dots! What did his mom do? She let her sense of humor take over. She went and got the washable markers and finished connecting the dots with him.

It would have been easy for Mom to scold and humiliate Richard. The entire event could have disintegrated into tears and misery. Instead, Mom made room for one of childhood's treasured moments. When Richard is a dad himself, sitting with his children around Grandma's table telling "Remember when . . ." stories, Richard and his mom will both laugh as they remember Richard's dot-to-dot chicken pox! And as they laugh, they can re-create that moment of fun and love shared long ago.

When three-and-a-half-year-old Elsie's dad picked her up from preschool one evening, he immediately noticed that Elsie's hair was significantly shorter in the front than it had been that morning. "Did someone cut Elsie's hair today?" the perplexed father asked Elsie's teacher.

"No, she did that herself," the teacher replied. "Elsie has been practicing a lot with the safety scissors lately."

Was Elsie misbehaving? When Dad entered Elsie's world, he realized that Elsie was actively exploring the wonders of using scissors. Today she had discovered that hair could be cut. Dad may not like his daughter's new hairstyle, and he will surely explain to Elsie that he would prefer that she not cut her own (or anyone else's) hair. He might also tell his intrepid daughter, "Let's find some things you can cut." This dad knows that Elsie's experiment was a learning experience. Hair grows back. Elsie made a mistake, and her dad helped her to learn from it.

Both of these children were behaving in ways that are developmentally appropriate—and quite creative. Yet it would have been easy to interpret both situations as misbehavior.

So how do you know when a behavior is misbehavior? The key is discouragement. Children who feel discouraged about their ability to belong are more likely to misbehave. Neither Richard nor Elsie was discouraged; instead, they were exploring the world around them (and their parents and teachers should probably supervise the use of permanent markers and scissors).

Richard's behavior might have been misbehavior if he had wanted his mother to play with him rather than talk on the phone. His behavior then might have been intended to get attention or power, as a mistaken way to feel belonging. As you have learned, one of the primary human needs is the need to belong, to feel a sense of worth and significance. When a child believes he doesn't belong, he feels discouraged. Out of that discouragement he chooses what Rudolf Dreikurs, author of *Children: The Challenge* (New York, 1991), called a "mistaken goal of misbehavior." They are considered "mistaken" goals because the child mistakenly believes the behavior will help him regain a sense of belonging. You may view misbehavior differently when you recognize that a misbehaving child is simply a discouraged child who wants to belong and has a mistaken idea about how to achieve this goal.

MISBEHAVIOR OR CODED MESSAGE?

Three-year-old Maggie is visiting her grandparents' house on Thanksgiving, with all the other aunts, cousins, and members of her family. When Grandma goes to see what's taking Maggie so long in the bathroom, she finds Maggie tearing a roll of toilet paper to shreds.

Is Maggie misbehaving? It would be understandable if her grandmother's first response was anger.

Getting into a child's world is a bit like looking through a kaleidoscope. Pretend that you are Maggie's grandmother. What do you see when you look through the kaleidoscope? You may see piles of shredded paper everywhere, tinged by the red glow of your own anger. Now turn the kaleidoscope slightly and look again. Look at Maggie, who has just been chased away from the kitchen because she was underfoot. Look at Maggie, who just got told by her big sister, Joan, that she was too little to play Monopoly with Joan and her older cousins. Look at Maggie, who wanted to show Grandpa how to do Itsy Bitsy Spider but was abandoned when he had to go help move chairs into the dining room. What might Maggie really be saying with her toilet paper? How is she really feeling? What might stop Maggie from further acts of destruction?

How do you suppose most adults would react to Maggie's behavior? What would you do? Does understanding what Maggie's world feels like just now influence your response?

Understanding Maggie's world does not mean that deliberately making a mess is okay. But understanding some of what Maggie is experiencing is likely to affect how her grandmother responds. Maggie will still have to pick up all the tiny bits of paper. Armed with love and understanding, Grandma may be more likely to help Maggie pick up the pieces and maybe invite her to help roll out pie dough afterward.

MISTAKEN GOAL CHART

The child's goal is:	If the parent/teacher feels:	And tends to react by:	And if the child's response is:	The belief behind the child's behavior is:	Coded messages:	Parent/teacher proactive and empowering responses include:
Undue attention (to keep others busy or to get special service)	Annoyed Irritated Worried Guilty	Reminding Coaxing Doing things for the child he/she could do for him/herself	Stops temporarily, but later resumes same or another disturbing behavior	I count (belong) only when I'm being noticed or getting special service. I'm only important when I'm keeping you busy with me.	**Notice me— involve me usefully**	Redirect by involving child in a useful task. "I love you and _____." (Example: I care about you and will spend time with you later."); redirect by assigning a task so child can gain useful attention; avoid special service; plan special time; set up routines; use problem solving; encourage; use family/class meetings; touch without words; ignore; set up nonverbal signals.
Misguided power (to be boss)	Challenged Threatened Defeated	Fighting Giving in Thinking "You can't get away with it" or "I'll"	Intensifies behavior Defiant compliance Feels he/she's won when	I belong only when I'm boss, in control, or proving no one can boss me. You can't make me.	**Let me help— give me choices**	Redirect to positive power by asking for help; offer limited choices; don't fight and don't give in; withdraw from conflict; be firm and kind; act, don't talk; decide

Goal	The parent/teacher feels	and tends to react by	And if the child's response is	The belief behind the behavior	Coded message	Parents/teachers can
		make you" Wanting to be right right	parent/teacher is upset Passive power			what you will do; let routines be the boss; leave and calm down; develop mutual respect; set a few reasonable limits; practice follow-through; encourage; use family/class meetings.
Revenge (to get even)	Hurt Disappointed Disbelieving Disgusted	Retaliating Getting even Thinking "How could you do this to me?"	Retaliates Intensifies Escalates the same behavior or chooses another weapon	I don't think I belong so I'll hurt others as I feel hurt. I can't be liked or loved.	**I'm hurting—validate my feelings**	Acknowledge hurt feelings; avoid feeling hurt; avoid punishment and retaliation; build trust; use active listening; share your feelings; make amends; show you care; act, don't talk; encourage strengths; put kids in same boat; use family/class meetings.
Assumed inadequacy (to give up and be left alone)	Despair Hopeless Helpless Inadequate	Giving up Doing for Overhelping	Retreats further Passive No improvement No response	I can't belong because I'm not perfect, so I'll convince others not to expect anything of me; I am helpless and unable; it's no use trying because I won't do it right.	**Don't give up on me— show me a small step**	Break task down to small steps; stop all criticism; encourage any positive attempt; have faith in child's abilities; focus on assets; don't pity; don't give up; set up opportunities for success; teach skills/show how, but don't do for; enjoy the child; build on his/her interests; encourage, encourage, encourage; use family/class meetings. Empathize with child.

Misbehaving children are discouraged children, and encouragement is like rain to their parched souls. It is important to create opportunities to help children feel encouraged and valuable, to let them know they belong.

Let's turn the kaleidoscope together and take a closer look at the four coded messages of discouraged children.

BREAKING THE CODE

If you can learn to read the code behind your child's behavior in different situations, you can deal effectively with his *beliefs* instead of just the behavior itself. There are three specific clues that will help you break the code. Let's examine the clues that help you decode the message behind a child's misbehavior—and, finally, what to do that will encourage your child and change his behavior.

Your Own Feelings in Response to the Behavior
How *you* feel in response to a child's misbehavior is the first important clue to understanding the child's mistaken goal. For instance, when the child's goal is undue attention, her actions invite adults to feel annoyed, irritated, worried, or guilty. When a child seeks misguided power, adults usually feel challenged, threatened, or defeated. When the child's mistaken goal is revenge, her actions invite adults to feel hurt, disappointed, disbelieving, or disgusted. When a child is so discouraged that she gives up completely (the mistaken goal of assumed inadequacy), adults also feel inadequate, despairing, hopeless, or helpless.

As you examine the Mistaken Goal Chart on pages 144 and 145, you can usually find one set of feelings in the second column that best describes your feelings when faced with a misbehaving child. Note that you don't need to *do* anything about your feelings; simply notice and use them to help you understand your child. Also notice that your child's behavior does not "cause" you to feel a certain way. Your feelings flow from your understanding of your child's behavior. When your understanding changes (and you understand the coded message), your feelings also will change.

Your Usual (Ineffective) Attempts to Stop the Behavior
Another clue is your usual response to your child's behavior. Adults often respond to the behavior of each mistaken goal in predictable ways. For instance, Dad and Ryan are constantly battling over something, whether it's what to wear, how much to eat, or how long Ryan can play at the computer. Their struggles reveal an ongoing battle for power: Dad gives a command, Ryan resists, and Dad reacts by fighting with Ryan, thinking, "You can't get away with this; I'll *make* you do it." Some adults just give in. In either case, there is a power struggle with a winner, a loser, or a slight pause while each side gathers strength and ammunition to continue the battle. The third column of the Mistaken Goal Chart lists the common reactions of adults to each of the four mistaken goals' behaviors.

Your Child's Response to Your Ineffective Action
The next clue in deciphering a child's mistaken goal is how a child responds when the adult tries to stop the misbehavior with punitive or permissive methods (instead of Positive Discipline methods).

When the teacher at his child care center tells five-year-old Matthew, "Behave yourself," Matthew usually responds by damaging his toys or knocking over other children's blocks. Sometimes he even yells, "I hate you!" Matthew's mistaken goal is revenge. The goal is revenge when a child reacts to an adult's actions by hurting others, damaging property, or retaliating in some other way, such as using insulting words.

The fourth column of the Mistaken Goal Chart lists a child's typical responses to ineffective intervention by adults for each mistaken goal behavior.

STICK TO THE SPIRIT OF THE PRINCIPLE

Sometimes it is hard to determine a child's mistaken goal. Don't be overly concerned about getting the "right" answer, and don't get hung up in "analysis paralysis." Observe carefully, and do the best you can. Remember, no one is perfect. Learn to see your mistakes as opportunities to learn and grow.

Behavior never happens in a vacuum (whether you're a child or an adult); there is a message behind the behavior, and the message involves some form of discouragement. No matter what the goal, it is always wise to use encouragement through unconditional love, hugs, patience, and letting children know you have faith in them.

SEEING THE POSSIBILITIES

No matter how hard you try, you will never force someone to change his behavior, at least not more than superficially. And when behavior is tied to deeply held beliefs, those beliefs will have to change before the behavior will. You may be able to make a child stop banging his spoon against his cup by removing the cup, but if that child believes he is important only when he is getting attention, he will surely be banging his leg against the chair within the next five minutes.

Stopping a symptom provides only temporary relief from the condition. When a child's deep need to feel belonging is satisfied, his mistaken method of reaching that goal is no longer necessary. One of the most powerful ways to create a sense of belonging is to spend special time together.

SPECIAL TIME

Since a misbehaving child is a discouraged child, the obvious solution for misbehavior is encouragement. Often it is not necessary to deal with the misbehavior. Instead, help the child feel encouraged and the misbehavior will disappear.

Each of us needs time with those we love. Quality time together affects the health of family relationships ("Family Strengths: Often Overlooked, but Real," by Kristin Anderson Moore, Ph.D., Rosemary Chalk, Juliet Scarpa, and Sharon Vandiver, M.P.P., Child Trends Research Brief, August 2002). What do we mean by special time, and what makes time together special? The three *As* of special time will help you create meaningful special time with your child.

The three *As* of special time are:

- Attitude

- Attention

- Alone

The first *A* is *attitude*. When you begin with an attitude that special time is valuable and worthwhile and you take time to really connect with your child (or other family member), the time you spend together takes on a truly special quality. It is this quality of specialness that will help you create long-remembered and treasured memories. Attitude (yours and your child's) makes special time a powerful tool in strengthening each child's sense of belonging, the sort of feeling that comes from meaningful connection to others. Special time tells a child that he is valued, loved, and appreciated.

The second *A, attention,* means that special time will be more effective when you can focus on being fully present with your child. Special time is a time to engage in an activity without any outside competition for your attention: no other family members, ringing phones, or scheduled commitments. Imagine filling up your child's heart and spirit, as well as your own, with this special sharing of attention and love. Even a trip to the grocery store can become special when you devote your full attention to being together.

The final *A, alone,* underscores the idea that special time is time spent away from other family members, a shared time between one child and one adult. No matter how big or small a family might be, time spent alone with a parent (or aunt, uncle, or grandparent) is a treat.

> *Kim, age five, and her dad call the special day they spend together their "me and Daddy date day." Twice a month Kim gets to spend the day alone with her dad while Mom and her little brother stay behind. Kim and Dad stop at the library, selecting and reading books together; then they head to the hardware store or lumberyard as Kim accompanies Dad on*

errands. They end the day with ice-cream cones at their favorite confectionery. Even though their activities are not focused only on Kim, the attitude they share toward this special time together, Dad's focused attention, and Kim's chance to be alone with Dad make this day one to which they both look forward.

Meanwhile, Mom is home with Kim's younger brother, Frankie, making cookies together. Without his older sister around to push him away or do things he can't do yet, Frankie has the opportunity to learn skills and enjoy special time alone in the kitchen with Mom. Special time can be both simple and wonderful, as Kim and her family's experience so beautifully demonstrates.

The other part of special time is *time*. For busy parents, this may be the most difficult part. Still, a wise person once said that *love* is spelled *t-i-m-e*. Where do we get it? How much or how little is needed? If something is important to you, chances are good that you will find time for it. Even in the busiest of lives, there is time for what matters.

One mother of five reads to each child for ten minutes every night, less than an hour of time spent reading. She cuddles with each child in the rocking chair in the corner of her bedroom while the other children help with after-dinner chores. Each child knows when her ten minutes are coming and is willing to honor the time Mom spends with the others. Interruptions are rare—and Mom gets to spend her evenings lovingly connected with her children instead of all alone in the kitchen, scouring the sink.

PLAN IT AND NAME IT

Special time does not require lots of time, but it is important that it be regarded as special by both of you. You can let your child know you look forward to this as much as she does: "I am glad we can have this special time together" or "It is a special treat for me to go swimming with you." You can validate your child's unique skills: "Isn't it great that you are older and can do so many things now that you couldn't do when you were a baby?" (For an older child still adjusting to the arrival of a new baby, such words will be balm indeed!)

When your child wants some attention and you truly are too busy, it can be comforting to your child when you say, "I can't right now, but I sure am looking forward to our special time at 7:00."

SATISFACTION

Misbehavior requires a lot of energy from both children and adults and generates some pretty intense feelings. Being chased around the playground or carried kicking and screaming to bed might just seem better to a discouraged child than feeling unimportant, unnoticed, and powerless. There are a number of ways to invite a child to form a new belief, depending upon the goal of her behavior. Possible solutions for each mistaken goal are shown in the last column of the Mistaken Goal Chart. (You may find this chart a useful addition to the front of your refrigerator.)

Getting into a child's world will help you interpret the meaning of your child's behavior, especially if you can remember that not all undesirable behavior will be *mis*behavior. When a discouraged child does misbehave, you can practice compassion and discover more effective ways to respond. In the next two chapters we will examine what each of the four mistaken goals looks like at home and in child care settings. When you understand the message behind a child's misbehavior, you will be better able to deal with it in loving and truly effective ways.

9

MISTAKEN GOALS
AT HOME

We've explored some of the reasons children occasionally misbehave. To understand the coded messages behind your child's actions and to work with him effectively, it is helpful to learn to recognize mistaken goals in real life. What do the goals of misbehavior look like in your home? Get out your kaleidoscope and let's give it a twist to see what happens when behavior is viewed from the perspective of the mistaken goals. (Refer to the Mistaken Goals Chart on pages 144 and 145 as you learn.)

UNDUE ATTENTION, OR "I'LL KEEP YOU BUSY WITH ME!"

Mom, Catherine (age seven), and Ann (age five) are in the doctor's office because Catherine has a fever and cough. Mom gets Catherine settled in the waiting room and gently tucks her coat around her. She feels her forehead for fever and tries to help her feel as comfortable as possible. Mom then sits down and begins to look through a magazine. Ann comes over with a children's book she has found and asks her mom to read it to her. Mom says, "Not right now." She reminds Ann that she was up most of the night with Catherine, and now she just wants to look at her magazine.

Ann wanders away, but a few minutes later she begins to bounce up and down on the couch. "Stop bouncing and sit quietly, Ann," Mom calls out. Ann stops bouncing but within minutes she asks if she can sit on Mom's lap. Mom says, "No, of course not. You are much too big a girl for that!" Mom gets up and goes over to Catherine to check on her fever again.

Then they are called into the examining room. As the three of them are waiting for the doctor, Ann complains of a stomachache. Mom looks at her anxiously and feels her forehead. When the doctor arrives to examine Catherine, Ann starts tugging on Mom's sleeve, saying she has to go to the bathroom. Mom sighs loudly, gets up, and takes Ann down the hall to the bathroom.

Ann's behavior certainly annoys her mother. What might Ann believe that prompts her to act this way? Well, Ann has noticed Catherine getting a lot of attention. Ann may have decided that Mom loves Catherine more. It certainly looks that way from her perspective.

How do you think Mom is feeling right now? Annoyed? Irritated? Guilty? She probably wishes she'd left Ann at home. How would Mom feel if she got into Ann's world? What might she do differently?

Ann's behavior is saying, "I want attention, too. I want to be noticed and to be a part of what is going on." Ann believes that she belongs or matters only when she is being noticed or when Mom is busy with her. This is the first of the four messages (or mistaken goals): undue attention.

IDENTIFYING THE GOAL OF UNDUE ATTENTION

Ann's mother felt irritated and guilty, feelings listed in the second column of the Mistaken Goal Chart. These feelings are significant because they are the first clue to what is going on in this situation. When Mom and her daughters were at the doctor's office, what sorts of things were taking place, and how did Mom react (column three of the chart)? Mom asked Ann to sit quietly and stop bouncing on the sofa. Mom coaxed Ann out of sitting on her lap by reminding her that she is a "big girl" now. Finally, she walked her down the hall to the bathroom, which Ann may have been able to do on her own. All of these were reactions to Ann's behavior. Children whose mistaken goal is undue attention successfully keep the adults in their lives busy with them most of the time. All children need their parents' attention, but they may not be seeking that attention in positive, encouraging ways.

Look at the next column on the chart. What was Ann's response to her mother's actions? Ann stopped each behavior when her mother told her to, but quickly discovered another. The feelings and reactions of Ann's mother and Ann's responses to her mother are clues that reveal the mistaken goal of undue attention.

The child who sends a coded message by seeking undue attention believes that the only way he is able to count or belong is to keep others busy with him or to receive some sort of special service. He is willing to accept any attention, even negative attention, to achieve this goal. Peer through your kaleidoscope and picture this child wearing a large sunbonnet covered with feathers, fruit, flowers, or flying dinosaurs. There is a colorful banner on this hat. It says, "Notice me; involve me usefully."

"But wait a minute," parents often say when they learn their children's behavior is focused on getting attention. "We give our kids lots of attention. We spend all our free time with them; we read to them and play with them. How could they possibly need *more* attention?" Actually, giving children excessive attention (even in the name of love) may be part of the problem. Children with special needs or children

Encouragement for Undue Attention Seekers

- Use active listening to deal with the belief instead of the behavior.
- Notice and compromise.
- Involve the child to gain useful attention through cooperation.
- Give a reassuring hug.
- Encourage the child's ability to entertain and soothe himself.

who simply are loved a great deal may receive huge amounts of adult attention. This is fine—as long as it continues. When something happens to deflect adult attention even momentarily (a telephone call, a doctor's appointment, a conversation with a friend), children perceive this as a loss and do whatever they can to regain the usual amount. In other words, it isn't necessarily true that children whose mistaken goal is undue attention aren't receiving enough attention; they may actually be receiving so much that it creates a need for special service all of the time!

Ann came to the conclusion that Mom loved her less than Catherine because Catherine was receiving most of Mom's attention. Not surprisingly, Ann's behavior reflects this belief. Attention becomes the measuring cup for love in Ann's world.

RESPONDING TO THE MESSAGE

How can you give your child the attention and feeling of belonging he needs without giving in to an endless stream of small annoyances? Now that you understand the belief that prompts your child's mistaken goal of undue attention, you can respond in ways that will encourage your child instead of reinforcing the mistaken belief. Here are some things you can do.

Use Active Listening to Deal with the Belief Instead of the Behavior
Let's go back to the doctor's office. Mom could have chosen to deal with Ann's *belief* that Mom loved her sister more rather than attempting to control Ann's behavior. One possibility might be to practice active listening with Ann.

Active listening means getting into a child's world and making guesses about what she might be feeling. It is important to check out your guesses. Mom could say, "It must be hard for you to see me giving so much attention to Catherine. You might feel that I don't have any love left for you." If Mom has guessed correctly, Ann will feel validated for her feelings. She may even cry from relief as she acknowledges the truth of her mother's guess. She might then be able to give up her belief that she doesn't have significance—and her need to misbehave.

Notice and Compromise

Mom might tell Ann that she will read her one book as soon as Ann agrees to look at another book quietly afterward and let her mother look at a magazine. This form of limited special time offers appropriate attention while setting a boundary on undue attention. By asking Ann to honor her need for some quiet time, her mother has not just given in to Ann's demands for attention but has understood Ann's needs, respectfully stated her own needs, and then reached a compromise.

Involve the Child to Gain Useful Attention Through Cooperation

Mom could invite Ann to help care for her sick sister. (Do you remember the "Involve me" sign on the hat?) She could ask Ann how they might help Catherine feel more comfortable, involving her in the process of caring for Catherine, Mom will be giving her a meaningful role and directly meeting her need to feel necessary and valued. Mom then might ask for Ann's support by explaining how tired she is, and Ann might offer to give her a neck rub or even read her mother a story. When adults ask children for their help and cooperation, children can be remarkably thoughtful. These choices would create a sense of caring and connection, rather than inviting further misbehavior.

Give a Reassuring Hug

Another choice might be to hug Ann and tell her that her mother loves her very much. It can be very powerful to forget about the behavior and give a reassuring hug that says, "You belong and you are significant in my life." This is often enough to stop the misbehavior. A hug feels much better for everyone than nagging and lecturing.

Encourage the Child's Ability to Entertain and Soothe Himself
None of us is born knowing how to amuse ourselves; it takes time and encouragement from parents and caregivers for children to learn this skill. Children usually expect adults to provide constant entertainment and diversion, but if adults comply, children may never learn how to occupy quiet moments or cure boredom for themselves.

Encourage your child to learn to entertain himself—and recognize that this is a process that will take time and patience. Provide story tapes and teach your child to operate the tape player himself; let him explore the world of puzzles, art projects, and quiet games. Then, when your child seeks undue attention, say, "I love you—and I have faith in your ability to take care of yourself for a little while." It does take time, but a child who has discovered ways to fill empty moments is less likely to demand that adults do so. The ability to entertain himself is one your child will use for a lifetime.

MISGUIDED POWER, OR "YOU'RE NOT THE BOSS OF ME!"

Four-year-old Beverly is standing beside the computer, gazing curiously at the keyboard. Interesting pictures and patterns move across the colored screen; Beverly has watched Mom and Dad do this and is determined to try. She's been warned not to touch the computer, so she looks carefully around her and, seeing no Mom in sight, gives the keyboard several taps.

Mom turns the corner just in time to see this. She flies across the room, grabbing Beverly firmly by the elbow, totally hooked by her small daughter's misbehavior. "I've told you not to touch the computer! Now you've messed up my work," she says angrily, and lightly slaps Beverly's hand. Beverly responds by twisting free of her mother's grip and smashing her small fist down on the keyboard.

Mom, exasperated beyond belief, picks Beverly up and puts her into her room for a punitive time-out. Beverly launches into a major tantrum; Mom storms out to repair her damaged files. Right now, Mom is feeling angry and provoked—she has been defeated by a four-year-old!

Beverly's behavior may have begun as a lack of impulse control. She knew she was not supposed to touch the computer—but that rule could not override her impulse to explore, touch, and learn. Mom's swift reaction changed things at once, triggering an intense power struggle. Beverly's discouraged message becomes her misbehavior: Beverly is saying, "I don't believe I am important unless I have power—or at least I don't let you boss me around."

IDENTIFYING THE GOAL OF MISGUIDED POWER

When Beverly and her mom were struggling over the computer, her mom first felt provoked and then defeated. Beverly's mother reacted with some power-filled statements: "I've told you . . ." and "You've messed up my work!" Beverly's response to her mother's ineffective interventions was to intensify her own behavior. And the battle raged on.

An important aspect of the mistaken goal of power is that both participants—and note that it takes two—are determined to win. Neither is willing to give an inch. When parent and child are locked in combat this way, the result is a power struggle. The problem with power struggles is that if there's a winner, there also has to be a loser. When the loser is a child you love, the victory may not be worth the price.

> ### Encouragement for Seekers of Misguided Power
>
> - Offer limited choices.
> - Turn misguided power to useful power by asking for help.
> - Shut your mouth and act—kindly and firmly.
> - Ask if a positive time-out would be helpful.
> - Make a date for problem solving.

There is another interesting thing going on here. It often surprises an adult involved in a power struggle to discover that as he or she becomes more and more irate, the child may in fact be deciding that all of this hoopla is—*fun*! That's right, fun! Power struggles generate a lot of energy, and the harder the adult tries, the more obvious it becomes just how much power the child has. This is a thrilling discovery for children just experiencing their own initiative.

If you have heard an impassioned "You're not the boss of me!" shouted by a child, you might well suspect that the goal involved is power. The child whose goal is power can be imagined wearing a bright orange hard hat. Printed in bold letters on this hat is the command "Let me help; give me choices."

RESPONDING TO THE MESSAGE

When four-year-old Beverly and her mom fought over the computer, they were involved in one of a series of power struggles that might set the tone of their future relationship. Fortunately, Beverly's mom learned about her own responsibility in fueling their power struggle. She changed *her* behavior first, and thus opened the way for Beverly to change her belief system and her behavior.

Offer Limited Choices
Beverly's mom sought out a parenting class and eventually learned how to empower Beverly by giving her power in appropriate ways. She learned to give Beverly limited choices and ask curiosity questions instead of demanding obedience: "Mommy's work is for Mommy to do. Would you like to read a book or play with your Legos?" or "What would you like to do while I work?"

Turn Misguided Power to Useful Power by Asking for Help

A power struggle can often be defused by asking a child for her help. Mom could let Beverly know how much she needs her: "Honey, we are a family and you are so important to me. I know you really want to touch the computer, but computers are easy to damage. Mommy and Daddy need to be the only people who touch the computer. But I'll bet there are ways you could help me with my work. Let's see what we can find!" Asking for help or involving a child in the solution redirects both the child and the parent away from a power struggle and toward the positive power of cooperation. Demands invite resistance. Curiosity questions usually invite cooperation.

Shut Your Mouth and Act—Kindly and Firmly

Another way to disengage from a power struggle is to be firm and kind *at the same time*. When Beverly pounded the computer keyboard, she was throwing down the gauntlet, challenging her mom to fight. Instead of picking up the gauntlet, Mom can stop talking and act. She can kindly but firmly pick Beverly up and take her into another room. There need be no further mention of the computer until after a cooling-off period, which is often necessary before a child will listen to a limited choice or an appeal for help.

By not lecturing or shaming her daughter, Mom does not invite further resistance. Even if Beverly chooses to have a tantrum, Mom has defused the power struggle by refusing to become engaged (or throwing her own mom-sized tantrum). Children's tantrums are less likely when children feel the energy of kindness along with firmness. This does not mean that tantrums can be entirely avoided, but avoiding a tantrum is not the goal. The goal is to kindly and firmly act upon what you have said. You can also help your child find ways to cool off when strong emotions erupt.

Ask if a Positive Time-Out Would Be Helpful

When adults and children engage in power struggles, both have stopped thinking rationally and are reacting irrationally. The neuronal

connections needed for logical thought and objectivity actually become unavailable when the brain is flooded by strong emotion. Until everyone can cool off, effective problem solving will need to be postponed; a positive time-out may be required before win-win solutions can be found. Invite your child to help you create a positive time-out area (see Chapter 1). Then, when power struggles occur, you can ask, "Would it help you to go to your cool-off spot until you calm down?" If your child has helped create a place to cool off and understands that this kind of time-out is not punitive, she will often choose this option. If your child says no, you might say, "Well, then I think *I'll* go to my room until I feel better." What powerful role modeling that would be! Remember, it takes two to have a power struggle. When you choose to calm down, your child can do so, too.

It is appropriate to follow up a positive time-out by working on a solution together. Beverly and her mom might agree that Beverly can play her own computer games when Mom is there to help, that Mom gets to have some uninterrupted time to work, and that Beverly must ask Mom when she wants computer time.

Make a Date for Problem Solving

Problem solving with preschoolers can be accomplished by using curiosity questions to help them explore what happened, what caused it to happen, and what ideas they have to solve the problem. Four- and five-year-olds are also very good at participating in family meetings (see Chapter 16). After a cooling-off period (or even at the time of conflict), it might defuse the power struggle to ask, "Would you like to put this problem on our family meeting agenda, or would you like me to?" Not only does putting the problem on the family meeting agenda give everyone a cooling-off period, but you can then work together on solutions at the meeting.

REVENGE, OR "I'LL MAKE YOU FEEL AS BAD AS I DO!"

It is bedtime, and Dad is helping three-year-old Alice get ready. Dad says it is time to put on her jammies, but Alice is having great fun playing with bubbles in the sink and doesn't want to stop. Just as Dad is becoming impatient, Alice spills a cup of water on the floor. Dad immediately becomes angry, thinking Alice spilled the water on purpose. He picks Alice up and spanks her. Alice begins to cry, and Dad has to wrestle her into the pajamas as she kicks and struggles.

When Alice is finally in her pajamas, Dad grumpily picks up a book for a bedtime story. Alice's lower lip juts out. "I hate that book," she pouts, "and I don't want you to read to me! I want Mommy!" What a blow! Dad feels terrible; his own daughter doesn't love him. He is hurt and disbelieving.

Alice may be saying, "Daddy hurt me, so I'll hurt him back" in the only way she knows. This is the third of the four mistaken goals: revenge.

IDENTIFYING REVENGE

Dad was shocked that Alice would deliberately spill water all over the floor. He was trying his best to get Alice to bed while his wife was working late, and now, on top of everything else, his feelings are hurt. He regrets having spanked Alice. He didn't like doing it, but he didn't know how else to respond to her behavior.

First of all, did Alice deliberately spill the water? Young children spill a lot of things. Their muscle control is still developing. If Dad had understood the developmental nature of Alice's action, he might have understood that Alice simply had an accident or made a mistake; he could have helped her get a sponge to clean up the puddle. Working together to mop up the spill might even have distracted Alice enough that the jammies would go on easily.

> ### Encouragement for Revenge Seekers
>
> - Deal with the hurt feelings.
> - Apologize if you caused the pain.
> - Listen to your child's feelings.
> - Make sure the message of love gets through.
> - Make amends, not excuses.

Even if Alice *had* deliberately spilled water, spanking is unlikely to help matters much. Spanking teaches children that might makes right. It can invite many responses, and few of them are what parents intend. In this case, a spanking invited revenge. Both Alice and her dad wound up feeling hurt.

Whenever an adult feels hurt by the behavior of a child, it is likely that the child is feeling hurt, too. As you examine Dad's feelings and reactions and Alice's response, you will see the clues that indicate the mistaken goal of revenge. When you picture the child whose goal is revenge, imagine a black baseball cap turned backward. On the back is written the plea "Help me, I'm hurting; acknowledge my feelings."

RESPONDING TO THE MESSAGE

When adults can begin to see a child who is hurtful as a hurting child, they feel motivated to respond to that child differently. Instead of giving in to the instinctive desire for retaliation and punishment, they can choose to offer care and support. If a child is feeling hurt, does it make sense to make that child feel worse?

Deal with the Hurt Feelings

First of all, Dad can move to the heart of the matter by dealing with Alice's hurt feelings. Dad could say, "It looks like you're feeling very hurt right now. I'll bet it hurt your feelings as well as your bottom when I spanked you." Getting into her world and acknowledging her feelings is validating for a child, and she is likely to feel understanding, belonging, and significance.

Apologize if You Caused the Pain

Alice's dad really does love his daughter, and he immediately regretted spanking her. His attitude will invite Alice to change her beliefs when he takes responsibility for his own behavior by apologizing. Dad can tell Alice that it was wrong of him to spank her. Dad can reassure her that it is wrong for people to hurt each other, even when they're angry or hurt.

Responding to the belief *behind* a child's behavior (instead of reacting to the behavior itself with punishment or lectures) will require that you give up the notion that you can or should control your child. You must also decide for yourself that teaching and encouragement are more effective responses than punishment. Making this change—especially if you were raised with old-fashioned ideas—will take some time. Be patient with yourself, acknowledge your mistakes, and be willing to learn from them.

If you have never had the experience of apologizing to a child, swallow your pride, admit that adults aren't always right, and apologize the next time you make a mistake with your child. Children are delightfully quick to forgive, and you may discover that the hugs that follow apologies bring you even closer.

Listen to Your Child's Feelings

Dad might take a moment to observe his small daughter closely. He may notice Alice's jutting lip, trembling chin, and the tears beginning to fill her eyes. And he can ask Alice—with genuine interest—how she is feeling. If she is too young to articulate her feelings, he can ask her if she thinks that Daddy doesn't love her. Alice will probably respond with a verbal (or nonverbal) signal that lets her dad know he has understood correctly. He could have asked Alice why she threw water on the floor in the first place. She might explain, "It spilled" or "It was an accident." Most likely Dad's irritation would have melted upon hearing answers like those. When Dad and Alice have this kind of conversation, they are developing a new sense of trust.

When a child is feeling hurt, it is difficult for her to move beyond her emotions to solutions. Therefore, it is important to address the feelings first.

Make Sure the Message of Love Gets Through
Dad has a chance to tell Alice how much he loves her and how important she is to him. When a child is feeling hurt, this message can do so much to heal the pain. Dad also can share how he felt. When Dad can listen to and respect Alice's feelings and then explain his own, each will learn a great deal about the other. The love connection is rekindled.

If Dad tries these new ideas, he just might find himself snuggling close to his precious daughter as they read a bedtime story together. Even a painful and damaging experience can be healed when the message of love and caring gets through.

Make Amends, Not Excuses
Whether or not Alice spilled the water intentionally, once she and her dad have dealt with their feelings they will need to address the mess. Dad might offer to help her wipe up the spill or supply her with a mop or sponge so she can do so herself. If Alice resorts to tears or retreats into hurt feelings again, her dad can make this encounter an opportunity to teach (rather than continuing the revenge cycle) by kindly and firmly continuing to help Alice clean up the puddle, and then wordlessly continuing with her regular bedtime routine.

ASSUMED INADEQUACY: "I GIVE UP"

Jean lives with her grandparents and today is her fifth birthday. When she enters the kitchen, her grandparents eagerly watch for her reaction to the brand-new bike proudly displayed in the center of the room. Jean looks anxiously around and doesn't comment on the bike. Grandmother impatiently asks, "Well, what do you think? Do you like it?" Jean doesn't respond. Grandma then says in a coaxing voice, "Jean, look at your wonderful new

"Help Me Put Things Right"

Q. My four-year-old threw his cup of juice onto the floor when I told him it was time for his nap. The cup cracked and broke. I think his feelings were hurt because he didn't get to go to the park this morning. I want to respond to his hurt feelings, but I don't think his behavior should go unpunished.

A. Sometimes adults take the approach that if a child misbehaves for a mistaken purpose, he is no longer responsible for his actions. Ignoring misbehavior does not teach life skills. Nor does punishment, which translated usually means "You must suffer." What does help is to give children the opportunity to make amends.

If an item is damaged, it is appropriate to work out a way for the child to replace or repair it. That might mean doing a few helpful tasks to earn the money—even small children can do some small job—or taking the money out of his piggy bank. Or it might mean helping come up with a plan to repair the damage, such as patching a tear in a book.

All of these solutions focus on teaching responsibility. Spanking, shaming, yelling, or taking away television for a week does not achieve the same life lesson. With those punishments, a child might learn fear of retaliation, escalate to more hurtful behavior himself, or decide that he is a "bad" person. None of these outcomes includes learning to take responsibility for his actions.

Children feel so much better about themselves when they are given a chance to put things right. If this is done in a spirit of love instead of anger, a child can regain a measure of self-esteem in the process. Few children feel pleased with themselves when they lose control of their behavior. They need encouragement to learn from their mistakes and tools to repair the damage, while parents need to change their attitude of shame and blame to one of support and true discipline.

bike." Jean shakes her head and mumbles, "I can't ride a bike." Grandpa rushes over to reassure Jean, "That's no problem, sweetie, you'll learn in no time." Jean says nothing and does not go near the bike. Her grandparents look at each other in exasperation and shrug. "What's the use?" they think, and Grandpa dejectedly begins to pour Jean's cereal and milk for her.

Jean's grandparents have been convinced to give up on her. They feel hopeless about themselves and about Jean. Somehow Jean has come to believe that she is not "good enough," that she is truly helpless. She acts upon this belief by convincing others of her inadequacy. Jean's grandparents love her, but they mistakenly believe that the best way to show that love is to do things for her, such as pouring her cereal and milk, that she could easily do for herself.

Of all the four goals or messages, children displaying assumed inadequacy are often the most overlooked—and the most discouraged. They usually don't create the havoc that children acting upon the other three goals do. Children communicating this message may become nearly invisible.

This goal is rarely found in children younger than age five unless they are given little or no opportunity to develop a sense of autonomy. It can be especially baffling when highly productive and goal-oriented parents see this behavior in their child. What parents value as personal drive and determination may overwhelm their children and convince them that they are truly incapable—that they can never measure up to expectations. This creates the fourth mistaken goal: assumed inadequacy, or giving up.

IDENTIFYING ASSUMED INADEQUACY

Jean's grandparents try not to feel hopeless, but Jean looks so discouraged. They do their best to protect her and to make up for the fact that her parents aren't around. Grandma and Grandpa react to Jean's helpless behavior by doing things for her. Grandpa pours her milk and cereal; Grandma dresses her every morning. They supply Jean's every need. They buy her things and make plans and choices in which she has no participation. Jean's response is to retreat further, to act passively, and to refuse to try anything new. The feelings, reactions, and responses all give clues that the behavior is assumed inadequacy.

Children who develop a belief in their own inadequacy may believe that because they cannot do things perfectly, they might as well give up. When children understand that mistakes are part of how everyone learns, they can break the power of the perfection myth.

It is easy to understand how a child who is constantly criticized might develop the belief that she can't do anything right. Criticism is not always overt. As a toddler, Jean was always dressed in beautifully ironed, frilly dresses. She was admonished to "keep clean" and her grandmother would become very upset when Jean got paint or food on her clothing. Jean's perception was that messy was "bad." Because she was often messy, Jean eventually began to believe in her own inadequacy. It seemed that every time she tried to paint a picture or pour her own juice, she made a mess. Jean decided that she couldn't do anything well.

The child who pursues this mistaken goal may be pictured wearing a drab-colored ski hat pulled far down over her face. What you will find stitched on the front (if you look closely enough) is "Don't give up on me—show me a small step."

RESPONDING TO THE MESSAGE

Feeling inadequate and giving up is a very lonely place to be. Since their goal is to be left alone, these children are rarely much trouble to others and are often overlooked. There are many things parents can do to meet this child's needs.

Have Faith in Your Child and Let Her Do Things for Herself
Parents may not realize that doing too much for children (usually in the name of love) is discouraging. A child may adopt the belief

Encouragement for Assumed Inadequacy

- Have faith in your child and let her do things for herself.
- Take time for training and encourage even the smallest steps.
- Teach that mistakes are wonderful opportunities to learn.

"I'm not capable" when adults insist on doing things for her that she could do herself. Another possible belief is "I am loved only when others are doing things for me."

It may be helpful to remember that self-esteem comes from having skills, and that pampering a child actually discourages her. Stop doing things for your child that she can do for herself and make room for her to practice—even when she does things imperfectly. When she says, "I can't," have patience; say, "I have faith that you can handle this task." Encouraging a child who believes that she is inadequate requires a great deal of patience, gentle perseverance, and faith in the child's abilities.

Take Time for Training and Encourage Even the Smallest Steps

It is not surprising that Jean does not know how to ride a bicycle; no one learns without teaching and practice. Instead of feeling frustrated, Grandma might share a story about her own experiences learning to ride a bike. Perhaps she could tell Jean how she felt the first time she fell and her brothers and sister laughed. When Grandma shares her own story, she is also telling Jean that feeling embarrassed is okay and that everyone has to learn how to do new things. Staying on a pedestal may be good for your image, but it can cripple the growth of closeness and trust.

How you react to your own mistakes and struggles is important. Your child is watching and may believe you always succeed easily (and feel inadequate because he does not). Or he may watch you try something and meet with repeated failure. How you react—whether you can laugh at yourself and keep on trying or whether you give up in discouragement—will give him clues about his own experiences. Never underestimate the power of role modeling.

Children who have already developed the belief "I'm inadequate" may resist attempts at training. This is why small steps are important. Grandpa might start by letting Jean sit on the bike inside the house. He might be sure the bike has training wheels and show Jean how they work. Before starting her down the block, he can reassure her that he will not let go until she is ready. He might also teach her how to pour her own milk (from a small pitcher). Remember that when teaching new skills, especially to discouraged youngsters, it helps to make every attempt to foresee problems—and to ensure a child's success.

Teach That Mistakes Are Wonderful Opportunities to Learn
What is your attitude toward your own mistakes? Most people learn much more from what they see than what they hear. Criticism (even "constructive criticism") is difficult to accept. For a child who believes she is inadequate, criticism only reinforces her belief in her inadequacy. One of the best ways to help a discouraged child is to stop all criticism.

If Jean messes her dress up with paint or mud, Grandma may consider dressing her in more durable clothes. What a great message it would send if Grandma could learn to say, "Wow, you are covered with paint! You must have had a great time painting today."

Family members also can share mistakes on a regular basis. During dinnertime each person can take turns sharing a mistake and what they learned from it. This can create a sense of fun and learning—and a much improved attitude about mistakes.

BE AWARE OF THE HIDDEN MESSAGE

"Whew," you may be saying, "I had no idea there was so much going on in my child's head when he acts that way." It is important to understand that children do not *consciously* decide to pursue one of the mistaken goals; they are only rarely aware of their own beliefs and are not out to baffle their parents with a game of "guess my goal." It also takes time to translate awareness of your child's mistaken goal into kind, firm, and encouraging action.

When parents can be aware of the message hidden in their child's behavior and when they can observe their own feelings and reactions, then they can take steps to encourage a discouraged child and to celebrate a child's willingness to take risks and make mistakes. In so doing, parents nurture children who believe they are capable, lovable, and worthwhile.

10

MISTAKEN GOALS IN THE PRESCHOOL

Misbehavior—the coded messages children send us about their beliefs—doesn't happen just at home with parents. Misbehavior happens everywhere young children go. Teachers and caregivers can also learn to decipher children's mistaken goals and respond in ways that teach and encourage. (For more information, see *Positive Discipline for Childcare Providers* by Jane Nelsen and Cheryl Erwin, Three Rivers Press, 2002.)

UNDUE ATTENTION IN THE PRESCHOOL

It should come as no surprise that where groups of children are gathered, the desire for undue attention appears.

> *There are twelve five-year-old children in Marcia's classroom at the Tiny Treasures Child Care Center this morning. At about*

10:00, Jamal finds Marcia; his shoe is untied and he asks her to tie it for him. Marcia does so, and Jamal goes off to play. Less than five minutes later, he needs help sharpening a pencil. Marcia helps him do that, too, but no more than two minutes pass before she notices that Jamal has begun to mess around with Ben's blocks. Marcia reminds him that these are Ben's blocks and Jamal needs to choose something else to do. By 10:15, Jamal's shoe is again untied.

By now, Marcia is longing for her break. In addition to feeling annoyed by Jamal's constant demands, she is also feeling guilty that she doesn't enjoy being around this child very much. These feelings, as you will see in the second column of the Mistaken Goal Chart (pages 144 and 145), are the first clue that Jamal's behavior is motivated by the mistaken goal of attention.

Marcia's reactions to Jamal's behavior are typical, and they are another clue to decoding his mistaken belief. She does things for Jamal that he could reasonably be expected to do for himself—or that he could learn to do on his own. She also spends a good deal of her time reminding Jamal to stop certain behaviors. A third clue that the mistaken goal is undue attention is that Jamal stops his behavior for a short while but soon finds other ways to keep Marcia busy with him. Every teacher will recognize a child she knows in Jamal.

What are Jamal and other children like him really saying by their behavior? Remember, Jamal, too, wears a large, colorful hat declaring, "Notice me; involve me usefully." When a child seeks undue attention, he is acting on a deeply held belief that he can belong or count only by being noticed or by keeping adults busy with him. When you learn to decode their mistaken goal messages, you will understand that what children who misbehave are really saying to you is "I'm a child and I just want to belong."

RESPONDING TO THE MESSAGE

Even when his teacher is able to understand that Jamal's behavior is a cry for attention, it is not always possible to give one-on-one attention in group settings. Still, a number of things can be done routinely with all of the children that will greatly diminish constant bids for attention such as Jamal's.

Help Children Get Attention in Useful Ways Through Meaningful Involvement

As you learned in Chapters 8 and 9, the message for the mistaken goal of undue attention is "Notice me; involve me usefully." It can be very effective to ignore misbehavior while redirecting a child to get attention in a useful way. Marcia might involve Jamal by asking him to help her with something—washing out paintbrushes, erasing the board, or blowing the whistle to let everyone know it's time to come in from lunch.

Teach Nonverbal Signals

Consider teaching children nonverbal signals to let you know that they need your time or attention. Marcia might have taught the children in her class to gently place a hand on her arm to let her know that she is needed. Marcia's signal that she notices that child's request for assistance is to make eye contact with the child, wink, and say, "As soon as I'm free." This gives attention in a reasonable way, while still allowing a child to feel acknowledged and important.

Give Special Attention Before the Child Seeks Undue Attention

Marcia could comment on something that makes each child feel special. She

> **Encouragement for Undue Attention in the Preschool**
>
> - Help children get attention in useful ways through meaningful involvement.
> - Teach nonverbal signals.
> - Give special attention before the child seeks undue attention.
> - Take time for training.

might greet Jamal and tell him she found a spider's egg sac and brought it in for the science table. She knows that spiders fascinate Jamal. Her special attention and recognition of his interests will help him feel included and cared about.

Another way to say "I notice you" is to greet children individually. Some teachers take the time to give every child a hug or a handshake as they enter the preschool or child care center. This gesture says, "I care about you and am glad you are here." You can find ways to inject effective doses of "special time" into a class full of children. When children feel belonging and significance, they are less likely to seek undue attention. Large centers may want to designate one teacher as the morning greeter.

Take Time for Training

What to do about Jamal's shoes, the ones that have the uncanny ability to come untied every ten minutes? Marcia could create a training plan to help Jamal learn to tie his own shoes. After an adequate amount of demonstration and practice, it would be reasonable for Marcia to tell Jamal that she would love to watch him tie his own shoes. Eventually Jamal could be encouraged to tie his shoes and come back to show Marcia when he has been successful. Jamal is being given attention but in ways that help him feel capable, not in ways that reinforce the constant flow of small annoyances or demands for inappropriate special service.

Just as children often make the mistake of trying to get undue attention, adults often make the mistake of getting hooked, instead of finding a way to redirect children into feeling a sense of belonging and significance in useful ways. Remember, encouraged children do not need to find mistaken ways to find belonging and significance—at least, not as often!

POWER STRUGGLES IN THE PRESCHOOL

It is a lovely, sunny day at the Silverport Preschool. Over by the apple tree, three-year-old Shama and her teacher, Julie, are glaring at each other. Julie says it's time to go inside. Shama refuses to go. Julie emphasizes that playtime is over: everyone else has gone inside and Shama must come in right now. Shama latches on to the side of the climber. Julie's face is turning pink, and she begins to threaten her small pupil: "If you don't come in this minute, you won't be allowed to come outside the rest of the day."

Shama sticks out her tongue. "You can't make me!" she taunts. Julie tries to pick her up and carry her inside, but first she has to chase Shama down.

Julie is angry (and a little embarrassed—after all, this is a three-year-old) and feels that her authority has been challenged. As Julie carries the writhing, screaming child inside, she says through clenched teeth, "When I say it's time to come inside, you will do what I say!"

What do you think? Will Shama meekly obey Julie next time? What is the message behind Shama's behavior? She may be saying, "I want to be the boss and have some power in my life!" Her invisible hard hat is saying, "Let me help; give me choices." Shama's way of achieving power is by proving that "you can't make me!"

IDENTIFYING MISGUIDED POWER

Julie felt angry; she also felt that her legitimate authority had been challenged. These are the typical feelings adults have when they are involved in a power struggle—and these feelings provide the first clue to identifying misguided power.

As we've mentioned before, a power struggle takes two. Shama needed Julie's reactions to engage in the battle. Julie reacted to the situation by using her superior strength to overpower Shama and carry her inside. She made Shama do what she told her to do. But did Shama ever give up her end of the fight?

Recall the way that Shama grabbed on to the play equipment to fortify her position. An additional clue that the goal is power is that the behavior intensifies. Shama's response is characteristic of the mistaken goal of misguided power.

The child who acts upon the mistaken goal of misguided power will spend a great deal of energy resisting cooperation. Shama had to clutch the playground equipment fiercely to maintain a hold that her teacher couldn't loosen. In the heat of battle, this ferocity may be described as "stubbornness." (When the same child is learning to do a complicated math problem, however, or running those last few miles of the marathon, this same trait may be seen positively as "tenacity.") The underlying belief of the mistaken goal of misguided power is "I belong only when I am in control. No one can make me do things."

RESPONDING TO THE MESSAGE

How might Shama's teacher give her power in appropriate ways? There are several possibilities.

Ask the Child to Help

If there is a pattern of power struggles between Julie and Shama, Julie could work to break the cycle by asking for Shama's help—which invites Shama to use her power in productive ways. Julie might say, "Shama, I need your help. Would you please tell the boys in the far corner that it is time to come in?" An opportunity to help often appeals to a child who is seeking misguided power, providing her with an opportunity to have power in a useful way.

Remember that few people—including little ones—enjoy feeling powerless or victimized. We all need opportunities to experience self-control

and to learn that personal power can be
used in helpful ways. It is not the need for
power that is mistaken; it is the misguided
use of power that creates problems.

Offer Limited Choices

One of the best ways to empower a child is
to give her limited choices in which all
alternatives are acceptable. Asking a child
if she is ready to come inside now implies

> **Encouragement for Misguided Power Seekers in the Preschool**
>
> - Ask the child to help.
> - Offer limited choices.
> - Do the unexpected.
> - Seek win-win solutions.

that she doesn't have to come in if she isn't ready. If that is not an
acceptable alternative, do not include it in your choices, stated or
implied.

Shama's teacher could ask Shama whether she would like to lead the
class inside at the end of playtime or hold the teacher's hand and follow the others. These are limited choices, both of which are acceptable. Staying outside is not one of the choices. If a child answers by
naming an alternative that was not given, such as staying outside, simply respond, "That is not one of the choices."

Another option might be to let Shama choose which equipment to
play on before going inside and to say that the bell would ring in two
more minutes. This requires planning ahead, which is a wise thing to
do when power struggles have become a pattern with a child.

Giving choices shows respect for a child; it is not a gimmick
designed to trick a child into compliance. (Remember, your attitude is
a powerful influence on how a child perceives your actions.) Choices
empower a child, meeting the need for power and belonging in acceptable ways. And meeting the underlying need will address the real cause
of the misbehavior rather than just the symptoms.

Do the Unexpected

Adults and preschoolers sometimes find that their behavior has become
rather predictable. Julie and Shama probably have enacted this little
scene (or a variation of it) many times before. Instead of responding to

Shama's challenge in her usual way, Julie could do the unexpected. When Shama refused to come inside, Julie could have said, "I'll bet you can't catch me," and then run away from Shama. What a surprise that would be for someone who is clinging fiercely to the railing! Shama just might let go to chase her teacher, and when she caught her, Julie could give her a big hug and walk peacefully inside with her. The stand-off evaporates; both are winners.

Seek Win-Win Solutions

Another secret to dealing with power struggles, as you learned with Shama, is to seek win-win solutions. It is when both people involved remain committed to being the only winner that the power struggle escalates. Why assert your own power when it inevitably means a child must be the loser?

REVENGE IN THE PRESCHOOL

It is a Tuesday morning, and four-year-old Eric has been thrown the toy dinosaurs across the room. His teacher, John, comes over and removes the toy dinosaurs, telling Eric he cannot have them for the rest of the day. Eric is furious. Eric remembers that when Zachary threw the blocks into the corner yesterday, nothing happened to him. This isn't fair! Eric stomps off.

A little while later, John makes the charming discovery that Eric has stuffed the toilet full of toilet paper and has clogged it up. John shows Eric the mess he has made and asks, "How could you do such a thing to our school?" Eric doesn't hesitate. "I hate this place," he says, "and I'm glad the toilet is broken." John tells the little boy that he will write a note to Eric's parents about this and that Eric will have to stay in at recess.

Before the day is over, Eric has also managed to rip the pages out of several books.

Right at this moment, John is deciding to call in sick tomorrow. He just can't take another day of this child. Eric's message is "I've been hurt, so I'm going to hurt others back. Life is unfair!" John is undoubtedly feeling pretty discouraged and hurt himself. He has devoted so much time and energy to becoming a teacher; what's the use? John also feels disgusted and disbelieving, and he is baffled by Eric's disdain for the school's property.

IDENTIFYING REVENGE

Adults (and children) often cover their hurt feelings with anger. John's reaction to Eric's behavior was to hurt back through reprimands and punishment. This created a revenge cycle.

Eric's response was to escalate his behavior by stomping off to stuff the toilet full of paper, to proclaim his hatred of his school, and to destroy the books. Children are very good at revenge cycles. They have many weapons to hurt adults who can't see the message behind the behavior and don't know how to get out of the revenge cycle. Eric's backward-facing cap declares, "Help me, I'm hurting; validate my feelings."

A child who has chosen the mistaken goal of revenge believes that if he can't belong (which must hurt a lot), at least he can get even. Unfortunately, it is difficult for most adults to love and enjoy a child who is hurting others and

> ### Encouragement for Revenge Seekers in the Preschool
>
> - Deal with the hurt feelings through validation and expression.
> - Teach the difference between feeling and doing.
> - Ask if a positive time-out would be helpful.
> - Allow the child to share his perspective.
> - Schedule a time (after the conflict) to work on solutions.
> - Repair the damage; make amends.
> - Work to help the child feel a sense of belonging.

destroying property. By acting upon his belief that he doesn't belong, this child behaves in ways that prove his point.

RESPONDING TO THE MESSAGE

It can be difficult to deal with a child like Eric, but once his teacher realizes that Eric feels he has been treated unfairly and is hurt, he can respond to Eric's real need. Eric wants to feel a sense of belonging, to be a real part of the group. How can that be achieved?

Deal with the Hurt Feelings Through Validation and Expression

Before Eric's behavior can change, he needs to have his hurt feelings validated and he needs help in expressing them in acceptable ways. John can spend time with Eric and help him find more effective ways to express his feelings.

Young children aren't consciously aware that their misbehavior is motivated by hurt feelings. However, when an adult correctly guesses what they are feeling, children feel understood and validated. The best way to start the learning process is through modeling. John could say, "Eric, when you behave that way, I feel hurt. My guess is that you might be feeling hurt, too. Can you let me know when you are ready to talk about our hurt feelings?" Eric may well need a little time to cool off before he is ready to discuss his feelings. If Eric still does not want to say anything, the teacher might tell a story about a time that he felt really hurt. Eric will probably feel more willing to talk with John about his own hurt feelings after hearing John's story. By spending this kind of time with Eric, his teacher can gain Eric's trust by showing that he accepts Eric, even when Eric is not feeling likable, and when Eric's feelings have been acknowledged and admitted, Eric can begin to feel (and act) better.

Teach the Difference Between Feeling and Doing

Learning to name the feelings inside of himself gives a child a new tool. By learning to stop, acknowledge, and name his feelings, Eric

When a Hurting Child Hurts Another Child

Understanding that a child's mistaken goal might be revenge for his own hurts does not make injuring others acceptable. Making amends for physical aggression involves three steps:

1. **Provide damage control.** Separate involved children or place one child out of reach of the offending child. Often this means placing both children in a cool-off area until they are calm enough to make better choices.

2. **Address hurt feelings.** Take the time to find out what might be causing a child to feel hurt and allow the feelings to surface. When you accept and validate a child's feelings, you encourage his sense of belonging by sending the message that it is safe for him to have all kinds of feelings. This is a form of unconditional caring. Sometimes you can do nothing to erase the cause of a child's pain. Parents fighting with each other, illness in a family, or other life events are usually beyond your control. But simply allowing a child a safe place to express his feelings and to feel supported and listened to can help him heal.

3. **Make amends.** Making amends is part of learning to take responsibility for one's actions—an ability all of us need to cultivate and practice. You might ask the aggressor if he needs solutions for ways he might help the injured child feel better. You and he might come up with ideas such as offering to provide a service (clearing the other child's place at the table for him, reading a story to him, or drawing a picture for him). A child may also choose to offer an apology, but you can't force him to say "I'm sorry"—this teaches a child to speak words without meaning them. If a child initiates a sincere apology, it will have more impact.

can slow down and take time to think before he acts. Eric needs to learn that there is a difference between feeling hurt and acting on those hurt feelings.

John could decide to tell Eric, "What you feel is always okay, but what you *do* is not always okay. Later let's brainstorm some things we can do when we feel hurt that doesn't hurt others or damage our school." John would be wise to postpone the brainstorming session, because Eric needs some time to recover.

Ask if a Positive Time-Out Would Be Helpful

If John has already taught his class about positive time-outs, he can ask Eric if it would help him to take a cool-off until he feels better. John could even ask Eric whether he would like company or if he would like to go alone. If Eric wants company and John has a few minutes, he could offer, "Would you like me to go with you or would you like a buddy to go with you?" Children who feel they don't belong usually jump at the chance to have someone go with them—they can cool off and feel they belong at the same time.

Allow the Child to Share His Perspective

After Eric has cooled off and feels better, John and Eric can talk about why Eric is feeling hurt and look for ways to help him feel better again. Eric could tell John how he felt about John's reaction to the block-throwing incident. Perhaps John could remind him that a solution for throwing blocks was decided at the morning's class meeting. That would explain why another child had been treated differently the day before. Or John could ask Eric to suggest a solution that would feel fair to him. By dealing with the hurt feelings first, John and Eric can move on to problem solving together.

Schedule a Time (After the Conflict) to Work on Solutions

Eric can be taught different ways to act when difficult feelings arise. Later that morning, John asked Eric to join him for a brainstorming session. Such follow-up encourages positive growth and also helps prevent future problems. John started by suggesting that next time Eric is feeling hurt, he can come to John and practice naming the feeling. John told Eric kindly that he will always try to be a good listener. John then asked Eric what ideas he had. Eric had been learning about "using his words" and said, "I could tell someone I don't like it when they hurt my feelings." John said, "That sounds good. Anything else?" Eric couldn't think of anything, so John prompted, "How about putting the problem on the class meeting agenda?" Eric said, "I could do that."

John ended their discussion by saying, "You have three good ideas. I have faith that you will choose the one that works best for you the next time you feel hurt." It is important to remember that this process may need to be repeated many times before Eric will learn to name his feelings, accept them as okay, and find acceptable ways to handle his feelings.

Repair the Damage; Make Amends

What about Eric's destructive actions? Remember, making a child feel worse is unlikely to encourage that child to act better. Retaliation and punishment are typical adult reactions to destructive behavior, but they often provoke a child to respond with more revenge. Instead, when a child destroys something, it is reasonable to expect him to take responsibility for replacing the damaged item or addressing the damage he's done.

When Eric stuffs the toilet with paper and causes it to overflow, he can be expected to help clean up the mess. Eric will be more likely to cooperate in the cleanup efforts when his feelings and the belief behind his behavior have been dealt with, and afterward, Eric and John can discuss how Eric could help clean up the mess in the bathroom. Notice that the focus is on the mess in the bathroom, rather than the mess Eric made. This is not the time for blaming but for working together to find a solution to the problem. It takes time, but this kind of respectful and caring approach is much more likely to lead to improvements in Eric's behavior.

Eric hasn't "gotten away with" anything; eventually, he and John will agree on a plan for repairing the damage he has done, and John will see that the plan is implemented. When the focus is on solutions, the result just may be a change in the behavior. Then the revenge cycle can be broken.

Work to Help the Child Feel a Sense of Belonging

We have explored a number of ways that John can help Eric deal with one day's behavior, but to make a lasting change in the way Eric sees himself, John must focus on ways to give Eric a sense of belonging in the classroom. During a class meeting or circle time, John could begin a discussion of how good we feel when others want to do things with us. John could then say that he has chosen Eric to pass out the morning snack. He could ask who would like to share this task with Eric. Several hands would go up and a helper would be chosen. By focusing on sharing the task with Eric, John has sent a different message than if he'd simply asked, "Who else wants to serve the snack?"

Afterward, John could spend a moment with Eric and comment on how many children raised their hands to do something with him. Did Eric feel good when so many children raised their hands to pass the snack with him? In this way, John would be helping Eric become a contributing member of his class, as well as helping Eric perceive himself as a likable person with whom others want to share tasks. This sort of processing is a crucial piece in helping Eric to form different beliefs about his experiences.

ASSUMED INADEQUACY IN THE PRESCHOOL

For Dale, it is just another day at swim class. Dale is five years old but he is still in the three-year-old group. The instructor, Tom, is trying to get everyone to blow bubbles in the water. Dale hates to get his face wet and blows little puffs well above the surface. Tom comes over and suggests that Dale pretend to blow out a birthday candle. Dale only folds his arms around himself, puts his chin into his chest, and gives a tiny shake of his head. After a minute or two, Tom gives up and goes on to the next child.

A little while later, the other children are holding on to the edge of the pool and practicing kicking in the water. Dale sits on the side, refusing to get into the pool. Tom offers to hold Dale while he kicks, but Dale refuses and turns his body away from the pool. Eventually Tom gives up and leaves Dale alone.

Dale has successfully convinced his swimming instructor to leave him alone. Dale believes that because he is not "good enough," he must be hopeless. He acts upon this belief by convincing others to give up on him, demonstrating to perfection the mistaken goal of assumed inadequacy, or giving up. Dale's imaginary ski hat, pulled low over his face, reads, "Show me small steps; celebrate my successes."

IDENTIFYING ASSUMED INADEQUACY IN THE PRESCHOOL

Tom must stay alert to the needs of all of the children in his swim class—he can't spend all of his time with Dale. Tom feels hopeless when he can't convince Dale even to try the various activities. Tom cannot force Dale into the water or make him blow bubbles. His only choice seems to be to leave Dale alone, to give up on him. What else can he do? Dale's response is to retreat further. He isn't fighting or being aggressive. In fact, he makes it pretty easy to ignore him and leave him alone.

If Dale could only try, he might prove to be a terrific swimmer. Where did he acquire his belief in his own inadequacy? As it happens, Dale has very athletic parents who excel in most sports. They run, they Rollerblade, and they bike. When Dale attempts to join them, it's difficult for his parents to hide their impatience at how much he slows them down. They love Dale very much; they just don't know how to adjust their activities to Dale's level.

RESPONDING TO THE MESSAGE

Dale believes that because he is not as good at sports as his parents are, he might as well not try at all. He can't seem to do anything well enough. They are "perfect" and Dale, obviously, is not. It is safer to be helpless. If Dale can convince others that

Encouragement for Assumed Inadequacy in the Preschool

- Encourage even the smallest steps.
- Focus on what a child can do.
- Break up the tasks into small steps and celebrate success.

they can't expect much from him, they will leave him alone. What can Tom do besides ignore Dale?

Encourage Even the Smallest Steps

How might Tom encourage Dale when he is backing away from the pool? Tom might say, "Dale, I know it took a lot of courage for you to join in the bubble blowing. I want you to know I really appreciate that kind of effort." A simple message, but a powerful one! Tom did not assume that learning to swim was easy; in fact, he acknowledged how hard it is for Dale. Tom took time to notice the small step that Dale was willing to take. Over time, this kind of gentle encouragement may help Dale to take additional risks.

Focus on What a Child Can Do

Adults can learn to focus on what a child can do, to help him to see his own abilities first through others' eyes and eventually, through his own. All too often, teachers are occupied by the attention seekers or are busy waging power struggles with defiant children. Yet the child whose mistaken goal is assumed inadequacy or giving up is the one who can least afford to be ignored.

Break Up the Tasks into Small Steps and Celebrate Success

Adults who live and work with small children can learn to recognize and encourage small steps toward success and to have realistic expectations. Rudolf Dreikurs said, "Work for improvement, not perfection." An important part of encouraging small steps is to break a task down into small pieces that don't seem so intimidating to a discouraged child. Dale's teacher can be instrumental in helping him believe in himself. The key words for a child with this mistaken goal are "Believe in me!" and "Encourage, encourage, encourage!" As difficult as it may seem sometimes, try to have faith in the discouraged child. He sees himself mirrored in your eyes, and the energy of your belief in him is contagious.

WILL IT MAKE A DIFFERENCE?

Teachers and caregivers sometimes feel frustrated by the enormity of the task they face each day. It is no easy matter to teach and manage dozens of small, active people—especially when so much of what they believe about themselves and their world is shaped at home, out of the teacher's control.

Still, each of us can only do his or her best. The hours that children spend with their caregivers each day may be the closest many will come to feeling a sense of belonging and significance—and every hour is worth the work it takes to create. Better still, when parents and teachers can work together to truly understand children's behavior and deal with it effectively, the results for children can be nothing short of miraculous!

11

"YOU CAN'T COME TO MY BIRTHDAY PARTY!"

Social Skills for Preschoolers

"Will you be my friend?" Every preschool teacher has heard this plea. It can cause a tug on the heart—or annoyance at what may seem like a bid for undue attention. Actually, a child's need for friendship and social skills is part of normal and appropriate development.

The preschool years are filled with astonishing growth, and that growth can be traced in the development of friendships. The acquisition of social skills happens in predictable phases, and it happens much less painfully when adults understand a child's developing abilities. Caring adults can offer training, patience, and encouragement during this period of social skill development, a time sometimes fraught with tear-streaked faces, thrown toys, and grim tugs-of-war.

WHAT DOES FRIENDSHIP MEAN TO YOUNG CHILDREN?

When children are two or younger, they don't really have friends, even though they may find themselves surrounded by classmates at child care, the children of parents' acquaintances, or neighbors with whom they are plopped down to "play" with while the adults socialize. Between the ages of two and three, children begin to interact with their peers as objects of curiosity or exploration, which could include poking, biting, grabbing toys, or throwing sand—not effective components of friendship. They may engage in parallel play—playing individually next to another child.

At three, friendships begin to emerge; they are often organized by adults and may be fleeting, but the seeds of real relationship have been

planted, and some children do begin to build real connections with peers. By age four, children will begin to build more lasting friendships, often with two or three favorite playmates.

Learning for preschoolers often seems to involve opposites—they learn one skill and its opposite at the same time. In the case of friendship, this means that the blossoming of connection through friendship also brings with it a negative side—that of exclusion. There is no greater statement of friendship from a preschooler than "You can come to my birthday party." She is saying, "I like you enough to share the most important day in my world: the celebration of me!" Unfortunately, preschoolers also learn that leaving another child out provides a sense of power or the opportunity for revenge.

Jenna is four and a half years old. It is June and her birthday is not until December. Even so, hardly a day goes by that Jenna does not invite—or uninvite—someone at her preschool to her birthday party. When a parent wandered in to discuss enrolling her daughter, Jenna immediately went up to the new girl and said, "I'm going to be five. You can come to my party." A short while later, however, when Jenna's friend Ilsa won't share the dress-up clothes, Jenna sticks out her lip and announces in a voice of doom, "You can't come to my birthday!" Ilsa trembles at such a threat and quickly hands over one of the scarves.

Birthday invitations (or the threat of their withdrawal) are an early social tool. They represent an offer of mutual companionship and acceptance—and its opposite, momentary rejection. Because children at this age are unskilled at identifying and saying how they feel, this birthday threat and others like it serves two purposes. It says, "I am mad, sad, or upset in some way." It also serves as a tool to manipulate others to do one's bidding: "If you don't let me use the swing, you can't come to my birthday." As children mature and gain social and emotional skills, they learn to interact in more cooperative ways.

By the age of five, stronger friendships develop. This stage of friendship coincides with the increasingly strong emotions young children experience and sparks can fly when such powerful aspects of development coincide. By age five, children may focus on one playmate with whom they have a special relationship or they may have a special circle of friends.

Sergio and Kenneth are best buddies. Each watches for the arrival of the other at the child care center in the morning. They greet each other by rolling around on the floor in mock combat, or they quickly run off to begin a new Lego tower. They want to sit next to each other at group time, and their teacher sometimes has to remind them that if they can't sit together quietly, they will have to sit apart. Sergio and Kenneth are together all through the day; theirs is a wonderful and important early friendship.

A common problem evolves when three children are friends and one gets left out. Lauren's parents will hear anguish in her voice when she tells them that Erin and May are going swimming together; being left out is very painful. (By the next day, the hurt feelings are usually resolved and the friendship continues to thrive.) Rejection can be a painful social tool, and these later years of preschool require adults to model and coach children in the use of problem-solving techniques to work out the differences that will arise and to encourage healthy social interactions. Interestingly, gender also appears to influence social interactions. Several studies have shown that girls are more likely to use relationships and rejection as forms of aggression, while boys are more likely to fight, argue—and make up quickly.

> *Hal, Allan, and Shelley are also pals. They chase one another around the playground and are an inseparable team. Shelley is the clear leader of this threesome; she is frequently the one who chooses the game to be played and makes the rules. The wise teacher knows that if he wants to get these three interested in a new activity, the one to convince is Shelley.*

Special friendships form important foundations for many of life's relationships and provide a way for children to experiment with different roles. Just because Allan chooses to follow Shelley's lead now, for instance, doesn't mean he will never be a leader. It's just one of the roles he's trying on for size.

Social skills do not come without practice, and there will be many yelps of complaint and tearful faces. If adults focus not on playing the rescuer or referee but on nurturing healthy children who feel influential and capable, they will be helping children acquire the social skills they need to achieve a sense of belonging in a world of relationships.

PLAYTIME: A STAGE FOR SOCIALIZATION

Children's play is actually a laboratory where intensive research about roles and relationships is taking place. Playing is an activity that will form the foundation of their future interactions with others—it definitely is not meaningless or wasted time. Still, there will be rough spots, and most parents and caregivers can tell stories like this one.

Four-year-old Sharon came home with a scraped and bleeding knee one afternoon; her best friend, Jamie, had pushed her off the swing. Her mother's first instinct was to call the preschool teacher and complain. After all, weren't they supposed to be watching the children?

Fortunately for Sharon, her mom was more interested in helping her learn life skills than in blaming others for social conflicts. She sat down next to Sharon and asked, "Honey, can you tell me what happened?"

"Jamie got off the swing and I got on," Sharon said, then added defensively, "She wasn't using it anymore."

Mom suppressed a smile, suddenly realizing where this story might be going. "Do you know why Jamie got off the swing?"

"To get her jacket," was the calm response.

As Mom suspected, when Jamie came back with her jacket she found Sharon on "her" swing and pushed her off. Mom took a moment to validate her daughter's feelings. "I'll bet it was scary when Jamie pushed you. Maybe you felt that she wasn't your friend anymore."

Sharon's lip quivered. "Uh-huh," she said, and burst into tears. When her crying had subsided and she felt better, Sharon and her mom explored what happened. Mom asked if Sharon might have done something other than get on the swing when Jamie got off. Sharon thought for a moment and decided that she could have held the swing for Jamie until she got back.

"What might have happened if you held the swing for Jamie?" Mom asked.

"Jamie would have gotten back on," Sharon said.

"Would Jamie have pushed you off?"

Sharon shook her head. She could see that the results would have been different if she had behaved differently. Mom agreed that it was wrong of Jamie to push Sharon and helped her daughter understand that she could have told Jamie clearly, "No pushing." Mom has helped Sharon understand that she has choices that can affect the outcome of a situation. In other words, Sharon has personal power and influence. By talking this through with Sharon rather than rushing in to rescue her, Sharon's mother has helped her to feel capable.

It is important that parents avoid training children to see themselves as victims, helpless to change or affect what happens to them. Sharon's mother could have rushed to call (and blame) her daughter's preschool, and in the process might have encouraged her daughter to develop a victim mentality. Sharon might need some help, but not through sympathy, blaming others, or being rescued. She is learning how to interact in social situations, and parents and teachers should help her explore for herself what is happening, how she feels about it, what she is learning from it, and what ideas she has to solve the problem. Adults can help children learn from these early friendship experiments that they are not powerless and that the choices they make in life affect what they experience.

VICTIMS AND BULLIES

As early as preschool, however, children learn to use exclusion and physical threats to gain and maintain control over others. These behaviors plant the earliest seeds of bullying. Children need the help of parents and teachers to learn that they do have choices and personal power, which makes them less likely to become the targets of bullies. If adults rescue children instead of teaching them skills and helping them recognize the power they do have, they may unintentionally encourage children to become victims. After all, bullies need victims to be successful.

Marcie learned that she could get lots of attention when she complained to her mother that another child had hit her. Her mother would hug her, call her "my poor baby," and then call the preschool or neighbor (if the incident had happened at a friend's house), enraged that there had not been adequate supervision to protect Marcie. The teacher or neighbor would promise to be more vigilant.

One week Marcie's teacher, Joe, saw something very different happen on the preschool playground. As Joe watched from a corner of the yard, he saw Marcie trip and fall. When Joe went over to help her, Marcie said, "Bruce pushed me." Joe was astounded. Bruce had not been anywhere nearby. Marcie had decided that she liked the pity and attention of being a victim and was prepared to lie to get it.

Of course, children do need adult protection and supervision; at some point, Marcie probably was hit by another child. It is appropriate for a concerned parent to speak to other adults about such a problem. But at this age it is equally important to empower children to solve problems.

Marcie can learn to say, "Stop! Don't hit me." She can ask an adult for help, and the adult can coach Marcie in expressing her feelings: "That hurt me. I feel angry." The adult can help Marcie say what she does want: "I want to play without being hit or hurt." By focusing on healthy problem-solving methods and teaching children to understand and express their feelings, you can prevent bullying by not reinforcing it. Other problem-solving skills include naming and expressing one's feelings in words and learning to have empathy for others. Children can also learn the important skill of focusing on solutions (rather than blame). Empathy and compassion will continue to develop throughout childhood and adolescence but can be encouraged as soon as your child enters the world of peers and friendship. Many of these skills are enhanced through family and class meetings (see Chapter 16).

The preschool years are a good time to talk openly about bullying. During a family or class meeting you can invite children to talk about how others feel when they are bullied, why they think someone might choose bullying behavior, and how they could solve the problem.

In one preschool, the children often expressed anger at Joshua for knocking down their block towers and stomping on their sand castles. One day Joshua was absent, and the teacher decided to use this as an opportunity to help her students practice compassion and problem solving. During a class meeting she asked, "Why do you think Joshua does things that hurt other people's feelings?"

One observant little girl said, "Maybe he doesn't have any friends." (Joshua was new to the school and the other children avoided him because of his aggressive behavior.)

Another said, "Maybe he hasn't learned to use his words."

The teacher then asked, "How many of you would be willing to help Joshua?" Every child raised his or her hand. (Children love the opportunity to help.)

The teacher said, "I'll talk to Joshua and ask if he would be willing to join us in brainstorming for solutions to this problem. Meanwhile, what could you do to help Joshua?"

Several children suggested that they would be his friend and would invite Joshua to play with them. They also decided that they could use their words and tell him how they felt when he destroyed things, to ask him to stop—or to help them rebuild if they were too late.

The teacher decided to see how their plan worked before talking with Joshua and found that the problem diminished so profoundly that she didn't have to bring it up again. Joshua's aggressiveness began to blossom into leadership; he offered many suggestions for solving other problems that came up on the class meeting agenda. He learned to feel a sense of belong-

ing through the children's efforts at friendship, and to use his power in helpful ways.

"BUT NOBODY LIKES ME"

As we've mentioned, children's friendships are social skills laboratories—and not all of their experiments turn out well. Scraped knees and hurt feelings come with the territory. When you can avoid playing superparent or superteacher and help children learn from their mistakes, you will be teaching them to feel capable and competent.

> *Carla is five. One day when her mother is getting her ready to go to preschool, Carla resists. She says she doesn't want to go because she has no friends and no one likes her.*

Carla's parents and teachers must figure out what is really happening. If, in fact, Carla does not have playmates, the adults in her life can help her understand why. A child who is hurting others or who refuses to cooperate in games is not a welcome playmate, but such children can be taught more effective ways of relating to their peers.

Children who are successful at social relationships often learn to watch a game in progress and then join in by creating a role for themselves. Angela, for instance, spends a few moments watching her playmates play house, then offers to bake cookies for the others. She smoothly blends into the game in progress.

Emma is less skilled at doing this. She bounces over to a group of children and says, "Can I play?" She is often told no because the others don't want to be interrupted by having to create a role for Emma. Helping a child develop social skills will help her find belonging in her peer group, a need that, if not met, can result in the mistaken goal behaviors of undue attention, power, revenge, and assumed inadequacy.

A child like Carla may actually be a welcome playmate who simply does not see herself that way. Class meetings may be helpful in dealing with this situation at preschool but a parent confronted with this dilemma might need a different approach. For instance, Carla's dad might ask her, "What makes you believe that the other children don't like you?" or "What do you think it means to be someone's friend?" Together they can explore Carla's perceptions of friendship and then examine her experiences. "I noticed that today Adrian asked you to play on the swings with him. Why do you think he did that?" Carla now has an opportunity to compare her perceptions with what has actually happened. Teachers may also be able to offer information about positive experiences that happened during the day.

PLAYDATES

The playdate has become part of modern life. Children today may not have lots of siblings or other children living nearby, and inviting a child over to play is a way of helping children form friendships and practice social skills. Children feel a greater sense of kinship when they share time together in different settings. Carla's parents could invite one of her schoolmates to go to the zoo with them or perhaps to spend a Saturday afternoon playing with Carla's new playhouse. The increased closeness that results often will translate into more playtime at preschool as well. When a child initiates her own playdate, it is a milestone of social development.

> Six-year-old Leyla burst through the door announcing, "My friend is here for a playdate!" She was breathless with excitement and so was her friend, Zoya. They raced through the house, and Leyla could hardly show her friend each room fast enough. Even Leyla's mom, Fauziah, was excited and a bit anxious. Zoya was in Leyla's kindergarten class at her new school. Fauziah usually knew Leyla's friends from their mosque, Leyla's old preschool, or because they were family friends; this was the first time Leyla had formed a friendship all by herself. Leyla's playdate with Zoya had a triumphant feeling for both mother and daughter, and it was an important benchmark in Leyla's social development.

THE LESS-THAN-LOVABLE FRIEND

Children sometimes choose friends who pose a problem for parents. Sometimes your child will actively dislike or quarrel often with another child—or you may not care for the way your own child behaves when with a particular playmate. If your child's friendship results in exceptionally rowdy behavior or aggressiveness, it is helpful to set clear expectations.

Caleb just loved to play with Derek, who lived down the street. Derek was a wild little guy who was very physical. The two four-year-olds inevitably wound up running recklessly around the house or wrestling on the lawn, and more than once toys were broken and Caleb returned scraped, bumped, and bruised. Caleb's mother wasn't very happy about this friendship, especially since Derek was the only child with whom this sort of play occurred. Caleb's mom decided not to rescue Caleb but to establish clear guidelines about what she would allow when the boys played at her house.

One quiet morning, Mom sat down with Caleb and explained her feelings and her concerns for the boys' safety. She then clearly explained her expectations to Caleb, gently having him repeat them back to her to be sure he understood.

She established three rules: no bad names, no making fun of people, and no rough play. Mom and Caleb agreed that when Caleb or Derek chose not to follow the rules, Derek would have to go home. Derek would wait in the den and Caleb would wait in his room until Derek's mother could come to get him.

The plan was discussed with Derek and his mother, who agreed with the rules. Now both moms needed to plan ways to follow through when necessary. It is the nature of learning (and young children) that Caleb and Derek would need to see if the plan was for real. They might play nicely once or even twice, but eventually the rules would have to be tested.

Sure enough, the day came when Caleb joined Derek in climbing on the countertop. Caleb refused to get down when his mother asked him and threw in a "You're a butt-head" for good measure.

Caleb was given the choice of walking to his room or being carried there. Mom pointed kindly but firmly to the sofa, where Derek could wait for his mother. There was no reminder or warning necessary, since both boys knew the expectations and consequences. Derek's mom arrived at the front door quickly and escorted Derek home. Now both boys had learned that their parents really meant what they said and that their behavior would have to change. If it didn't, Caleb and Derek would lose the opportunity to play at each other's houses.

"HEY, LOOK AT ME!": SHOWING OFF

Some children seem to have inherited "peacock genes." They act as though strutting their stuff is the best way to succeed with others.

Q. My four-year-old son seems to totally forget everything we have taught him when he gets together with his peers. He is so excited to be with them that he tries to show off by misbehaving intentionally in their presence. He turns a deaf ear to all grown-ups and will stop goofing off only if we raise our voices very loud. What action can we take to stop this behavior?

A. Your son is becoming more interested in interacting with his peers than in paying attention to adults, which is developmentally appropriate. Understanding this fact will help you decide how to respond to your young show-off.

It would probably be a good start to stop using the very loud voice. When you want your son's attention, kindly and gently take him aside, get down to his eye level, and establish eye contact. Explain the problem, what you would like him to do, and what *you* will do. In other words, explain that the yelling indoors must stop. If it continues, you will have to take him home. (If you are not willing to actually leave, perhaps you can go into another room with him where he can calm himself before rejoining the play.) This plan will work only if you can speak to him respectfully and privately, so that he is not tempted to continue misbehaving out of embarrassment—and if you follow through.

"WHERE DO I FIT?": THE SOCIAL SIGNIFICANCE OF BIRTH ORDER

The family is often the laboratory where children first experiment with social skills—and brothers and sisters are the guinea pigs. Where children fit in their families is one factor in how they approach relationships with each other, and with the wider world outside the family.

In these preschool years children are making many of the decisions about themselves and others that will influence the rest of their lives. They are asking themselves, "What must I do to find a sense of belonging and significance in this family—and with my friends? Am I cute and adorable, or less than lovely? Am I good enough or must I keep trying harder—or should I just give up?" Preschoolers will carry the answers to those questions with them into the world around them, and they will practice what they are learning as they explore social relationships. (For more information on birth order, see Chapter 3.)

SIBLING FIGHTS

Are brothers and sisters a blessing or a curse? Most children occasionally wonder. Brothers and sisters are forever; most of them will outlive their parents, and children usually learn their first lessons about friendship through their relationships with their siblings.

It is heartwarming to see eighteen-month-old Timmy go up to his four-year-old sister and say, "Wuv you, Bef." It isn't so heartwarming to watch Timmy pull Beth's hair when she tries to rescue her favorite book from his clutches. When children are three to six years old, sibling fighting is the result of their immature social skills, mistaken ways to find their place in the family, and the reactions of the adults involved.

Social skills training is important for siblings, especially because of the unique aspect that sharing (and vying for) a parent's love and

---

A Parent with Arguing Children Can Use One of the Following Three Options

- **Beat it.** You can choose to leave the area. It is amazing how many children stop fighting when they lose their audience. Don't be surprised if they follow you. This is why Rudolf Dreikurs suggested that the bathroom is the most important room in the house—it's sometimes the only room with a lock on the door. If your children pound on the door, you may want to jump into the shower or stuff your ears with Kleenex while you read a good novel. (If you choose these methods, it is a good idea to tell your children, in advance, that this is what you will do when they fight.) You then may want to discuss fighting and problem solving at a family meeting.

- **Bear it.** This is the most difficult option because it means staying in the same room without jumping in to stop the fight or fix the problem. When children are fighting in a car, bearing it may mean pulling to the side of the road and reading for a while, telling your children, "I'll drive as soon as you are ready to stop fighting." The hard part is keeping your own mouth shut until they say they are ready.

- **End the bout or boot 'em out.** If things are simply getting too heated and you're worried about their safety (or your house's), you can send both children to cool off somewhere, or they can go outside if they want to continue their fight. Or they can "end the bout," an option they have at any time. (See Raymond Corsini and Genevieve Pointer, *The Practical Parent*, Simon & Schuster, 1984.)

attention brings to their conflicts. (Keep in mind that sibling fighting is not the same as sibling rivalry. Sibling rivalry is about the decisions each child in the family makes based on his or her birth order and role in family life—and can be a hidden basis for sibling fights.)

It is helpful when parents learn to see sibling fighting for what it usually is. Young children sometimes tussle as they investigate their relationship with each other. Parents can stay out of the rescuer role simply by leaving the room. Taking a quiet moment elsewhere eliminates the audience—and sometimes the struggle.

If the noise level and fear of mayhem is too great to ignore, try giving the children a big hug. "What?" you may say, "reward them for fighting?" Not exactly. If your children are competing for your attention, try giving it in an unexpected way. While hugging them, say, "I bet the two of you would like my attention right now. Next time, try telling me with your words instead of hurting one another." Acting in an unexpected way can cause children to pay more attention to your words—and it's always great to be hugged!

Since both children are involved, treat them the same way. Invite both children to take a positive time-out to cool off. Don't try to be judge and jury; worry about whodunit when you read a mystery, not when you raise a preschooler. When your children are ready to get along, they can come out. You have shifted the message from "Who is loved more?" to "Hurting each other is not okay."

THE SOCIAL SKILL OF SHARING

Sharing isn't easy. Most of us know adults who struggle with the concept, and for preschoolers, sharing is an ongoing challenge in the development of social skills. As we have pointed out, sharing is also affected by societal and cultural attitudes. In Western cultures, we expect little people to take turns, to welcome new siblings, or to be willing to give up playing with a favorite toy. These skills are counterbalanced by attitudes of "mine" and the high value placed on individualism. Expectations often accelerate during the late preschool years.

More Possibilities for Peacemaking

- Invite children to put the problem on the family or class meeting agenda.

- After a cooling-off period, use curiosity questions (which often begin with "what," "why," or "how") to help children explore what happened, how they feel about it, what they learned from the experience, and how they can solve the problem now.

- Teach children to use their words. This means that adults act as coaches—not lecturers or referees.

Older preschoolers are beginning to suspect that they are not the center of the universe—and the idea is not entirely welcome.

Many adults do not have much patience with children who have not mastered the social skill of sharing, and in many cultures such selfishness would be unthinkable. Still, learning to share is an ongoing, developmental process that requires skill training, lots of practice, and lots of patience from adults.

Q. My three-year-old has been acting up lately in child care, fighting with the other kids. He doesn't hit them, but he can't agree about sharing toys. He is not listening to his teacher. One day he seems okay, but the next day he refuses to allow any children near "his" playthings. How can I get him to understand that what he is doing is not acceptable behavior?

A. It sounds like you have a very normal little boy. Three-year-olds are just learning how to share, and sharing is a difficult skill to master. Most of us are unhappy when we do not get to have what we want when we want it.

A child needs clear and firm guidance, and he needs teaching rather than lectures or punishment. Remember, he does not yet know how to negotiate, compromise, and discuss problems with others. When children argue over a toy, adults frequently take the toy away from both children. There is more, however, that parents and caregivers can do to help children learn this important skill.

Children need to learn how to use words to ask for what they need. The adult can take two children aside after a dispute. When everyone is calm, try practicing how to ask to play with a toy. For instance, a child may ask, "May I use the blocks?" One possible response to a playmate's request is, "I am not done with them yet." You can then teach negotiation skills: "You can play with them in five minutes" or "Would you like to play with me?" Such training is vital to learning to share.

QUARRELING

Have you ever watched a litter of puppies wrestle, nip, and fight? You probably laugh at puppies and see their aggressive behavior as normal and even cute. When children argue and fight, however, parents are a bit less enchanted. Yet testing limits and disagreeing are as normal for young children as for puppies.

When children between the ages of three and a half and six quarrel, it may be effective to ask if it would help them to visit their feel-good place or to put the problem on the family meeting agenda, not as punishment but as an opportunity to cool off and calm down. Later you can then ask them to explore and name their feelings, and invite them to identify ways they could handle the situation next time. It is not helpful for adults to lose their own tempers, offer blame, punishment, and lectures, or leap into the fray themselves.

Teaching social skills with the same attention you give to other types of skill development will produce children who can play together peacefully—at least most of the time. When children experience continuous modeling and training, they can learn to get along quite well with other members of the world around them.

Mr. Conners found another creative way to deal with fighting when he saw two five-year-olds wrestling with each other at their preschool. He grabbed a toy microphone, rushed up to the boys, and said, "Excuse me. I'm a reporter for the six o'clock news. Would you each be willing to take thirty seconds to tell our listening audience your version of what this fight is all about?" He handed the microphone to one boy and told him to look into the make-believe camera.

The boy caught the spirit of the game and started telling his story. When thirty seconds were up, Mr. Conners took the mike and handed it to the next boy. When his thirty seconds were up, Mr. Conners looked into the imaginary camera and said, "Well folks, tune in tomorrow to find out how these boys solved their problem."

Then Mr. Conners turned to the boys and said, "Would you boys be willing to come back later and tell our listening audience how you solved this problem?" With big grins on their faces, both boys agreed and went off together to work on a solution—which was then reported then to the imaginary camera. Mr. Conners turned an argument into an opportunity to learn social skills.

RECOGNIZING AND NAMING FEELINGS

For preschoolers, a big part of learning social skills involves learning about feelings. It helps to know that often children hit because they are acting out their feelings of frustration and anger. After all, there are so many people who get in the way of a child's impulses and urges. It's important to teach children that there is a difference between a feeling and an action, and how to identify and cope with feelings. (See Chapter 7 for more on feelings and communication.)

Three-year-old Jack was on a rampage. He had been hitting the other children at the preschool, knocking over their towers of blocks, and kicking gravel on the playground. One afternoon, Jack got angry when another child ran in front of him. He pushed her down, causing her to scrape her knee.

Miss Terry, Jack's teacher, gently led the raging Jack away from the other children and toward the book corner. As Jack calmed down, Miss Terry brought him a book that had a picture of a sad-looking boy on the cover.

"Why does he look like that?" Jack asked Miss Terry.

"Well," his teacher replied, sitting down to look at the picture, "he looks sad to me. Why do you think he might be sad?"

This question planted that first small seed of empathy, inviting Jack to experience the world through another person's perspective. Jack began to explain that the boy in the picture was sad because his favorite babysitter had gone away and he wasn't going to see her anymore—attributing his own feelings to the child in the picture because his experience of the world is his only reference point. Understanding this, Miss Terry asked Jack if he would like a hug, and he scrambled gratefully onto her lap. "That little boy must feel very lonely and sad," she said. Jack began to cry in his teacher's arms.

When Jack's sobs had slowed to sniffles, Miss Terry asked if he could think of a way to help the child he had pushed feel better again. "I bet she's sad, too," Jack said. "Maybe I could play a special game with her and help her put away her lunch stuff."

Miss Terry wrote a note to Jack's parents explaining what had happened and mentioning Jack's sadness over the loss of his babysitter. Jack helped by making a mark at the bottom to serve as his signature.

Jack had an opportunity to explore his feelings in safety. He also learned that he was responsible for his behavior toward other children. Identifying and accepting feelings can help children learn effective social skills.

HITTING AND AGGRESSION

Older preschoolers who are hitting or pulling hair should be firmly separated. A parent or teacher can say, "I can't allow you to hurt others," and can help the combatants explore other ways of acting when they feel angry or frustrated. It is important to understand that behavior often contains a coded message about how a child is feeling; while some behaviors are inappropriate or hurtful, the feelings themselves are not wrong. Interpreting the beliefs a child has about himself will provide clues about how parents and teachers might respond.

It will take more than one such occasion to teach children to play cooperatively together. Patient repetition, modeling, and guidance will help children learn more quickly the pleasures of getting along; it won't turn them into angels! Remember that social skills mistakes can always be turned into opportunities to learn.

WHEN CHILDREN HURT ADULTS

Sometimes a child's aggression and anger aren't directed only at other children. Some preschoolers have learned to hit, kick, bite, or yank the hair of their parents and caregivers when life doesn't go their way. And even little fists and feet can hurt. Parents often do not know what to do with an aggressive child and may inadvertently reinforce the very behavior they are trying to change.

Q. I'm the mother of a three-and-a-half-year-old boy. My son has been calling me names and hitting me when he doesn't get what he wants. I think he picked this up at his preschool. We've always tried to use the most humane methods of discipline; we don't hit, yell at, or humiliate him in any way. We always try to reason with him. I'm at a loss in this situation. Please tell me the best way to deal with such behavior.

A. It is unlikely your child picked up this behavior at preschool. Preschool simply exposes him to more children and adults with whom he must share, to whom he sometimes has to defer his demands, and over whom he tries to establish his right to territory. At home he may simply redouble his efforts to get his way, where the odds are a bit more to his liking.

There are several things a parent can try to help a child change aggressive behavior. The following sections provide suggestions; choose the one that fits you and your child.

Decide What You Will Do

Let your son know that every time he hits you or calls you a name, you will leave the room until he is ready to treat you respectfully. After you have told him this once, follow through without any words. Leave immediately.

Hold the Child Kindly and Firmly

If you are concerned that your child will tear up furniture, break things, or hurt herself, try sitting down and holding her firmly so that she cannot hit or kick, without lecturing or yelling, until the moment passes. Rocking gently may help her to calm down more quickly.

Share Your Feelings

Tell him, "That really hurts (*or* that hurts my feelings). When you are ready, an apology would help me feel better." Do not demand or force an apology. The main purpose of this suggestion is to give a model of sharing what you feel and asking for what you would like. People don't always give us what we would like, but we show respect for ourselves by sharing our feelings and wishes in nondemanding ways.

Use a Positive Time-Out

As you learned in Chapter 1, it can be a good idea to create and name a positive time-out area with your child—a place that can have teddy bears, books, or a soft cushion. When your child hits or hurts, ask, "Would it help you feel better to go to your cool-off place for a while?" It is important to teach your child that people do better when they feel better and that sometimes everyone needs time to calm down and cool off. If your child doesn't want to go, you might model for him by saying, "I'm very upset right now. I think I'll go to a quiet spot until I feel better."

> **When Children Are Disrespectful to Adults**
>
> - Decide what *you* will do.
> - Hold the child kindly and firmly.
> - Share your feelings.
> - Use a positive time-out.
> - Ask curiosity questions.
> - Offer limited choices.
> - Put the problem on the family or class meeting agenda.

Ask Curiosity Questions

Curiosity questions help a child explore the consequences of his behavior. "What happens when you hit people or call them names? How does it make you feel? How does it make others feel? What could you do to help them feel better? How else could you get what you want?" Be sure to ask these questions in a kind and firm manner and with a sincere desire to hear what the child has to say. Don't turn the conversation into a lecture.

Offer Limited Choices

You can calmly let your child know what he *can* do by offering limited choices. You can say, "Hitting and hurting others is not okay. You can stop hitting and stay here with me, or you can go to your room and have your feelings in private. You decide." Be sure that all of the choices you offer are respectful and are acceptable to you.

Put the Problem on the Family or Class Meeting Agenda

When the problem of hitting and name-calling appears on the family or class meeting agenda, it can be discussed during a regular family or class meeting when everyone is feeling calm. Everyone can work together for solutions. (More on meetings in Chapter 16.)

Stopping Violent Behavior

Q. How do you handle a child who feels that violence is the only way to solve a problem?

A. This question raises several more: What is going on in this child's life? Where is this child learning violence? Too much television? Too many video games? Too much punishment? A child's environment and the role models he encounters provide many clues about that child's violent behavior.

As a wise person once said, if you want to understand the fruit, look at the tree. Children do indeed learn what they live, and changing angry, aggressive behavior is best accomplished through kind, firm teaching about respect, nonviolent ways of solving problems, and watching adults practice what they preach.

DISRUPTIVE BEHAVIOR IN THE CLASSROOM

It is especially important in group settings to provide opportunities for learning about social skills. Teachers face the ripple effect of behavior daily. For example, everyone sits down to group time and one child starts to make raspberry noises. Within moments, the entire group is buzzing and spitting.

Sit quietly until the class calms down. Model the behavior you want. Some teachers decide to join in the noise making, which usually makes everyone laugh—and which may be the easiest way to help children settle down. When disruptive behavior causes repeated problems, ask the children for help.

Use a class meeting to explain that it causes a problem for you when children continue to make noise after the group gathers together. Discuss what happens, invite the children to comment on what they notice, and then come up with a proposed solution. A hand signal, clapping pattern, or lights out might be decided upon as a way to indicate that classroom noise should stop.

Class meetings can be used to explore many possible problems. Ask, "What would you do if . . . ?" or describe a situation and ask the children what they think went wrong. Storytelling, flannel boards, and books are other ways to introduce social skills. Help children identify the skills you are teaching, and take time to discuss what happened and why.

SOCIAL INTEREST

Alfred Adler described "social interest" as a real concern for others and a sincere desire to make a contribution to society. As children enter into the lives of their families and schools, they want very much to feel that they belong. And one of the most powerful ways to achieve a sense of belonging is to make a meaningful contribution to the well-being of others in the family or group. When adults can help preschoolers care about and participate in their community, everyone benefits. In the family or preschool, a wonderful way to encourage social interest is by sharing chores or the work the family does together.

For young children there really is no difference between play and work, so adults can use everyday tasks as opportunities to teach social interest.

While Charlene fixed the hamburger patties, three-year-old Sean happily unwrapped cheese slices and placed them on the buns. When the family sat down to dinner, imagine how pleased Sean felt when the family mentioned how good their cheeseburgers tasted, thanks to Sean's efforts.

Five-year-old Becky reminded her grandma to use her eye-drops every evening during her visit. When Grandma returned home, Becky wanted to call her every night so she could continue to remind her.

These examples show social interest at work; it is meaningful involvement that benefits others. There are many simple tasks preschoolers can do that not only build skills and cooperation but also give them opportunities to practice getting along with others. Invite your child to help you with one of the tasks in the table on page 215. These are some ideas to get you started. For more information on age-appropriate tasks, see *Chores Without Wars* by Lynn Lott and Riki Intner, Taylor, 2005.

RELATIONSHIPS: THE TIES THAT BIND

Like it or not, relationships form the fabric of our lives. We live in families, we go to school with peers, and eventually we work, live, love, and play with other people. Helping your young child get along pre-

AGE-APPROPRIATE TASKS

Age	Self-Care	Food	Household
Age 3	Undress self Wash hands Take off shoes	Set table (napkins and silverware, except knives) Feed self (with hands and spoon) Put on coat (with some help) Pour milk from small pitcher Serve fruit Oil potatoes for baking Peel bananas Stir batter (pancake, etc.) Rinse lettuce and other produce Slice hard-boiled eggs (with a special slicer)	Pick up toys Put own clothes in hamper Dig in garden Harvest berries and other garden produce
Age 4	Select clothes Dress and undress self (with some help) Put on shoes	Squeeze fruit for juice Grate cheese Butter toast Scrub mushrooms Slice bananas, pickles, etc. (with butter knife) Knead dough Measure water to reconstitute juice Frost cupcakes	Straighten bedcovers Arrange cut flowers Stack newspapers Crush cans for recycling Set table Sort laundry
Age 5	Help pack lunch Comb/ brush hair Wash hair Tie shoes (with some help)	Slice soft fruit or vegetables (with sharp knife, under supervision) Roll out dough Put together a cake mix Spread peanut butter and jam on crackers or bread Help plan menus "Smash" cooked potatoes with hand masher	Fold washcloths Care for pet Put away laundry (with some help) Wash windows Help grocery shop Polish shoes Wash car (with help)

pares him to experience the best that life can offer: connection and contentment with friends and family. Disagreements and conflict are inevitable, but he can learn to handle those, too, with dignity and mutual respect. Taking the time to teach and encourage social skills now will pave the way for a happier life as your child grows and matures.

12

ENDING BEDTIME BATTLES

Preschoolers and Sleep

It is nap time at the preschool, and all of the children are asleep—except Anita. The teacher has read a story and offered back rubs, but in spite of her best efforts, Anita is still awake.

Tasha is a different story. Tasha's mother worries that Tasha sleeps too long at nap time, which makes it difficult to get her to bed at night. The teacher promises to keep Tasha awake longer or to wake her up earlier, but despite her best efforts, Tasha is usually the first to fall asleep and the last to wake up.

The bottom line is that you can't make a child sleep, and you can't control when he will wake up. Sometimes parents feel so in need of time to themselves that they try to establish a bedtime or nap time that just doesn't match their child's needs.

During the preschool years, most children give up taking a long, regular nap—if they ever did! Parents often miss those peaceful afternoon hours during which they could get something accomplished or rest a bit themselves. It becomes very tempting to try to coerce a child into taking naps—but unfortunately, making him fall asleep (whether at night or during nap time) is simply beyond adult control.

Most parents have experienced the frustration of a child who is happily wide awake long past bedtime, tumbles out of bed at awkward moments, or refuses to wake even when Mom and Dad have urgent business to attend to. Is there anything parents can do to help children settle into a sleep cycle that works for everyone?

ROUTINES: EVERYDAY MAGIC

Children in the preschool years thrive on routines. Routine and consistency (while occasionally boring for adults) work well with a young child's brain development and encourage cooperation and learning. Children thrive when their lives are clear and predictable, and they enjoy the security of comfortable repetition.

Routines are also a first line of defense and a unique safety net when children and families experience traumatic events. Reestablishing a familiar routine in the midst of change or chaos will help children feel safe and protected. Whether a child has been uprooted by a national disaster, political upheaval, or a family crisis (divorce, death, or a move to a new home), the sooner a routine is back in place, the sooner that child will be able to cope and begin healing.

According to "Family Strengths: Often Overlooked, but Real," by Kristin Anderson Moore, Ph.D., Rosemary Chalk, Juliet Scarpa, and Sharon Vandiver, M.P.P., Child Trends Research Brief, August 2002, children who live in families in which daily life is predictable do better at school and acquire high levels of self-control. This self-control has a bounce-back quality, most commonly referred to as *resiliency*. Everyone experiences stressful and difficult times, but resiliency allows us to get beyond those tough times—not just to survive, but to thrive.

Taking part in regular daily routines may even lead to lowered risk of marijuana, alcohol, and tobacco use, as well as fewer school suspensions during later adolescence.

A familiar routine in the morning, at mealtimes, and at bedtime can eliminate the need children often feel to test their boundaries. Clear expectations and predictable activities can smooth the rough spots out of a youngster's day (and that of his parents and teachers).

As children grow older and begin school, using routines can eliminate many of the hassles surrounding chores or homework, especially when the child is old enough to help create the routine. Issuing commands often invites resistance from children. How would you feel if someone was always telling you what to do, how to do it, and when to do it? If you and your child create routines, the routines can then become the "boss." You have only to ask, "What is next on our routine chart?" and children love to tell you (instead of being told).

The best way to help your children maintain a strong sense of self and to develop a desire to contribute and cooperate is to involve them in age-appropriate decision making as much as possible. Involving children in the creation of routines is a great way to help them maintain their sense of self and their desire to cooperate.

Routines will vary from family to family, from preschool to preschool, but they are useful ways to take the struggle out of the terrible trio of sleeping, eating, and toileting. In this and the following chapters, you will discover basic guidelines that are helpful when planning any type of routine.

THE ROUTINE CHART

Brainstorm a list of bedtime tasks with your child and then let her help make a routine chart. Try to keep the list to three or four (but no more than six) tasks. Remember, a routine chart is not for rewards or stickers; it is simply a map to help your child remember what comes next. Children love it when you take pictures of them doing each task so pictures can be pasted on the routine chart. Some prefer to draw pictures of themselves doing the task, or simple symbols to represent each task. Images cut from magazines can also be used. Help your child personalize the chart with her name, glitter, or other decorations. The chart can then be placed where it is easy to see and follow. Remember the magic words: "What is next on your bedtime routine chart?" so she can tell you instead of being told.

BEDTIME ROUTINE POSSIBILITIES

Having a predictable, familiar routine can take the struggle out of bedtime. But how do you find a bedtime routine that works for your family? The following ideas for bedtime routine activities may help you build a routine for your child that helps him (and you) enjoy sweet dreams.

Playtime

A family playtime is a good way to begin your nighttime routine. One family enjoys playing board games, while another likes a rousing game of tag or a pillow fight. It is best to place more active games at the beginning of your routine. The idea is to move steadily toward quiet, calming activities.

Time for Choices

Planning ahead can eliminate many a power struggle. For instance, allow your child to choose between two pairs of pajamas *before* getting into the tub. She can lay them out on her bed so they are ready as soon as bath time is over.

Choosing clothes for the next day is also important. Successful mornings usually begin the night before. Power struggles and meltdowns often occur in the morning when your child can't decide what to wear, wants to wear something she can't find, or puts on something you think is inappropriate (such as shorts in the middle of winter). We think it's important to let children have some autonomy in choosing what they wear, but children often choose to test boundaries when parents' time is in short supply. Choosing clothes the night before will eliminate at least one potential morning power struggle. (This may sound obvious, but another simple solution is to put winter clothes away in the summer and summer clothes away in the winter. Inappropriate choices for clothing are then less likely.)

Bath Time

A soak in the tub can be wonderfully soothing—and it can be a time for closeness and play, too. There are many wonderful bath toys available (although your kitchen measuring cups and spoons will probably do quite nicely), and the sound and feel of warm water helps relax most children. An evening bath time should probably follow any active games and begin the "settling down" part of your routine.

Toothbrushing

Did you know that brushing teeth can be fun? Some families put toothpaste on each other's brushes and all scrub happily away together, not only teaching good oral hygiene but having some good, clean fun as well. Instead of creating power struggles over toothbrushing, use it as an opportunity for creating traditions and connections.

Story Time

Telling or reading stories is a familiar part of bedtime, for good reason. Young children love to hear stories; in fact, some never tire of hearing the same story over and over—and woe to the lazy parent who tries to leave a paragraph out! And story time really helps children learn: a child's earliest "reading" experience may consist of reciting a book to you, even turning the pages at the right spot. Children's poetry and simple rhymes are wonderful, too, and help your child learn language.

As your child grows older (or if she often has difficulty falling asleep), you may want to let her look through books as she lies quietly in bed. A variation on this theme is to play a story tape and let your child follow along in the accompanying book. Or you might tape yourself reading or telling a favorite story; then, if your child lives in more than one household or if you must be away for a while, he can hear your reassuring voice even when you can't be with him.

Do beware of manipulation: some children beg for "just one more story," and then "just one more, pleeeeeease." This can be prevented by agreeing together on one or two stories when creating your bedtime routine. Then, when the begging starts, you can ask, "What does our routine chart say?" Another possibility is to give your child a hug and say, "Nice try" (with a warm smile) as you leave the room or move on to the next part of your routine. Simply reflecting this request ("I can tell that you really want to hear another story") followed by reassurance ("Let's put this book beside your bed so we'll remember to read it first thing tomorrow night") demonstrates kindness without allowing manipulation. Children know when you mean it and they know when you don't. Being kind and firm at the same time will let them know that you mean what you say.

Special Activities

Since children often feel cozy and willing to talk just before they fall asleep, bedtime can be one of the best parts of your day together—if you let it be. You may want to pray together or sing a special song. One dad carries his small son around his room to say good night to each stuffed animal and picture. A tape of soothing lullabies or soft music can create a relaxing atmosphere.

Some parents enjoy asking their children to share the happiest and saddest moments of their day and then letting their children ask them the same questions. (Because children's grasp of time is a little fuzzy, you may hear about things that happened this afternoon, last week, or even last month!) You will be amazed at how much you and your children learn about each other. Such moments go far beyond helping a child sleep; they are filled with shared love, trust, and closeness.

Hugs and Kisses

There are families where hugging, kissing, and saying "I love you" happen daily. In other families, these things rarely happen. Not surprisingly, researchers have discovered that a daily ration of hugs encourages emotional health, and if you haven't been dispensing regular hugs and kisses, you might consider giving it a try. Bedtime is the perfect time for hugs, kisses, and gentle reassurances of love.

> *Every night, Cissy's aunt Elaine loves to sit on the edge of three-year-old Cissy's bed and say, "If we were to line up all of the three-year-old girls in the world, guess which one I'd pick? I would say, 'I want that one!'" Aunt Elaine then points at Cissy, who giggles happily and launches herself into her aunt's arms for a hug.*

Hugging Rather than Hitting

A recent study at the University of Miami's Touch Research Institute discovered that going through the day without a hug, a pat on the shoulder, or even a handshake can be harmful—and some researchers believe that American children are dangerously touch-deprived.

The institute's studies have shown that touch can reduce pain and stress, alleviate symptoms of depression, and help premature infants gain weight, among other benefits. Lack of human touch appears to increase the risk for aggression. Touch should always be welcomed and appropriate, but back rubs, hugs, and other loving touches may become a valuable part of your child's routine.

The glow from a child's face during moments like these can illuminate an entire room!

PRACTICE YOUR ROUTINE

A bedtime routine does not guarantee that your child will never have difficulty falling asleep. If a child says he "can't sleep," tell him it's okay. He just needs to lie quietly in bed and look through a book or think quiet thoughts. Keep in mind that falling asleep is your child's job. You can only provide him with the opportunity. The hardest part of your job may be to ignore (with kindness and firmness) demands for more drinks and stories after you have completed a loving bedtime routine.

A bedtime routine may make it possible for you and your young child to enjoy sharing a special part of the day together rather than rehearsing for World War III. The possibilities are endless. Pick out some ideas that appeal to you—or use your own creativity to find a routine that works for you and your child. Whatever you decide on, practice it often enough that it becomes a familiar, predictable part of your day—and a peaceful way to help and encourage your child to fall asleep. A special quality of routines is that they guide us to the development of healthy (and desirable) habits through consistent, comfortable repetition.

PRESCHOOL ROUTINES FOR NAP TIME

Teachers can follow a similar procedure to create nap-time routines in the preschool or child care setting. Include soft music, muted lighting, or gentle back rubs. Involve children by allowing them to help set out nap things, take off and line up shoes, and use the potty before and after lying down to rest. Calm caregivers invite children to enjoy a restful atmosphere.

THE IMPORTANCE OF COMFORT

Even though we stress the importance of getting children involved, there are many things adults can do on their own to help children sleep cozily. You can make sure children are comfortable in pajamas that fit, in beds or cribs that are secure, and with the appropriate number of blankets. You can also remember to consider your child's temperament. Is the sleeping area warm or cool enough? Does your child need absolute quiet or a steady hum of activity? A night-light or complete darkness? Like adults, children have different needs regarding light and dark, noise and quiet. There is no right or wrong; finding out what works best for your child will take patience and a bit of trial and error.

If your child spends time in more than one household, special smells and textures can make bedtime much less stressful. A pillow or blankie that travels with your child from home to home or a special cuddly toy at the child care center can be very helpful. Children have been known to curl up with their jackets tucked under their heads when nothing else was available or the preferred item had been left behind, drawing comfort from the familiar feel and smell.

An evening snack containing calcium, such as milk or yogurt, may help your child relax enough to sleep. Some people believe that sugar stimulates children. Although research is inconclusive, avoiding sugary food late in the evening or before naps may prove helpful. (Be sure to read labels; you may be surprised at the sugar content of some so-called healthy foods.) Use trial and error to discover what works best for your child.

TESTING TIME

How many times have you heard the plaintive cry "Mommy, I'm thirsty"? It may be helpful to agree with your child on how many drinks of water she will get (and put the allotted number on your routine chart). Whatever your agreement, follow through with kind and firm action. There are several ways to do this. You might say, "I hear you, and I'm sure you can make it until morning." You could offer a simple "Uhmmmmm." (Children often stop testing when they don't get a response.)

If the testing escalates and your child gets out of bed, kind and firm action without any words is usually most effective. It looks like this: your child gets up; you take her by the hand and lead her back to bed with a kind manner and your mouth shut; you give her a kiss and leave. If she gets up again, you take her by the hand and lead her back to bed with a kind manner and your mouth shut; you give her a kiss and leave. At times, if she refuses to walk beside you, you may need to pick her up and carry her. Again, do this in a calm, matter-of-fact manner, with a firm but loving touch. If you repeat this process

as many times as it takes (usually quite a few the first night), your child will get the idea that she can count on you to mean what you say—and she can count on you to treat her with dignity and respect even when she is testing you. Summon all your patience—and don't get discouraged. When you are consistent, the testing usually does not last longer than three nights—five at the most (although they may feel like five *very* long nights).

One mother shared that on the first night they tried this new plan, her daughter was put back to bed twenty-four times. The second night, it was twelve times. The third night, it took only twice before the daughter knew her mother meant what she *didn't* say. By the fourth night, her daughter was happily following the bedtime routine—to the letter.

CONTROL YOUR OWN BEHAVIOR

Perhaps it is time for a reminder that the only behavior you can control is your own. The magic that occurs is that children usually change their behavior in response to you.

Q. We have a three-year-old daughter who has been having a very difficult time going to bed at night. We have a bedtime routine—we give her a bath with her baby sister, read her a story, get her a glass of water, and say prayers. As soon as it's time for us to leave, she starts acting up. We tell her that if she keeps yelling or crying that we'll have to close her door because she's going to wake up her sister. She doesn't care about this and will call us stupid, stick her tongue out at us, and so on. When we close her door, she goes absolutely crazy—banging on the walls and doors, messing up her blinds, dumping her toy box, or yelling by her window, "Somebody help me—I need my mommy and daddy."

We wait for three minutes (one minute of time-out for each year of her age) and then open the door and ask her if she's finished being mad and ready to get back in her bed and behave. She'll say no and go through it again for another three minutes. We give her one more chance and then tell her that we'll have to close her door for the remainder of the night. The other night we had to stand by her door until 1:30 A.M. with her going crazy for four hours! We let her sleep in in the morning and she also takes a nap, but we can't do that. We're exhausted. Help!

A. It sounds like no one is getting much rest except your daughter. Four things will help to close the curtains on this nighttime drama: help her feel sleepy, respect her needs—and yours, quit battling and work toward cooperation, and use kind and firm follow-through.

Help Her Feel Sleepy
It seems that your daughter is able to marshal all her physical and emotional reserves for bedtime. She just isn't all that sleepy, especially after sleeping in and taking her nap. She may not be getting enough active exercise during the day to make her feel tired at night. Try making active play part of your bedtime routine. Consider taking a trip to the park, engaging in some rough-and-tumble play, or even signing up for evening swim classes. Once she is tired, you will have nature on your side. You might also consider giving up naps so that she is ready for an earlier bedtime. Although you can't control when she will or will not sleep, by eliminating the nap rituals you at least make it less convenient for her to take a nap.

Respect Her Needs—and Yours
Your daughter is feeling dethroned by her baby sister. Babies and toddlers take up lots of adult time and energy. What is left over for the older child? Your three-year-old has discovered an effective way to get her parents' attention. You can replace this negative attention with positive attention at other times of the day.

Carve out time to enjoy a moment with her alone. Be sure to point out to her that this is a time for just the two of you, that you are glad to have time alone with her, and that you enjoy having an older child with whom you can do special things. Such time can be as simple as a trip to the grocery store or library or a walk around the block. When her need to feel included, noticed, and special is met in this way, she will have less reason to seek attention through bedtime battles.

You have needs, too. Your children will be more likely to respect you if you demonstrate that you respect yourself. Give yourself time to unwind, relax, and focus on the evening together. A late-afternoon shower, a cup of tea, or a short exercise routine might make a real difference in your energy level. Remember that meeting your needs means you are better able to respond to the needs of other family members.

Quit Battling and Work Toward Cooperation

Where does your daughter get her amazing tenacity? Two parents who are willing to wait at her door for hours must have some genetic connection to the howler on the other side. It is time to start building cooperation, and the only people in this power struggle you can control are yourselves. In other words, you may not be able to control your daughter's sleep habits, but you can decide what you will do. Here are some suggestions:

- Ask for her help. (You might be surprised at how well this works.)

- Explain that you do not like to hold her door closed at bedtime. Ask her if she has any ideas about ways you could stop doing that.

- Work out a bedtime routine together.

- Decide what you will do instead of what you will try to make her do. (You may decide to take her back to her bed, give her a kiss, and leave.) Let her know your plan. Some possibilities are to go to bed yourself, read a book, and keep your own door closed rather than stand guard over her door.

- Seek solutions that work for all of you.

Use Kind and Firm Follow-Through

It may be comforting to know that you are not alone in your bedtime hassles. If you have tried all of the above and your child is still getting out of bed, simply put her back in bed. This is effective when you remember the following:

- Don't say a word. Actions speak louder than words—and they are much harder to argue with.

- Be sure your actions are both kind and firm. This means you eliminate even the nonverbal lectures (i.e., your angry body language).

- Be consistent. If you put your child back in bed five times and then give in, you have taught her that she only has to be more persistent than you are.

- Be sure you are spending special time with your child at other times during the day. (For details about special time, refer to Chapter 9 on mistaken goals.)

WHAT ABOUT NAPS?

Young children may resist sleep, not because they don't need it but because they don't want to miss out on anything as they explore their exciting world. All children do not need the same amount of sleep. Quiet time may work better for some children than nap time. Some are through with napping by two or two and a half years old. Others need naps until they start kindergarten (or, like one of the authors of this book, forever).

Whether it is nap time or quiet time, follow these guidelines:

- Don't tell your child she is tired. Admit that you are tired and need some quiet time.

- Get your child involved in planning for his nap time or quiet time. Allow your child to choose a special nap-time stuffed animal, a different bed, or a blanket different from the one he uses for bedtime.

- Teach your child to use a simple CD, cassette, or other player. Let her choose from a collection of nap-time music and start the player herself. Do not use earphones but allow the music to play softly nearby.

- Give her a limited choice: "Do you want to start your nap (or quiet time) at 1:00 or at 1:15?"

- Avoid the use of television to put your child to sleep. A study in the journal *Pediatrics* suggests that the longer children sit in front of a TV, the less likely they are to sleep well.

One mother we know lets her child choose a special sleeping bag that can be used only at nap time. During family meetings, her three-year-old daughter chooses the room she wants to take a nap in. To avoid manipulation she could choose between only two designated rooms: her bedroom or the playroom. She also agreed that whichever room she chose would be the one she would use for that week. She and her mom then set a kitchen timer for one hour (so she won't miss out on too much, and so she'll be sleepy at bedtime). Mom has promised that if the "ding" doesn't wake her up, Mom will.

Taking naps in different beds can work for nap time, but bedtime routines require the consistency of the same bed. This raises the question of whose bed a child will sleep in.

WHOSE BED?

There are many people who believe in the family bed. Usually, this is a happy time for families who choose it. However, many parents have small children in their bed not by choice but by default—and they are begging for help about how to solve this problem. They may have enjoyed snuggling with their little one for a while, but now they want their privacy back.

Parents need to decide what they truly want and be ready to follow through with kind and firm action. The reality is that like all habits, breaking this one can be painful for everyone. Children ready your unspoken messages quite well. If a child senses you are ambivalent about where he should sleep, he will recognize your doubts. When you are sure of your decision that he should sleep in his own bed, he will sense that as well.

Marissa and her husband want their bed back. Jonathan slept with them until he turned three. For the past six months, Jonathan has had his own bed but has refused to use it unless his mom or dad lies down with him until he falls asleep. They often fall asleep before he does and the rest of their evening is lost. When they do wake up and go to their own bed, Jonathan usually wakes up and cries until they take him into their bed.

This issue is a bit more complex than it may seem. Since Jonathan shared his parents' bed for quite a while, it isn't surprising that now he wants to continue. Being with his parents at night probably has many meanings for Jonathan. He gets attention, security, and lots of cuddles. On the other hand, being alone in his bed feels lonely and a bit scary at times. Jonathan's feelings may be logical, or they may provide an excuse for him to continue seeking undue attention—a habit his parents have unwittingly reinforced. He may be missing an opportunity to learn self-soothing, an important life skill. Now the real question is what his parents want to do—and what they are willing to do to change their son's habit.

Jonathan's parents must decide what they want, as must all parents. Opting for the family bed has some long-range implications. The biggest one is what will happen when you decide you want your child out of your bed? What if you are a single parent who decides to remarry? Is your child (or new partner) going to be willing to share you in bed?

If you have decided that it is time for your child to sleep in his own bed, follow through as described above. Please remember to do lots of deep breathing, because this plan requires patience.

Learning to go to sleep on her own will not create lifelong trauma for your child; it is usually more traumatic for parents than for children! Your attitude is the key. If you feel confident that you are doing the right thing by teaching your child that he is capable of getting to sleep on his own, he will feel the energy of your confidence. On the other hand, if you feel guilty, angry, or ambivalent, that energy will be communicated and will invite manipulation, helplessness, or power struggles.

CODDLED OR CAPABLE?

Kindness and firmness at the same time are the keys to effective parenting. Giving in to a child's continuous demands is not loving behavior. Children do not feel safe when adults fail to establish clear boundaries. Allowing a child to learn to fall asleep on her own is a lifetime gift.

The suggestions in this chapter can help parents use bedtime as an opportunity for teaching their children important life skills instead of manipulation and power struggles. Children can learn thinking skills, problem-solving skills, self-control, and trust—that when parents say something, they mean it and will follow through with dignity and respect. They can also learn to trust themselves and to believe "I am capable." Bedtime truly can be heaven instead of hell. Sweet dreams!

13

"I DON'T LIKE THAT!"

Preschoolers and Eating

Imagine for a moment that you're sitting down to dinner with some friends instead of your family. Suppose you've invited Joyce, her husband, James, and your neighbor Sam over for a meal. As you pass around your favorite lasagna and a bowl of broccoli, the conversation goes something like this:

> You: "I'm so glad you're all here for dinner. I'll pass around the lasagna."
>
> James: "Just a small serving for me, please. I'm not very hungry tonight."
>
> You: "Oh, nonsense! A big man like you needs lots to eat. Here— I'll give you a proper serving. Sam, have some broccoli."
>
> Sam: "No, thanks. I'm not much of a broccoli eater."
>
> You: "Sam, broccoli is good for you. You have to try a little bit

or there will be no dessert for you! Now, Joyce, I expect to see your plate all clean; there are still some yummy veggies there."

How do you think James, Joyce, and Sam would feel? Would this be a successful dinner party? Does this sound a little bit like the conversation around your own dinner table?

All too often, the dinner table becomes a battleground for parents of young children. Parents worry about what their children eat—or refuse to eat. Have they had enough? Did they get enough vitamin C? Too much sugar? Enough calcium and protein?

Eating under surveillance is not relaxing, and children don't enjoy it any more than adults do. Listen to your own mealtime comments and ask yourself, "Would I say this to an adult guest?" Children treated with respect learn to treat others the same way. Just because they are small people doesn't mean they aren't entitled to opinions about food. It may help to remember, though, that those opinions often change as they grow and mature.

During the 1950s, 1960s, and 1970s, many university early childhood programs conducted studies to see what foods toddlers would eat when all kinds of foods were placed on the lunch table. The children were allowed to eat whatever they wanted. Sometimes children would eat dessert first. Sometimes they would eat broccoli first. The main finding of this program was that the children did not fuss. And the results were always similar—when children were left to follow their own "instincts," they chose a balanced diet over time. We wonder how these studies would look today if the choices were fast-food hamburgers, french fries, and soda pop. In order for children to make nutritious choices, they need to be given healthful options. The subtler flavor of a real orange can seem less appealing if a child has become accustomed to the chemically enhanced fruit flavorings used in overly sweetened fruit drinks and snack products. Sugar can really disrupt the body's natural craving for good foods.

Later in this chapter we will discuss how parents sometimes invite power struggles and how they can instead create an atmosphere of cooperation about food. First, it is important to point out some serious problems young children face today.

HEALTH PROBLEMS AND YOUR KIDS

Research is now showing that many children have more brittle bones than in past years, making them more susceptible to breaks. The theory is that drinking too many sweetened drinks and not enough milk is contributing to this problem. The rate of obesity among children is also rising, due largely to too much fat and salt in their diets (such as fast food and snacks) and not enough exercise. Many children spend a great deal of time sitting in front of the TV or computer, or playing video games. Following are some statistics from the Institute of Medicine's report "Preventing Childhood Obesity: Health in the Balance," released on September 30, 2004 (http://www.iom.edu/?id=22623).

- Since the 1970s, the prevalence of obesity has more than doubled for preschool children age two to five years and adolescents age twelve to nineteen years, and it has more than tripled for children age six to eleven years. At present, approximately 9 million children over six years of age are obese.

- Childhood obesity involves significant risks to physical and emotional health. In 2000, it was estimated that 30 percent of boys and 40 percent of girls born in the United States are at risk for being diagnosed with type 2 diabetes at some point in their lives.

- Young people are also at risk of developing serious psychosocial burdens due to societal stigmatization associated with obesity.

- Obesity-associated annual hospital costs for children and youths more than tripled over two decades, rising from $35 million in 1979–1981 to $127 million in 1997–1999.

- Obesity prevention involves a focus on energy balance—calories consumed versus calories expended—so taking action against

Gratitude and Attitude

There is an important truth about food, eating, and young children: you provide the food, and the children do the eating—or not, as the case may be. It is significant to note that children raised in many cultures don't experience eating problems, especially cultures in which food is scarce. But even more important, in such cultures food is always treated as valuable. Coaxing someone to eat is not necessary—what one person does not eat, another will. Food is simply never wasted. For example, students from Singapore and other parts of Asia who have come to America for internships in early childhood programs are consistently shocked at seeing food thrown away. In other cultures, nutrition and taste are outweighed by the pressure not to waste precious food. We sometimes forget the abundance we enjoy, but it is always wise to demonstrate gratitude and appreciation for food—and to encourage our children to do the same.

childhood obesity must address the factors that influence both eating and physical activity.

Research confirms that social pressure can affect one's food choices, so what you as parents model through your own eating habits is as crucial as the foods you provide to your children.

PICKY EATING

It is important to offer children a wide selection of nutritious food, but remember that special menus only reinforce finicky eating. And you can increase the odds that your child will eat the food you serve: be sure that at least one food on the table is familiar and something your child enjoys, then serve whatever else you wish. Remember, the more often a child is exposed to a food, the sooner it, too, will become familiar. Also remember that you can't force your child to eat something he or she doesn't want to eat; that will only invite a power struggle, and at that point everyone loses.

Martha was convinced that her son needed a warm bowl of oatmeal to start his day off properly. When three-year-old Lex refused to eat his oatmeal one morning, his mother decided she'd better teach him how important it was to eat the right foods. Martha got out some plastic wrap and covered the bowl of oatmeal. When Lex came in for lunch, Martha microwaved the oatmeal. After half an hour, it had turned as cold (and as hard) as stone. Lex glared at it but refused to taste it, so Martha resolutely covered it up again. Can you imagine how appetizing that oatmeal looked at dinner after another trip to the microwave? Lex would willingly have starved before letting a spoonful pass his lips. What do you suppose Lex has learned about oatmeal? And what has his mother learned about Lex?

There are a number of things parents can keep in mind to encourage healthy eating habits in their children and to make mealtimes together pleasant for the entire family.

Timing

Young children see no reason to get hungry on anyone's schedule but their own. Infants nurse on demand, toddlers want food when they're hungry, and preschoolers often just can't make it from one meal to the next without something in between. These are normal variations; try to be flexible. The key is to be certain that the choices available to your children are healthy ones. If your children aren't eating full meals, their snacks should provide them with the nutrients they need. A pile of carrot sticks or even a baked potato, for instance, is much better than french fries and a soda.

A child who doesn't eat his entire lunch at the child care center can snack out of his lunch box on the way home. *When* children eat is not as important as *what* they eat. Nutritious lunch food is just as good eaten at 5:00 as it would have been at noon.

Simplicity

Your church group may have raved about your prawns in Cajun sauce, but your preschooler is unlikely to be equally impressed. Children are often suspicious of unfamiliar foods or unusual mixtures. A cheese sandwich with lettuce and tomato may be spurned, while a piece of cheese, some tomato slices, and a few crackers will be consumed quite happily. If your little one looks askance at the pasta and vegetable salad, try serving the ingredients to him separately. You certainly don't need to provide a separate menu, nor should you, but being aware of your child's natural preferences will help you find ways to encourage cooperation and experimentation.

Choices

Allowing children to develop their own eating habits requires mutual trust. Children will eat foods their bodies need, and if you provide a variety of healthy and appetizing foods, they will be more likely to choose foods that are nourishing. Remember, though, that even adults need a splurge now and then; thousands of children have been raised on occasional doses of fast food, pizza, and hot dogs without suffering permanent damage. The key, as always, is *balance*. Providing a regular diet of nutritious foods will help you feel better about the Easter jelly beans, chocolate Santas, and Halloween tummyaches that seem to be an inevitable part of childhood. However, if you have jelly beans, potato chips, cookies, cupcakes, and soft drinks around the house all the time, you are inviting poor eating habits and food battles.

Avoid becoming the food police. Families committed to special diets often defeat themselves by creating a vigilante atmosphere around food. If you want your child to avoid foods with sugar, do not become frantic when a stray cookie passes his lips. Your overreaction is more likely to invite food-related problems, now and later.

Portion Size and Hunger

One recent study has shown that when children are served extra-large food portions, they eat larger bites of food and cumulatively more food. If children choose how much to eat or are given smaller portions, they tend to eat more appropriate amounts. Preschoolers are capable of dishing up their own food (with training). An important part of training is to teach them to take small helpings. (They can always take more if they want it.) It is not helpful to make your child eat everything on her plate when she makes a mistake and takes too much. It is helpful to help her explore, through curiosity questions, what happens when she takes too much and how she can solve the problem.

When you insist that a child eat everything on her plate or eat only at specified times, you teach her to ignore her body's cues. This is why snack time plays such an important role in these preschool years. Little tummies need frequent fueling, so snack choices are important.

Hunger is a better guide to eating than the clock—and one all of us would benefit from tuning in to. Focusing only on when or how much your child eats invites her to ignore the messages her body sends. It is better to ensure that food is nutritious, whenever it is eaten.

CHOOSE YOUR BATTLES

It may be absolutely imperative to you that your four-year-old eat her lima beans. Or you may feel comfortable watching your child eat a steady diet of salami slices, raisins, and crackers. But be aware that if you *in*sist, your child may feel compelled to *re*sist—and it's doubtful that staring at a plate of cold lima beans after everyone else has left the table has ever persuaded a child to love veggies.

Some parents gloat about making their children sit at the table until they finish their dinner—and claim it works. If you talk to the children, you get a different story. Either they figured out how to feed most of the food to the dog or hide it in their napkin (weren't the parents suspicious when their children offered to clean up the table?) or they developed eating problems as adults. Someone will always lose in battles over food, short-range or long-range.

Help for Picky Eaters

- Avoid becoming a short-order cook. Teach children older than four how to make their own peanut butter or turkey sandwiches.

- Offer choices. When children complain about a food, say, "You can eat what is on the table or fix your own sandwich. What is your choice?"

- Invite solutions. If a child complains about the food served, ask, "What do you need to do about that?" This invites children to use their thinking skills and problem-solving skills. It invites them to use their power in positive ways (instead of in power struggles) and to feel capable.

- Invite children to help plan menus during family meetings. Kids are more cooperative when they have been included. Get them involved in creating the shopping list.

- Share tasks. Let children help with shopping. Many grocery stores now have small carts that can be pushed around by preschoolers. Let children find certain items on the shopping list to put in your cart. When they want something that isn't on the list, kindly and firmly say, "That isn't on our list."

- Let children help with cooking. During the family meeting, let them decide which nights they want to help cook. Again, they are more likely to eat what they help cook and to be more cooperative when it is not their turn if they have been involved in the planning process.

- Respond without rescuing. Simply avoid the sparks (bids for undue attention) that become bonfires when you feed them. Use active listening ("I guess you don't like that") and avoid engaging in debates. And allow your children to handle the problem. ("You don't have to eat it. I'm sure you can make it until our next meal.")

- Ease your own anxiety about nutrition. Give your child a good multivitamin. Then relax. She'll eat when she's hungry.

MEALTIME ROUTINES

Yes, routines work for eating, too. Mealtimes in busy families often become hectic, rushed, and stressful occasions that no one truly enjoys. Parents arrive home tired after a long day's work; children are often both hungry and cranky. The milk of human kindness does not make it to the dinner table. Comfortable routines can make mealtimes proceed far more smoothly. The elements are simple; here are some suggestions that may help you create routines for your own family.

Take Time to Relax
If dinnertime is often rushed in your home, try beginning the process differently.

> *Todd always packs an extra-large lunch for his four-year-old daughter, Katie. During the drive home after work and preschool, Katie opens her lunch box and enjoys whatever is left over from lunch. When they arrive home, Katie is not urgently hungry and her dad doesn't feel pressured to serve dinner immediately. Instead, they usually manage time for a cuddle and story before Dad tackles the dinner preparations.*

Taking time to wind down at the end of the day is almost always worth the investment. You may want to spend a few minutes curled up on the sofa with your child, reconnecting and sharing moments from your day. A warm bath or shower might refresh you for the evening ahead, or you may want to take time for a walk or a quick game together. Slices of fruit or a bag of crackers may satisfy the hunger pangs long enough for the entire family to catch its breath. "But I don't have time," you may be saying. "I simply have too much to do!" Regardless of how busy your lives may be, taking time to relax and reenter your family's world will eliminate the hassles and bids for undue attention that often consume even more time.

Prepare the Meal Together

Nothing wins a finicky eater over better than helping plan and prepare the meal. And most parents fail to recognize the wonderful little helpers they have right there beside them. Get a big apron, pull up a stool to the sink, and invite your child to slosh and tear the lettuce for tonight's salad. Even a two-year-old can use a brush to scrub vegetables, and at three, your child can place silverware and napkins on the table. (See the chart on page 215 for more ideas.)

Mr. Parker, a preschool teacher, invited a group of children to help prepare a smoothie made with kale and pineapple. Now, most adults would cringe at this particular flavor combination, yet every one of the children who helped wash and tear up the kale and took part in the preparation process not only tasted this concoction but pronounced it delicious and went back for more. Then Mr. Parker filled a tray with samples of the smoothie and brought it out to share with the children in another classroom. Guess what? Not one of them would so much as try it. It would be difficult to find more persuasive evidence of the value of including children in food preparation.

Giving your children a way to contribute encourages the growth of their sense of initiative, teaches them life skills, invites them to see themselves as contributing members of the family or community, and builds their sense of belonging.

Create Moments That Draw You Together

Lunch at the Roundtree Child Care Center is a special time—the children join hands around the table, one child is invited to share something she feels grateful for, and then they take turns squeezing the hand of the person on their right, so the "squeeze" goes all around the circle before the children begin their meal. Ezra is from a traditional Jewish family, and before each meal in his home, he recites special Hebrew prayers. In Jenny's family, each person stands at his or her place at the table, and when all have gathered, they sing grace together. At Maia's home, the whole family meditates in silence for several minutes before beginning each meal.

In our busy families, meals are often eaten on the run—everyone has somewhere to go, and the moments of communication and togetherness can be lost if we're not careful. Rituals—spiritual or not—can be wonderful ways to preserve the sense of family and teach your children to value it, and to create warm and loving moments with your children. The National Center on Addiction and Substance Abuse at Columbia University has linked family dinnertime to such diverse issues as a reduced risk for alcohol and drug abuse, lower suicide rates, and improved school performance. Those are pretty compelling reasons for making time for family meals—and for making mealtimes with our families pleasant. These times spent gathered around the table offer priceless opportunities for connection and closeness—times to create memories that feed our souls as much as Grandma's home-baked bread once fed our bodies. Food is for eating (not for force-feeding), and it should never become fuel for family feuds.

Set Guidelines for Finishing Up

Should children be expected to sit quietly until everyone has finished eating? Or should they be allowed to leave the table to play quietly? There is no "right" answer, but it may be wise to decide the matter beforehand rather than arguing over the cold mashed potatoes.

Even young children can be involved in some aspect of cleaning up after a meal. If your child can walk well on his own, he probably can clear away his plate, scrape off uneaten food, or load his utensils into the dishwasher. Many child care programs will set out small basins for mealtime leftovers and provide different bins where children can sort

Allergies, Medications, and Special Diets

Many a battle is being fought to "make" children take their medications or to "make" them avoid foods that create serious problems. It is amazing what children are willing to suffer to avoid being controlled. We emphasize over and over how important it is to engage children in the problem-solving process so that they develop thinking skills and problem-solving skills— and so that they feel empowered and capable. Here are some suggestions.

- Avoid lectures. Instead, engage children in self-exploration by asking "what," "why," and "how" questions: "What happens when you don't take your medication [or when you eat this food]?" "How do you feel when that happens?" "What ideas do you have to solve this problem?" (This will not be effective if children sense even a hint of a lecture instead of true curiosity about their thinking and ability to learn and solve problems.)

- Involve children in creating a medication routine. Decide together on a time of day that works best for both of you. Work together on creating a reminder chart and on reminder methods (such as an alarm watch that goes off at the same time every day).

- Take your child to the library to explore food allergies—and exactly what happens to the body. (Be sure your goal is education, not fear.)

- Decide what *you* will do. This could mean that you are willing to take responsibility to kindly remind your child every day at medication time, or that you will stay out of it because you have faith in your child to handle the problem or to learn from mistakes. (If the problem is life-threatening, choose the former, and do it without lectures or the display of overconcern.)

- Recognize that you may not always be around to supervise your child's diet or medications. In age-appropriate ways (and with kind, firm supervision), allow your child to take responsibility for measuring, mixing, and remembering. Remember that confidence and competence come from practice.

their dishes, cutlery, and cups. Some centers go a step further and allow children to take turns bringing the food scraps to a worm bin or the center's compost container, thus adding a new level of learning as children come to appreciate the relationship between food and the environment.

OVERWEIGHT CHILDREN

More and more children are becoming overweight, with serious implications for their long-term health. The seeds for this problem are planted very early on. There are genetic causes as well. When overweight is genetic, it is very important to help children feel accepted just as they are—and to work with them (if they want help) on how to manage their challenge in life.

Being overweight can create a vicious cycle when children also feel low self-esteem. Low self-esteem may invite overeating to fill the emptiness. Children will do better when they feel better. Offer lots of unconditional love and encouragement by stating that you have faith in them to deal with the challenge of being overweight—if they want to. Offer your support, not your control. Many of the ideas suggested to avoid power struggles over medications and food allergies are also effective for overweight children.

Of course, modeling is very important. Don't expect children to do something you have not done. Take care of your own weight issues (you might even work together on this). Together you can prepare healthy meals and avoid putting junk food on the shopping list.

EXERCISE

Here it comes again: turn off the TV. We have discussed the reasons that too much television is not healthy for brain development, but of course you know that it also is not healthy for the rest of the body.

Children need your guidance. It is much easier to enjoy the peace and quiet while your children watch TV, but it will be healthier for all of you if you go outside and play ball. Consider teaching children some of the pastimes people enjoyed before TV took over. Make your home movement-friendly. Designate spaces where running or tossing soft balls is allowed, such as a long hallway or a playroom with minimal (and unbreakable) furnishings. Try to get your apartment complex to sanction an area for active (supervised) play.

Television, Advertising, and Obesity

The Institute of Medicine recently released a summary of 120 studies on children and food marketing. They found that advertising scattered throughout children's commercial television programming is saturated with plugs for fat-, salt-, or sugar-laden treats with little nutritional value. This advertising heavily influences what children younger than twelve pester their parents to buy. The institute found that children younger than four cannot distinguish between an advertisement and entertainment programming and do not understand that advertisements are intended to sell products.

The report also notes that U.S. companies spent an estimated $10 billion in 2004 to market food, beverages, and meals to children. Such studies led the American Psychological Association in 2004 to conclude that advertising to children younger than eight exploits them and should be restricted—by law, if necessary.

Go for walks, which are both fun and practical, especially if the family dog or pot-bellied pig needs exercise, too. Cap off an evening with a family swim night once each week. Turn technology into part of the solution by renting child or family exercise videos and using them to exercise together. Play music and dance around the house, or have a basket of bells, tambourines, and other noisemakers to make your own music. Have fun, and everyone will reap the benefits.

If the school your child attends is eliminating recess (and many are), become an advocate for reinstating it. Share the statistics about childhood obesity and how important regular exercise is for a child's brain and body.

BON APPÉTIT!

Remember that allowing children to be involved, encouraging mutual trust and respect, and having realistic expectations will take much of the struggle out of eating and may make mealtimes together an event the entire family looks forward to. No matter how tempting the foods on your table, your child must choose to eat them. Remember: you can't make 'em do it!

14

PRESCHOOLERS AND POTTIES

The Ongoing Saga of Toilet Training

"Wait just one moment!" you may be thinking. "Surely preschoolers have mastered toilet training. Aren't kids supposed to be trained by the age of three?" Well, not necessarily. Bathroom habits and hygiene remain issues of concern for young children and their parents well beyond the age of three—or even four. Few topics arouse such strong emotions as potty training.

RELAX!

Your child is still in diapers, and more and more of the neighbors' kids are becoming potty trained. What should you do? Should you love your child just as he is? Should you avoid power struggles? Should you engage your child in joint problem solving to figure out what will work for him—and how to clean up messes when he makes mistakes? Or should you feel embarrassed and competitive, and try to make him do what he is "supposed" to do?

If you answer yes to the last of these, it is likely that you are engaged in a power struggle. It might be helpful to review the section on power struggles on pages 159–162. Toileting is one of the areas where a child can be most stubborn as he proves to you that "you can't make me."

> Q. I have a son who needs to be potty trained. He turned three a couple of months ago. He does not like to use the potty. He does not show me signs when he has to go, but he will tell me when to change him. I feel so discouraged. Please, I need some advice!

> A. We can hear your desperation. It is so hard to keep changing diapers as children grow older. Children develop on their own schedules where toileting is involved. Your son's delay in using the toilet is magnified by your own discouragement. He will succeed eventually, but it may take more patience than you knew you had.

Difficult as it may be, try to deemphasize the whole issue. Your son can read your nonverbal messages and knows that his toilet habits are extremely important to you—which is an invitation to a power struggle. Meanwhile, when he needs to be changed, show him ways he may help out. He can help wash or wipe himself off, help empty the stool into the toilet bowl, and wash his own hands afterward. In the meantime, enjoy him and his other life successes. Express your confidence that he will use the potty successfully one day. He, too, needs encouragement.

You will be amazed at how quickly time passes when you detach emotionally from the potty-training issue. Your detachment will eliminate power struggles and may actually speed up the process. Children are much more likely to become interested in potty training when allowed to do so according to their own timetable—and when there is nothing to rebel against. A big part of detaching and relaxing is to know that a number of things can cause a temporary setback.

SETBACKS: "WHOOPS!"

When a child is experiencing new things—a new preschool, a new house, or a new sibling—it's common for potty training to suffer a setback. A new environment or an especially exciting activity can cause a child not to pay attention to his body's signals; other major life events, such as death, divorce, illness, or travel, can interfere with toileting. All of these events represent major adjustments in a child's life, and toilet issues often take second place to coping with change.

Your attitude as a parent or caregiver will make all the difference in how your child handles accidents. Imagine how confused and discouraged a child might feel when she not only loses control of her body but faces a parent's anger and disappointment as well.

> *Tara was four years old when she was asked to be a flower girl in her aunt's wedding. She wore a lovely long white gown made especially for her with a lacy veil and a tiny pearl necklace. People smiled and nodded at her as she walked down the aisle scattering rose petals, and Tara glowed with the attention and excitement.*
>
> *The reception was beautiful, and Tara was thrilled by the festivity around her. She had crawled under a table and was listening to the adults talking when she became aware of*

What Time Is the Right Time?

A study at Children's Hospital of Philadelphia recently found that children acquire toilet skills more readily when their parents choose the right time to begin training. When children began toilet training before twenty-seven months, the process took a year or more; when children began training between twenty-seven and thirty-six months, training took five to ten months. According to this study, the optimal time for speedy toilet training is when a child is just shy of his third birthday. It takes approximately five months to toilet train a child when he begins between the ages of thirty-three and thirty-six months.

something she'd been ignoring all afternoon. Before she could get up, it happened: she had a bowel movement, soiling her lovely white dress.

When Tara's mother discovered her, she was horrified. "I can't imagine what got into Tara," she told the assembled aunts and grandmothers. "She never does this anymore." Turning to her crying daughter, she said coldly, "You should be ashamed of yourself." Tara was changed into her old play clothes and spent the rest of the day hiding from everyone.

When children have toileting accidents, the last thing they need is a disapproving audience. Tara's mother could have taken her quietly aside, helped her to change, and explained to her daughter that excitement can sometimes make us forget to do the things we should.

It may be wisdom to keep a change of clothing nearby when your child is learning to use the toilet. It is also immeasurably helpful to be patient and to offer your child unconditional love and acceptance. Once you have taken into account your child's personal clock, provided him with appropriate clothing and accessible facilities, and taken time to train him in the skills he needs, it is time to relax, celebrate his successes, and sympathize with his disappointments.

CONSTIPATION

Bowel control is another issue where a parent's desire to speed training may cause complications. Some children will not release their stool, sometimes to the point of physical damage.

Quentin's grandma had a lot to say on the issue of toilet training, most of it to his mother. "My children were all trained by the time they were two," she said disapprovingly, glaring at three-year-old Quentin while his diaper was being changed.

So Quentin's mom embarked on a full-scale assault. Quentin was placed on the toilet several times each day while his mom knelt nearby and urged him on. Quentin grew to hate the bathroom, and so did his mom. She would encourage, threaten, and scold; he responded by refusing to produce the desired result—anywhere or anytime. Before long, Quentin even lost the ability to respond to his body's signals and could no longer tell when he needed to have a bowel movement.

One day at his regular checkup, his pediatrician gave Quentin and his mom the news: he had a severely impacted bowel, with stool backed up well into his intestines. Daily doses of mineral oil and enemas were prescribed to relieve the problem, and both mother and son shed many a tear until the problem—which need never have existed—was resolved.

It is never helpful to force toileting issues. If your child is resistant, first look for natural or environmental causes. Does your child eat sufficient fiber to produce soft, regular bowel movements? If not, switch to juices containing fiber, such as peach or apricot nectar. A spoonful of prune juice mixed in with other foods might help. Serve kiwi fruit daily, and your child's stools should improve quickly. Children may reject cereal such as raisin bran or other high-fiber choices unless they are baked in muffins. Serve fewer dairy products and apple juice, which tend to be constipating. But do be careful: don't set up a new power struggle trying to get him to eat these foods! Offer them, as in make them available—don't force-feed them.

It is also possible that your child is experiencing excessive stress. Major life changes affect all family members. One parent, concerned over her own father's terminal illness, did not make the connection between her struggle to face this crisis and the toileting problems her son experienced. Although he had been totally potty trained, he began having daily accidents. When the family crisis resolved itself, his problems disappeared.

What about the expectations placed on a child?

The Mackey family deferred all kinds of decisions to their four-year-old. "Where should we eat dinner?" they asked. "Should

Mommy and Daddy go out tonight?" "Do you want to go to preschool this morning?" The list went on and on. This child experienced severe constipation because she felt overwhelmed by all the decisions placed on her shoulders. Her parents worried that setting limits would restrict her too much. They went so far in the other direction that she experienced enormous distress.

Pushing a child to master too many tasks by signing him up for an endless string of classes may create stress. Similarly, expecting perfection from your child invites anxiety. Though some children may show interest in learning new skills early on, forcing them to do so takes an emotional toll. One of the areas where children display the results of such stress is in toileting problems.

Finally, control issues play a role in stool retention problems. Avoiding power struggles, empowering your child in positive ways, and encouraging cooperation are as effective in solving bowel problems as they are in other areas of family life.

OTHER CHALLENGES

Children with other problems, such as attention deficit disorder, often have a high percentage of associated bowel control problems. Other physical or biological conditions can also affect toileting. Here are a few tips that may help.

A child who is having difficulty defecating may loosen up and relax his muscles if he blows bubbles while sitting on the toilet. It is difficult to squeeze and blow at the same time! Playing a harmonica offers the same benefits.

Some children need a gradual approach to mastery. When you notice your child having a bowel movement, accompany him to the bathroom (but leave his diaper on). This may create a positive, comfortable association with being near a toilet while pooping.

If your child appears anxious about the toilet itself or is frightened by the loudness of the flushing sound or a fear of falling in, find opportunities to talk gently about his fears. Wait to flush the toilet until after he leaves the bathroom and help him to see that his body is bigger than the toilet opening (or provide a potty chair if that feels safer). By tuning into your child's feelings, you may promote and improve potty success without creating power struggles or inviting him to feel shame and discouragement. Toileting can be harder for some children to master than it is for others. Simply knowing that your child is not the only one experiencing such difficulties may help you cope with this troubling behavior.

THE IMPORTANCE OF PATIENCE

Sometimes the passage of time is all that is required for children to master the toilet. We heard from one set of parents who were at the end of their rope. They had tried everything with their three-and-a-half-year-old and nothing worked; he was still wetting his pants several times a day. Six months later, we heard back from the same parents, who were relieved that their child had become fully toilet-trained. "It's amazing how time works wonders," they wrote us. Be patient; your child will learn.

The reality is that a child will use the toilet when he is ready to do so. You can cheer, beg, and threaten, but hang on to your diapers. Each child has his or her own unique schedule—and absolute control.

HOW CAN YOU SET YOUR CHILD UP FOR SUCCESS?

There are six important factors that can help parents set the stage for this important developmental milestone: physical readiness, ease of wakefulness, understanding your child's perspective, logic versus power struggles, inviting cooperation, and detach, relax, and enjoy.

Physical Readiness
Many children become potty-trained before they reach the preschool years. This fact adds to the frustration of parents whose preschoolers

have not yet reached this important step in the socialization process. The delay could be due to power struggles between the child and his parents, or it could be because the child is not yet physically ready to perceive and respond to the signals sent by his body. He also must have a bladder large enough to allow him to wait for increasingly long periods of time before urinating, especially for overnight control. The reality is that some children simply don't develop bladder control as soon as others.

> *Bridget was very familiar with the level of bladder control of her three children. This knowledge helped her know how quickly they needed to stop the car when the children requested a bathroom stop on long trips. In response to seven-year-old Kenny's request, Bridget would remind her husband, "We can keep driving for about twenty minutes." When three-year-old Lori would ask for a bathroom, Bridget would say, "Well, we have about ten minutes to find a good stopping place." However, when five-year-old Jacob said, "I have to go," Bridget would say, "Pull over immediately. If we can't find a bush, Jacob will just have to settle for the side of the road."*

Important Factors and Attitudes to End Toilet Battles

- Physical readiness
- Ease of wakefulness
- Understanding your child's perspective
- Logic versus power struggles
- Inviting cooperation
- Detach, relax, and enjoy

Ease of Wakefulness

Another important factor in toilet training is ease of wakefulness. Many children who remain bed wetters during and even beyond their preschool years are the same children who have difficulty waking up. Even sheets with alarms that go off when urination begins sometimes do not wake these children. When parents try getting their heavy sleepers up in the night to take them to the toilet, they are like limp rags who cannot stand or sit. They simply cannot wake up. Lighter sleepers may fuss and complain when awakened for a night trip to the toilet, but boys can still stand up, though seemingly half asleep, and girls can sit on the toilet without falling off. Some children cannot wake enough to do either.

All children should always be treated with dignity and respect, but it is especially discouraging to use punishment with children who don't have the physical capacity to do what is expected of them. An understanding of readiness may inspire more patience.

Understanding Your Child's Perspective

Imagine for a moment that you are a very small child. You know that Mom and Dad are eager for you to learn to use the potty, to be a "big boy" and wear "big-boy pants." Suddenly, you feel that strange tingly feeling that you are beginning to recognize as meaning that you have to go. So you head toward the bathroom, becoming aware as you trot down the hall that there may not be a lot of time. You know you have to get your pants down, but the buckles on your overalls are stiff and your fingers are so small. Then you glance at the toilet, which looks very tall from your point of view. Maybe, you think, a little assistance is called for. But by the time you alert Mom, Dad, or the teacher, it's too late.

No wonder children often decide that it's easier just to stay in diapers! Understanding the occasionally overwhelming nature of the task can help parents set the stage for their child's success. Remember, toilet training is vitally important to diaper-weary adults—but rarely does it matter that much to a child. As with eating and sleeping, creating a toilet-friendly environment with easy-off clothing and kind training is a parent's job; deciding when (and where) to go is a child's!

Logic Versus Power Struggles

Parents often rely on logic in their attempts to resolve problems, but issues such as potty training are sometimes based on illogical power struggles. The more determined parents become to have urination and defecation take place in the toilet, the more determined many preschoolers become to have it take place somewhere else—usually in their pants.

Remember, your child is still developing a sense of autonomy and probably has an "I can do it" attitude. When parents try taking control of a child's bodily functions, they often meet with resistance. It could be that the child is deciding (at a subconscious level), "I'd rather walk around in urine-soaked pants than give up my sense of power."

In other words, when parents insist on winning power struggles, the only option for the child is to become the loser . . . and children will fight diligently to avoid being the loser. So the power struggles continue. Since parents are the "mature" ones, it is up to them to end the power struggles and find ways to invite cooperation.

Q. I'm at my wits' end. I have a four-year-old boy who, after a playdate with an older cousin, learned the joys of peeing off a bridge. Now he is peeing everywhere: on the carpet, in the trash can, off the porch, and so on. It seems to be an act of rebellion, often happening after I tell him to do something he doesn't want to do (like get dressed). We've tried time-outs (which only precipitate a tantrum) and taking away privileges (TV, computer time, or dessert). I have to admit I spanked him in frustration when I caught him in the act last time. I've tried talking to him about this problem, but I get nowhere. I'm at a loss. Help!

A. What a great opportunity for you to make some changes that could redirect these power struggles into useful power. Four-year-olds are ready to use their personal power in ways that contribute to the family. When parents use controlling methods and punishment, children resort to destructive power instead.

Our crystal ball suggests that when you say, "I've tried talking with him," what you really mean is, "We've sat down and I talked, and talked, and talked, and lectured, and lectured, and lectured." Maybe our crystal ball is wrong, but "talking" often means "telling"—over and over again. Our first suggestion is for you to stop telling and start asking curiosity questions. You might ask, "What happened? How do you feel about what happened? How does this create a problem for you or for others? What ideas do you have to solve this problem?" It is essential that these questions be asked in a calm and friendly tone of voice and with a sincere curiosity about your child's point of view (instead of trying to convince him to share your point of view). You may have to wait awhile between finding a stain and talking to your son so that you don't sound angry. Inviting discussion (rather than lecturing) will help your child develop thinking skills, awareness of the consequences of his choices, and problem-solving skills. Telling invites your child to become defensive or even more rebellious.

Another possibility is to get him involved by teaching him to use his power to engage in problem solving in all the areas of his life, not just where toilet habits are involved. This can take many forms:

- Ask him what he needs to do in a given situation. If it is morning and time to get dressed, ask what he needs to do when he finishes eating.

- Work together to create routine charts. You might be surprised by how well this invites cooperation instead of rebellion.

- Stop using any form of punishment, including punitive time-outs. Your child will feel positive power if he chooses the time-out. He will feel rebellious if you make him go.

- Start having regular family meetings so your child will learn respect and problem-solving skills. If your son has many opportunities to use his power in useful ways, he is less likely to be rebellious.

- Teach him to clean up any mess he makes. With a kind and firm tone of voice say, "You'll need to clean that up. Would you like my help or do you want to do it by yourself?" If he resists, say, "Would a hug help you feel better? I know you will want to take care of this problem when you feel better." (When doing this, always be sure to help a child wash with soap and water afterward.)

All of the methods we suggest create positive long-range results. Ask yourself, "Do I want to make my child pay for what he did, or do I

Be sure to train your child to wash his hands thoroughly. Have a stool available so he can reach the sink, with soap and a towel for drying within easy reach. One preschool teaches children to sing this song (to the tune of "Skip to M'Lou") while they wash their hands (when repeated twice, the song lasts about twenty seconds, just the time it takes to kill *E. coli* bacteria).

Wash, wash, wash your hands
Wash your hands together.
Scrub, scrub, scrub your hands,
Till they're clean and sparkly.

want to help him learn to do better in the future?"

Inviting Cooperation

Not surprisingly, potty training is just that: training. And there are many things parents can do to make it easier. The first involves your attitude. Knowing your child's temperament and abilities will help you keep your expectations reasonable. If you are relaxed and comfortable, your child is likely to feel the same way.

Pressure to succeed will only frustrate both of you. If accidents happen—and they will—be patient. If your child is wet, change her. If she is old enough, buy pull-up diapers so that she can change herself (which often encourages a child to be more aware of her body's signals). Be sure, however, that you never humiliate or shame a child about toileting setbacks. Dry pants aren't worth damaged self-esteem.

It can help to train your child in the steps he must master along the road to the successful use of the toilet. It's a good idea to provide clothing that is easily pulled down (and up); elastic waistbands are perfect. If the weather is warm, wearing underpants alone (or nothing at all) may simplify the process.

Having regular toilet times may encourage youngsters to develop the habit of using the bathroom regularly. When leaving for an outing (even a short one), it is wise to invite a young child to use the toilet beforehand. (Most parents quickly learn where the restrooms at the neighborhood grocery store are located.)

Miss Ellen decided to take her preschool class on a field trip to pick blueberries. They blithely sailed out of the preschool together and into a nearby field. Trouble soon arose, however; Ellen had forgotten to remind the children to use the toilet before leaving, and now the only option was a well-used outhouse. Ellen spent most of her field trip holding one child after another over the outhouse toilet, and she never forgot pre-outing reminders again!

Pull-ups and extra-strength diapers are now available for children two and a half, three, and even four and five years old. Unfortunately, extra-dry diapers may actually discourage toilet training because children remain comfortable and never feel wet. It may be wise to consider using less effective diapers, or those specially designed for training.

Detach, Relax, and Enjoy
When readiness and training have been taken into account, it is time to relax and trust that successful toileting will result in due time. Perhaps the best advice is simply this: relax. Using the toilet on his own is a very significant thing for your child to do. When he's ready, he'll do it—and probably not a moment sooner.

MAKE SURE THE MESSAGE OF LOVE GETS THROUGH

There are many ways to get the message of love through to children. One of the most important is to offer your trust. Sleeping, eating, and toileting can be battlegrounds where parents and children oppose each other, or they can be opportunities for sharing respect, kindness, and encouragement. Healthy sleeping, eating, and toileting habits are gifts that will serve your children well. You may not be able to make 'em do it, but there is much you can do to set the stage for success.

15

SELECTING (AND LIVING WITH) CHILD CARE

Jim has two children. The oldest is four and the youngest is eighteen months old. His marriage has just ended in divorce; he has sole custody of his children and cannot afford to give up a career that provides him with a way to support his family.

Bethany is director of research, midway through a ten-year project. If her research produces the results she expects, it may provide treatment for a type of cancer that has been considered hopeless. Bethany just turned thirty-four; she and her husband have decided that they can wait no longer to begin their own family. Bethany knows that continuing her research and having a baby will mean using child care or employing a nanny.

Lani's three-year-old daughter, Mitra, is lonely and wants play-mates, but there are no other children in their neighborhood.

Lani does not want her daughter to watch television all day. A preschool has opened on the next block, but Lani isn't sure if it's the best thing for Mitra and worries that placing Mitra in preschool while she stays home will make her seem like a neglectful mom.

Keiko was such a devoted parent that she didn't leave her first baby until he was six months old. Then she left him with a sitter for only two hours and called three times to make sure everything was all right. The baby slept soundly the entire time, but she still was not comfortable leaving him.

Linda and Miguel have two children, both younger than five. Miguel's schedule as a firefighter changes every two months, making it impossible to predict when he will be home to watch the children. Money is tight, but Miguel's job leaves no feasible way for Linda to work to supplement their income.

CHILD CARE: A MODERN NECESSITY

If you are the parent of a preschooler, you have undoubtedly heard the debate raging around the subject of child care. There are those who claim that children should always be at home with parents during their early years and others who claim (just as loudly) that children always benefit from child care or preschool programs.

We believe that a child's parents are the best people to make decisions about whether to work or stay at home, whether to place children in child care, and whether to enroll children in preschool programs. For many families, child care is a fact of life; it is not financially possible, whether parents wish it or not, to be at home with their children all of the time. Leaving a young child in someone else's care can be agonizing for parents. Most wrestle at least occasionally with guilt and doubts: "Am I being a neglectful parent if I don't stay home with my child?" "I don't have a choice—I have to work—but will my child be scarred for life?"

It may help to know that reputable university studies have demonstrated (even though many political groups do not like the results) that children do very well in a quality child care situation (NICHD Early Child Care Research Network, "Characteristics of Infant Child Care: Factors Contributing to Positive Caregiving," *Early Childhood Research Quarterly* 11, 1996, 267–306). One review of childhood early education studies determined that participation in such programs can actually strengthen a child's positive attitude toward school, develop improved health practices that continue into adulthood, and even enhance the parenting skills of participants' parents. These studies and others have found that family factors (primarily maternal sensitivity and responsiveness) appeared to be more powerful predictors than child care regarding child outcomes (except when dealing with poor-quality child care).

Child care today often replaces the extended family of aunts, uncles, grandparents, and cousins that past generations grew up with. These days, there may be no sister or cousin to compare notes with when Belinda pulls a neighbor's hair or Jeff wakes up with a fever in the middle of the night. Parents need other adults as their own support system when raising a child. Today's child care center can be such a resource. It is a place to meet other parents, share concerns, and learn from one another.

This knowledge may help you feel confident about your decision to find quality child care, whether you need it for a night out, a special event, or full-time work. It is important to note that children absorb the energy of your attitudes and react to them. If you feel fearful, so will your child. If you feel guilty, your child may sense an opportunity to use manipulation. It is ironic, but both working parents and stay-at-home parents seem to feel some degree of guilt and regret about their choice, whatever it is. Guilt rarely does anyone any good. The key is to make the best decision you can in your own special situation—and then to relax. You will find this easier to do when you know how to find quality child care.

WHAT IS THE BEST WAY TO PREPARE YOUR CHILD TO LEARN?

There is a growing tendency for parents to seek child care centers that offer academics, such as reading, writing, and arithmetic. This concerns most early childhood experts, and you need to know why.

Kathryn Hirsch-Pasek, Ph.D., director of the Temple University Infant Lab and coauthor of *Einstein Never Used Flash Cards: How Children Really Learn and Why They Need to Play More and Memorize Less* (Rodale, 2003), directed a research project where 120 four-year-olds in a middle-class Philadelphia suburb were followed as they progressed to kindergarten and first grade. The research confirmed that the children who attended academic preschools did know more numbers and letters than the children who went to play-oriented preschools. However, by age five, the kids from the play-oriented preschools had caught up, while those attending academic preschools felt less positive about school.

Parents mean well when they push their children to learn academics as soon as possible. They want their children to have every advantage and to feel successful. But this push may do more harm than good. When children are pressured to excel in academics, they may miss out on more developmentally appropriate and effective ways to learn.

Take a moment to get into the world of your preschooler. How would you feel if you were pushed into learning something and you knew learning it would make your parents proud? How would you feel if learning these tasks was difficult (even though you could do it)? Might you have feelings of inadequacy? Might you feel only conditionally loved? On the other hand, how would you feel if your parents allowed you to explore and experiment in a nurturing environment filled with enticing equipment that allowed you to feel capable with every accomplishment? How would you feel if

you were learning to be creative and mastering social and problem-solving skills instead of regurgitating facts and figures?

Does this mean academics should be eliminated entirely during the first three years? No. The key is to follow the interests of the children. (Maria Montessori knew this fifty years ago.) Some three-year-olds want to read, and feel excited rather than pressured to learn. Some enjoy learning to sing the alphabet song (even though they don't have a clue what it means). Be aware of what your child is learning and how he feels about it. You child may not have the words to tell you he is feeling pressured, but you will know if you are paying attention.

SELECTING CHILD CARE

Perhaps the most important question of all is "What is quality child care and how do I find it?" It is extremely important not to bargain-hunt when it comes to child care. Although cost must be considered, it should not be the most important factor in your decision. Many extremely important hours of your child's life will be spent in the child care that you choose.

Simply put, find the best care possible. If quality care is unavailable, make what you find into quality care by providing the caregivers with information, such as this book. A quality child care provider will appreciate the gift of a book such as this one or *Positive Discipline for Childcare Providers,* by Jane Nelsen and Cheryl Erwin, Three Rivers Press, 2002. Work to bring early childhood training to your area if it is lacking.

Don't be in a rush to choose: be sure to visit several different child care programs. Take notes on what you see. Are the children happy? Do they move around the center confidently? Do the teachers get down on the children's eye level to talk with them? Is the artwork displayed low enough for children to see it, or is it only at adult eye level? Is the building clean? Are there visible safety hazards? Do the teachers look cheerful or frazzled? (Of course, do remember that even the best teachers can have tough days!) Does the equipment provided allow

How to Select Quality Child Care

Identify quality child care using the indicators on this checklist.

1. The center or home has:
   - Licenses displayed and current
   - Low rate of staff turnover
   - Local, state, and/or national accreditation
   - Loving, child-centered environment

2. The staff is:
   - Well trained in early childhood development and care
   - Working as a team
   - Staying up-to-date through training programs
   - Adequately paid

3. Discipline is:
   - Positive rather than punitive
   - Kind and firm at the same time
   - Designed to help children learn important life skills

4. Consistency shows:
   - In the curriculum
   - In the way problems are handled
   - In day-to-day center management

5. Safety is demonstrated by the:
   - Physical setting
   - Program health policies
   - Preparedness for emergencies

6. Curriculum, equipment, and activities are:
   - Varied and age-appropriate
   - Well-maintained, planned, and supervised
   - Child-sized and accessible to all

children to play freely, to dress up, to learn, and to be active? Or are children expected to be quiet, sit still, and "be good"?

Parents sometimes look at lists of qualities and requirements for good child care and feel overwhelmed. You may be wondering how you will ever know if the facility you are considering meets these standards. There is a relatively simple solution: ask. Child care is an important decision, and your confidence as a parent will influence your child's comfort with and response to her new setting. Don't hesitate to ask for all of the information you need to make an educated decision. If a center or provider seems reluctant to answer your questions or to allow you to observe them in action, it's probably wise to look elsewhere. One of the most important criteria is to find a center or home that welcomes parents anytime. These centers have nothing to hide and will treat you as a respected partner in your child's care. If you feel like an intruder when you visit your child's preschool, child care center, or licensed home, find another where you feel welcome. Quality care is a must. Child care centers should be safe, pleasant, nurturing places for children to be.

The Child Care Center or Home

Most states or cities require centers and homes to meet a variety of licensing requirements. Seeing licenses posted tells you the requirements were met. Be sure to check dates to be sure that licenses are current (although many states are so backlogged that long intervals between licensing are common).

Centers with low staff turnover indicate that the staff are well treated, receive fair compensation, enjoy their work, and feel supported by the center's administration. When staff do not receive decent wages, they go elsewhere, often leaving the child care field.

Look for special licensing. The best-known is the NAEYC (National Association for the Education of Young Children), which takes a multifaceted approach. Centers spend several months doing self-assessments and correcting any weak areas; they then are visited by independent accreditors, usually on several occasions. This accreditation is valid for only two years, then must be repeated. Programs displaying this type of accreditation truly have earned it.

The Staff

Training and experience make it more likely that caregivers will truly understand the needs of young children, provide activities that meet those needs, and have developmentally appropriate expectations. Education added to low turnover creates experienced caregivers, a winning situation for everyone involved.

Look for the types of training staff receive. Are there special training requirements? Montessori, Waldorf, High/Scope, Creative Curriculum, and many other programs have specialized training curriculum for their teachers. Community college, undergraduate, and master's-level degree programs in early childhood studies exist in many states.

It is also helpful to examine consistency in the center's management. Are expectations (of staff and parents) made clear? Are events well organized? Are finances handled in a businesslike, respectful manner?

Doctors, stock market analysts, child care teachers—all professionals must keep up with current information in their fields. Do staff at the center you're considering attend workshops? Are there in-house training programs, or are employees encouraged to take part in additional educational programs? Do staff stay current by taking part in seminars, workshops, and special topic trainings such as Positive Discipline? Teachers learn about new research, get inspired by and reminded of basic concepts, or feel encouraged when they hear others share solutions to common dilemmas.

Look for harmony. When there is discord at a center, the children feel it. Remember, young children can "read" the energy of the adults around them and respond to what they sense. Centers that encourage cooperation (among children and staff members) model the value of teamwork. Look for regularly scheduled staff meetings, in-house communication tools, and an atmosphere of camaraderie.

Discipline

Is there a written discipline policy? In what manner are problems handled? Are there texts on discipline recommended by the center? Ask what teachers do about a child who hits, bites, or grabs toys. Find out if teachers receive any training in how to deal with problems that arise. Does the center condone spanking? Is the attitude at the center positive or punitive? Are children being shown what to do more often than being reprimanded about what not to do?

Notice how teachers interact with children. Do they speak to children in a respectful way? Does the teacher get down to the child's eye level when talking to him, or do teachers yell instructions across the room? One-to-one communication indicates more appropriate and effective caregiving.

Are boundaries made clear, or does a teacher giggle uncomfortably when children run up and slam into her? Is there follow-through? Do teachers do what they say? Does the teacher call out to a child, "Put down that stick!" and then proceed to chat with a coworker while the child brandishes the stick overhead? Or does the teacher walk over and calmly remove the stick after giving the child a moment or two to put it down?

What lessons do children learn about their own abilities? Do the teachers put on everyone's coats, socks, and shoes, or do they help children do so themselves? Are children encouraged to wash their own hands before lunch? Look for programs where skills are being taught and children are not simply objects to be fed, dressed, and carted around.

What type of atmosphere do you sense when you visit? Happy, peaceful children are a good sign. (Please note: this doesn't necessarily mean quiet children!) The level of activity should indicate that the children are involved in and enjoying whatever they are doing.

Consistency

Consistency in the curriculum means that certain activities are provided regularly. Show-and-tell, daily story time, and singing are examples. Children thrive on routine at their care facility as well as at home. Consistency also means that learning objectives exist and are implemented. Contrast a well-defined program to a place where children are given some old egg cartons to cut up, plopped down in front of the same container of blocks every morning, or left to watch endless videos and television programs. In the context of a clear curriculum, some of these activities may be fine. Just be sure that your caregiver values hands-on learning, healthy activity, and developmental growth—not just silence and obedience.

Is there consistency from teacher to teacher or class to class in the way problems are handled? Does one teacher refuse to allow children to help prepare snacks while another turns snack time into a yogurt "finger paint" free-for-all?

Centers with consistent programs encourage children to develop trust, autonomy, and a healthy sense of initiative. These traits are important at home, and they are also important where your child will spend so much of his time.

Safety

Safety includes the physical setting, the program health policies, and the emergency preparedness of the center. A program with exposed electrical cords, unimpeded access to a laundry cupboard, or broken-down play equipment does not provide an environment that is safe for little ones.

Look for everyday preparedness. How are emergencies handled? Are there regular fire or other emergency preparedness drills? Do teachers have CPR, HIV/AIDS, and first-aid training? How are medications stored and administered? What about allergies? (Many centers are now nut-free due to an increase in severe nut allergies.) What is the center's policy on illness and exclusion? Ask how injuries are handled.

If you are in an earthquake-, flood-, or tornado-prone area, what provisions have been made in case of such an emergency? Are food, water, and clothing set aside? Are out-of-area emergency contact numbers listed in case local services become unavailable? What evacuation site or route is designated?

Reassure yourself that the staff knows how to care for your child under a variety of circumstances. The more satisfied you are that these details have been addressed, the more comfortable you can feel about leaving your child at this center.

Curriculum, Equipment, and Activities

What curriculum guidelines does this program follow? Are there posted themes or a daily schedule of activities or learning objectives? As we've said, much learning takes place during play. Setting out toy kangaroos and Aboriginal art designs while learning about Australia; including woven African cloth, batiks, and child-sized tunics to promote multicultural appreciation; or providing a variety of sponges, brushes, and textures for painting will enhance the type and quality of children's play and exploration.

A room designed for infants should have child-safe, unbreakable mirrors at floor level, as well as rails or small, sturdy furniture that a child can use to pull herself up as she learns to walk. Balls and rolling toys on the floor will help your child with eye-hand coordination and encourage him to move and crawl.

Outdoor access and equipment such as climbers that encourage large-muscle development should be available for use. Be sure these areas are maintained and are safe and clean. Be sure there is regular outdoor time daily and that supervision is provided at all times. On outings, high adult-child ratios must be met.

Any equipment that children have access to should be scaled to their use, such as low-level sinks, easy-access shelves, and displays at a child's eye level. Whenever possible, there should be child-sized equipment. Small pitchers, drinking cups, and child-sized tables and chairs are very helpful for young children. If child-sized items aren't available, then some adaptation of adult-sized equipment will help. An example would be to make sinks or toilets more accessible by providing sturdy step stools.

Look for puzzles that have all of their pieces, a varied and changing supply of blocks and art supplies, and music, singing, or rhythm experiences. If all you see are stacks of paper and pencils and children sitting at desks or tables for long periods, beware. A program that engages all of the senses as well as encourages active play and movement promises the most appropriate learning balance.

LIVING WITH YOUR CHILD CARE DECISION

Once you have made your decision, you still may have feelings of sadness and anxiety about leaving your child in any kind of child care arrangement. Several things may help. The first step is to recognize that this is a necessary choice for you and your child. When a parent can accept the need for (or see the value of) child care in the life of the family, other concerns begin to fall into place.

The next step is to deal with the many questions you may have about handling the details of daily life when child care is part of your family's routine: "How can I handle leaving my child in the morning? How do our home routines change or alter when we are away from our child all day? What about my child's friends? Will my child be safe? Will my child be loved and feel loved?" Many of these questions will be resolved once you feel confident that you have selected a quality child care situation.

SEPARATION

Parents often feel not only sad but guilty when they leave their child in child care. Many children cry in the morning at child care or in the evening when a parent goes out with friends. How parents react to this has everything to do with a child's ability to be content in child care. The parent who, though sad, believes that her child will be well cared for and secure while she is absent communicates that confidence to her child.

The other side of separation is connection. While you and your child are apart, whom will your child connect with? Take time to help your child begin a relationship with his new caregiver(s). Both he and you need to know that he can trust that person to be there for him when you cannot be.

Provide tangible ways for him to feel connected to you and his more familiar world by supplying a nap blanket or cuddly toy from home. Set up playdates with the other children in his class to broaden and strengthen the connection he feels with his new friends. The more connections he feels, the better he will handle his time away from you.

THE CHILD CARE DAY

Your daily routines will be influenced and altered by the schedule, commute, and details of your child's care. Some families have to include food preparation time if they bring in all or part of their child's food. Getting dressed and out of the house, coping with nap time, establishing departure routines, and keeping up with your child's budding and shifting friendships are common issues that may overtake the whole family.

Even the most effective and smoothly functioning lifestyle can be derailed by a weeklong bout with an ear infection! Remember that everyone has a bad day now and then, and how smoothly your day goes depends on many different elements. These include the mood and condition of parents, children, and caregivers; traffic; and maybe even whether anyone remembered to put the milk back in the fridge the night before. With so many opportunities for disaster, make it a daily habit to celebrate what goes right.

It can be difficult to remember in the midst of rushing out the door, but even though two-year-old Nick insisted on wearing one purple sock and one orange sock and five-year-old Denise dropped the jar of honey on the kitchen floor, do take a moment to rejoice in the fact that

Nick dressed himself at all and that Denise was helping set out breakfast things without being asked. There will always be imperfections, so use your energy to focus on the daily victories—no matter how meager they may sometimes seem.

MORNING HASSLES

Routines are critical for getting out of the house in the morning. We've discussed children's differing perceptions about time and the "process versus product" thinking that prevails in early childhood (see Chapter 3). These traits sometimes work against a smoothly flowing morning. Remember that young children thrive on routines and predictability. Establishing clear routines for getting your little one to child care can prove to be the difference between a calm or hectic morning.

The Jasper family has four members. Dad has to be at work by 8:30 A.M., Mom begins work at 9:00 A.M., and their four-year-old twin daughters, Ada and Amy, must be taken to child care. Since they have only one car, the family commutes together and both parents deliver the girls to child care each morning. They have found several things that work well for them.

Each evening the twins help pick out the clothes they will wear the next day. At first Amy still wasn't happy because she hated to take off her warm nightgown in the chilly mornings, but then Amy and her mom agreed that Amy could sleep in the shirt she would wear the next morning. Either Mom or Dad would pack lunches the night before, with occasional "help" from the twins. Whoever packed the lunches also helped the twins make sure that all coats and shoes had been located and were laid out near the door so there would be no last-minute panic over missing items. Advance planning and preparation the night before eliminated a lot of decisions (and opportunities to get into struggles) in the morning; the established routines kept things running smoothly.

The twins knew that they had to be dressed before they could have breakfast. Mom or Dad was available to help with difficult buttons or shoe tying, but the girls usually did a good job of getting their clothes on each morning. Both Mom and Dad had begun training and encouraging their daughters' efforts at dressing themselves when the twins were two years old. Amy liked to pour the milk, and her parents kept a small pitcher in the refrigerator that she could manage. There was a sponge by the sink that the girls had been trained to use when the occasional spill occurred. Both Ada and Amy were given things to do each morning to help with breakfast: setting out napkins, putting salt and pepper on the table, mixing the juice, and so on. Ada and Amy felt good about the contributions they made each day. While the twins helped one parent clear up the breakfast things, the other parent got the car out and everyone's gear loaded up. Then, relaxed and smiling, out the door they went.

Does this sound like a fairy tale? Yes and no. It is possible to set up careful routines and achieve this kind of morning harmony. It did not happen overnight. First Mom and Dad hassled with each other over who should be doing what each morning. When they finally worked things out, they clearly understood each other's expectations and weren't spending lots of energy bickering.

Then Amy and Ada had to conduct a few tests to see if their parents really meant that they had to be dressed before they could come to breakfast. This meant that once or twice Amy and Ada did not have time to eat before leaving in the morning. (Their parents knew that they could survive an hour or two until morning snack.) It also meant that on at least one occasion, one or both of the twins arrived at their child care in pajamas with Mom or Dad carrying a paper bag of clothing. Amy and Ada's parents did not mistreat their daughters; they gave them the opportunity to become responsible in ways that were respectful by learning from the results of their own choices. It also meant that

Ada and Amy soon believed that their parents meant what they said, and both girls peacefully participated in the morning routines.

Usually the result was a hassle-free morning routine. Notice the word *usually*. The day did not always begin smoothly. Sometimes Mom or Dad overslept and got a late start or was just plain grouchy in the morning. Other times, no amount of routine would get Amy into her clothes. They learned to celebrate improvement instead of looking for perfection.

No morning routine works perfectly all the time. With training, thoughtful planning, and respect—both for one another and for agreed-upon rules—mornings can proceed much more smoothly, at least most of the time!

ARRIVAL

No matter what happened before you got there, the moment arrives when you and your child are at the child care center. Some things will help both of you feel better about the day ahead. Arrive early enough to create a smooth transition. Take a moment to look around the center with your child. Find out what the teacher is planning for the day. Prepare your child if you find out there is a substitute; meet the substitute and make sure you introduce your child to any new person she will be with that day.

Notice any changes in the environment. If a new toy or easel is out, explore it with your child. Sometimes you may have time to read a story or do a puzzle with your child before you leave. If time does not allow that, ask him what he will play with when you leave. This will allow you to feel more connected, and you and your child can visualize what he will be doing after you have gone.

When it is time to leave, go quickly (dragging out the farewell leaves you, your child, and the caregiver emotionally drained), but never just disappear. Tell your child that you are leaving. Tears may follow your announcement, but if you are respectful and honest, your child will learn that she can trust you. If your child clings to you, gently hand her into the caregiver's arms so that she can be held and comforted as you leave. It helps to have a special place for children to stand or be held to wave to parents as they leave.

Even when parents leave in a respectful and loving way, children still may cry. Remember that your child will learn that she can trust the adults in her life—and that she can trust herself. This is reaffirmed every day by the fact that you do, in fact, return (and that she does survive these separations). Eventually the tears will disappear and the routine of morning departure for parents and children will be smooth and happy. (If you feel the need, call the center midmorning to reassure yourself that the tears were brief and all is going smoothly. Your peace of mind will be worth it.)

DEPARTURE/EVENING PICKUP TIME

When you arrive to take your child home, allow time for a friendly greeting and a bit of reentry. You are both about to begin a new segment of your day.

When Madelyn arrives at closing to take her three-year-old daughter, Brie, home, she finds her playing with some dress-up clothes. Madelyn gives Brie a hug and comments solemnly on the orange wig and flowered purse that Brie has chosen. Madelyn then tells Brie that she may play for five more minutes.

During that time Madelyn gathers the notes about Brie's day that have been left by the morning teacher. She also signs up to bring a casserole to next week's potluck. When she returns to the dress-up area, Brie is still wearing the orange wig. Madelyn comments on how much Brie must enjoy that wig; perhaps she will be able to wear it again tomorrow. She then tells Brie that it is time to leave. Brie pouts a bit but puts on her coat and takes her mother's hand. Together they hunt down Brie's missing shoe. Madelyn signs Brie out for the day, and mother and daughter leave the center together.

Madelyn feels comforted that her daughter is so happy at her preschool that she doesn't want to leave. By taking time to reconnect with her daughter and giving Brie time to conclude her play, Madelyn has set the stage for a calm departure. Brie may fuss anyway—after all, she was having a lot of fun—but she is likely to fuss less than a child who is dragged away from her play.

The school staff has contributed to a smooth departure by taking time half an hour before departure to have the children find everything they need to go home—coats, lunch boxes, art projects, and notices for parents about the upcoming potluck. In spite of all this preparation, some children may not be as cooperative as Brie when their parents arrive to pick them up.

There is a good reason children are fussy at the end of their day. An important element of child care is that young children must cope with a highly social environment all day. That means that a certain amount of tension and stress may build up in your child. When a child falls apart at her parent's arrival, it may be her way of saying that you are the person she can trust to love and accept her, no matter what side of herself she shows to you. Social expectations can be relaxed in the warmth of a parent's arrival.

A major transition in a child's day takes place when he is about to leave the child care setting, and young children appreciate gentle support to get them through this transition. Devoting time to your child and his needs will ultimately benefit you both.

FAMILY SUPPORT

Whatever a family's configuration, resources, or location, all need support from time to time. Parents of young children need other parents with whom to share concerns, ideas, and stories. Children need both other children and adults in their lives to learn about the variety of people that populate their world.

Parenting classes, books such as this one, and other resources provide valuable tools for parents today. Many communities boast groups where parents can gather to share ideas and allow their children to play. In addition, the Internet has opened a vast world of information, including sites with forums for conversation, advice, and even opportunities to ask questions of recognized experts in a variety of fields. Caregivers also have access to an array of resources. Raising children involves the whole of society. What happens to children on every level matters to all people, young and old alike.

NANNIES AND SITTERS AS CAREGIVERS

Q. I have a wonderful sitter who is great with my two-year-old girl and four-year-old boy. My only concern with her is that she does not discipline her own three-and-a-half-year-old; consequently, her child is a tyrant and my two-year-old is starting to behave like the sitter's daughter. This child screams, hits her mother, and tells her mother "no" or "shut up." My daughter is starting to act this way at home, and it takes at least an hour to settle her down to our rules. I don't want my children to become tyrants as well. In all other aspects this sitter is wonderful. What do I do?

A. Your sitter's daughter did not develop such behavior in a vacuum. Although you feel satisfied with your sitter's treatment of your children, we suspect she is not very effective at setting limits. The behavior of her daughter is a big clue. Does her daughter act this way all the time? It could also be that her daughter is jealous of sharing her mom's attention and so devotes her energy to misbehaving in order to keep her mom busy with her. Talk over your concerns; ask the sitter how she feels about her daughter's behavior and see if the two of you can come up with a win-win solution. If this does not resolve the problem, you may face a decision about whether or not to change your child care arrangements.

Choosing a sitter or a nanny requires careful consideration. Always check references, interview candidates (without children present), and set up a trial visit where you, the caregiver, and your child can get acquainted. Conduct transactions in a businesslike manner; provide sitters with emergency and medical information, and honor agreements paying for a sitter's time in the event of a last-minute cancellation.

The advantages of employing a sitter or nanny include not having to take your child out of the home for care. Children sleep, eat, and play in a familiar and consistent environment. There is often more flexibility if parents must work varied schedules or if jobs include traveling. On the other hand, a child at home with a nanny misses opportunities to develop social skills unless she plays regularly with nearby friends and relatives or attends a part-time preschool program. Most parents worry about the danger of abusive or neglectful care. Nannies and sitters are alone with children. The only protection available is caution, careful screening, and a thorough checking of credentials.

No matter whom you select to watch your children while you're away, be sure you've talked with him or her enough to feel comfortable—and to be sure that person shares your philosophy of raising children. It may be helpful to take a parenting class together. If your child is old enough to communicate easily with you, check her perceptions occasionally to be sure everything is going well. And always listen to your heart; your instincts will help you know when changes are required.

GRANDPARENTS AND OTHER RELATIVES

Many children spend their time with grandparents or other relatives while parents work. In fact, many grandparents today are actually raising their grandchildren because the children's parents are unable to do so. Being cared for by relatives gives children opportunities to forge strong family bonds, and many of us have fond memories of times spent with our extended families. There may also be problems, disagreements, and clashes between the generations.

Q. How can I raise a well-mannered four-year-old if his grandmother lets him get away with murder and spoils him rotten? He stays with her while I work part time in a nearby office. I feel like I always have to be the bad guy since she won't discipline him. I'm even afraid that he loves her more than me. I need help.

A. Parenting disagreements with grandparents are often more about the relationship between the parents and the grandparents than about what goes on between young children and their grandparents. Such conflicts can stem from your need to move to an adult-to-adult relationship with your own parents, who sometimes continue to see you as that adorable chubby-cheeked darling they dandled on their knee only yesterday—or as the problem child who hasn't learned anything in the years since childhood.

Love is not a contest. It sounds a bit as though you and your child's grandmother are using your child as a way to prove superiority over each other. Children love their parents. They also love their grandparents. It is possible to love both without diminishing the love for either.

Children can learn what behavior is acceptable in different circumstances. If Grandma lets young Hunter decorate her kitchen table with marshmallows, Hunter will still be able to remember that marshmallows have a different function at home. He may, of course, try to talk you into this modification while whining about how "Grandma lets me do it." Just smile and remind him that the rules at home are different.

Unfortunately, when child-rearing philosophies, expectations, and rules clash, tolerance may not be enough. If parents make a sincere attempt to achieve a healthy relationship with in-laws or other family members, and differences cannot be resolved, different care arrangements may be necessary.

"WHAT IF I HAVE DOUBTS?"

Whenever a parent feels truly uncomfortable with a caregiver, related or not, the situation must be addressed. Suspicions of abusive treatment, exposure to harmful conditions, widely differing philosophies regarding discipline, or concerns about children falling behind developmentally merit immediate attention. If you believe your child is at risk, do not hesitate: remove him from the environment and find a caregiver you can trust and feel comfortable with.

If the concerns are not threatening to your child's safety or health, work toward solutions. Communicate your concerns and voice ideas, wishes, and requests in a respectful fashion. Listen nonjudgmentally to your caregiver's ideas. Work on solving problems together. As with any care setting, when adults work together, children benefit.

Your child will, in all likelihood, spend at least part of these important preschool years in the care of someone other than his or her parents—a nanny, relative, or child care provider. The time and energy you invest now in making child care arrangements that work for all of you will be repaid many times over in peace of mind, enjoyment, and learning. The environment and the teachers who work with young children help shape their future—and the future we all share.

16

FAMILY AND CLASS MEETINGS FOR PRESCHOOLERS

It is class meeting time at the ABC Preschool. As the young-sters settle into a circle, Mr. Scott, the teacher, consults the agenda. "It sounds like we've had a problem on the play-ground with people throwing wood chips at one another. Does anyone have something to say about this problem, or can someone offer a suggestion of how we might solve it?"

Five-year-old Girard raises his hand. "Whoever throws wood chips could take a cool-off!" Four-year-old Natalie waves her hand, and when called upon, she offers, "We could not have wood chips anymore and have grass instead."

The teacher looks toward three-year-old Cristina, whose lit-tle hand has been patiently held aloft, and calls on her. "Guess what?" Cristina says with a bright smile.

"What, Cristina?" Mr. Scott asks.

"I had bananas in my cereal today."

"Mmmm, that must have tasted good." Mr. Scott smiles and thanks Cristina for her comment, then asks for more suggestions about the wood chip problem. Although Cristina clearly is not thinking about wood chips, she is still a valued member of the group.

When children are old enough to participate actively in group or circle time activities (usually around the age of three and a half), they are ready for class meetings. Class meetings are a wonderful way to help children learn cooperation, contribution, and problem-solving skills. This class agreed that they wouldn't throw wood chips anymore—a suggestion that had never worked when teachers pleaded, but was very effective when suggested by a child and agreed upon by the whole class.

WHAT IS A CLASS MEETING?

Class meetings are far more than group problem-solving sessions. In a class meeting, children gather on a regular basis to help each other, encourage each other, learn communication skills, focus on solutions, and develop their judgment and wisdom. By far the most powerful effect of class meetings, though, whatever the age of the child, is to create a sense of belonging. Because the need for belonging lies at the heart of all mistaken goal behavior (see Chapters 8, 9, and 10), it makes sense that addressing this need will have the greatest long-range effect on the behavior of children in the group.

Class meetings provide many opportunities to learn and strengthen skills. They aid in the acquisition of social skills and promote language development. The meetings foster a sense of both group and individual responsibility and empower young children with positive attitudes about their own capabilities and significance—attitudes that not only help shape their behavior but also build their self-esteem.

In this chapter we will take a look at ways you can begin class meetings for the preschool set. For a broader discussion of class meetings, see *Positive Discipline in the Classroom* by Jane Nelsen and Lynn Lott, Three Rivers Press, 2000.

HOW YOUNG IS TOO YOUNG?

"I can see the value of class meetings for elementary school children," you may be saying, "but aren't preschoolers a bit young?" The answer really is no—children three and a half years old and older can work together in productive and encouraging class meetings. Even the younger members of your preschool group can begin to cultivate the attitudes nurtured by the class meeting process. The younger children can learn from their older role models, and the older children can learn to consider and include the needs of the younger ones. Three-year-olds like Cristina will certainly have different contributions to make than will older children. Still, there is real value in including the little ones, the greatest being that their sense of belonging to the group is established.

Even if your entire class consists of two- or three-year-olds, you can still enjoy class meetings together. The teacher becomes the role model when there are no older children; he may need to generate most of the suggestions and help the children learn to make choices. Even toddlers can get into the act, although the main purpose of meetings for them may simply be planning an outing or fun activity together rather than solving problems. Taking into consideration the social and language skills of the children you work with will help you know how much you can expect to accomplish.

By the time children reach the age of four, they learn the elements of class meetings by jumping right in and participating. For example, the concept of helping others can be taught by finding someone to help. In Chapter 10, we included an example of children who helped a bully learn to redirect his misbehavior. Children of four and older warm quickly to the idea of solving problems—and are very good at it when taught the skills and given the opportunity to practice.

ELEMENTS OF SUCCESS FOR PRESCHOOL CLASS MEETINGS

There are four main goals for class meetings with preschoolers. Listing these elements on a brightly colored chart can provide a stable agenda for every meeting and help focus children's attention on the project at hand. Once you have established the routine, preschoolers can take turns running the meeting. They love to call the meeting to order, call on people who have their names on the agenda (sometimes with a little prompting from the teacher), ask for suggestions to solve problems, and close the meeting.

Compliments and Appreciation

Compliments are clearly influenced by the age of the children offering them. Four- and five-year-olds may say things like "I compliment Jane for being my friend" or "I compliment Eddie because he played dress-up with me." You may even hear an occasional "She pushed me off the swing!" (Well, they don't have it perfected yet!)

Three-year-olds don't always understand the concept of compliments. They are more likely to say "I love my mommy," "I have a teddy bear at home," or "I get to have pizza for dinner." These little ones usually say whatever is on their minds, but teachers can smile and thank them for their comments. The feeling of having contributed is no less because the "compliment" was a bit off target.

Teachers can ask some helpful questions to guide children in learning how to give compliments. "What is something that you like about our school?" for instance, or "Is there someone who helped you feel good today?" They can also model giving compliments: "I want to compliment all of you on the delicious cake you made yesterday. And I loved how all of the tables were

> **The Four Elements of Class Meetings for Preschoolers**
>
> - To give compliments and appreciation
> - To empower children to help each other
> - To solve problems that affect the group
> - To plan future activities

washed and cleaned up after we finished mixing the batter." "Madison, I want to compliment you on letting us help you with the problem you were having about not liking your lunch. I appreciated the ideas that I heard because I can use some of them, too."

"I love you, but . . ." You've heard it before: the compliment that simply sets up the criticism. "You did a good job, but . . ." "Thanks for picking up your toys, but . . ." Children will do this, too. "I appreciate Maggie for playing with me and not pushing me down." Such compliments are like alligator tails that whip forward to knock us down. Children may even develop a "compliment flinch." They've learned that whenever an adult says something nice, it means something not-so-nice is sure to follow. When that happens, whatever power our encouragement and appreciation might have had is gone.

Modeling how to tell others that you appreciate what they do can be great practice for all of us. Let your smiles, thanks, and appreciation stand alone; find a quiet moment another time to give that helpful hint. Children will learn from your example.

Helping Each Other
Next up at the class meeting is helping each other. This time in your class meeting is an opportunity for children to ask for help with something that is a problem for them.

> *It is Tuesday morning at the Hill Harbor Child Care Center. The class of three- and four-year-olds is just beginning their class meeting with their teacher, Mr. Silk. He asks if anyone needs help from the group today.*
>
> *Matthias raises his hand and announces, "I can't wake up in the morning." Many of the other children agree that it's hard for them, too. Mr. Silk asks if anyone has a suggestion for Matthias. The children offer all sorts of helpful ideas: "Go to bed earlier." "Just get up anyway." "Come to school in pajamas." Mr. Silk turns to Matthias. "Do you think any of these ideas will help you, or should the group think of*

Kid of the Week

A special variation on compliments at one child care center is called Kid of the Week. Each week there is a special Kid of the Week circle time, and every child in the class will be selected at least once during each year.

The teacher brings a large sheet of paper and an assortment of colored pens to the circle. At the top of the page she writes the child's name. Then each of the children take turns saying what it is they like or appreciate about the child while the teacher writes their comments on the sheet of paper: "I like her because she's my friend." "She plays with me." "She has a sparkle in her eye." (Wow!) "She jumps like Tigger."

If the children seem to be a bit stuck about what to say, the teacher can offer some guidance by asking questions. "Who wants to say that Maureen can come to his or her birthday party?" "Who remembers a game you played in the dress-up area with Maureen this week?" The teacher can also add comments to show appreciation for the child and to model the skill of complimenting others. If some of the children still have trouble thinking of something to say (or are just a bit shy), the teacher can ask, "Who would like to have his name written on the paper as one of Maureen's friends?"

When all who want a turn have finished, the teacher rolls up the paper and ties it with a bright ribbon. Another child is chosen to present the scroll to Maureen, and the circle finishes with another song, perhaps a variation on "For He's [or She's] a Jolly Good Person." Not a bad way to

some more?" Matthias pauses to consider, then says he is going to "get up anyway."

Next, Julian raises his hand and says he needs help because "my mom doesn't have enough money." After sympathizing with Julian, other children volunteer that they have that problem, too. Julian's friends are eager to help. Some of the children offer to bring in money. Brandon suggests that Julian could do some jobs to get money. Crystal says, "My mom will help." Devon recommends, "Your mom can get a job that makes more money."

start a child's day, is it? Being Kid of the Week can be a special treat for every child—but remember to focus on creating a sense of belonging. It is easy to slip over the line of encouragement into praise, which teaches children to depend on the evaluation of others.

One teacher, who had seen Kid of the Week demonstrated during an internship at an American school, brought the concept back to her home classroom in Asia, renaming it Star of the Week. In her culture, families were not involved in the school's activities except for fundraising events, but they responded with interest and curiosity when she proposed her Star of the Week idea.

One week, a child whose father was poorly educated and whom the teachers had tended to look down upon took part in his son's Star of the Week event. Together he and his son had constructed an elaborate representation of their small home, creating this model entirely out of toothpicks and plastic straws. The resulting product was a true work of art. Watching this man's obvious pride and love for his son, the teachers felt humbled by his talent and the amount of time and labor he had devoted on his son's behalf. Their attitude toward the family was transformed: taking part in this Star of the Week circle had awakened their compassion. A new sense of respect between the teachers and all the children's families began to develop. In fact, the beautiful sculpture was kept on display for the rest of the term. Sometimes simple ideas can result in extraordinary transformations. Class (and family) meetings invite such connections by inviting children and adults alike to honor the contributions of each member of the group.

It is unlikely that Julian's mom will have more money as a result of this discussion. But Julian was genuinely concerned about money, and his concern was treated respectfully. He has also learned that his classmates care about his needs and that some of them share similar worries. Helping each other can become a very powerful part of class meetings.

Parents may be invited to place items on the agenda, too, and to visit and join in the class meeting. Seeing firsthand the experience their child is enjoying may encourage them to try similar meetings at home.

"Put It on the Agenda!"

An agenda is a list of topics written in a class meeting agenda notebook or posted on the wall where everyone can reach it, where children and adults can list things they wish to discuss at the next meeting. In addition to providing a list of things to discuss, an agenda can serve as a cooling-off device as well.

When Jon comes stomping over in a rage to tell the teacher, "Parker just killed a beetle," the teacher can share his concern and suggest that "how insects should be treated" would make a very good topic for their class meeting. She asks Jon if he would like to put it on the agenda. He readily agrees, and together they write "bugs" on the agenda, with the teacher sounding out the word; then Jon writes his name next to it. If Jon is very young, the teacher may write down Jon's name and topic for him. Or she may encourage Jon to draw a picture of a bug and either trace over his own name or make his own mark. Involving Jon in some way is respectful and creates a sense of responsibility and influence.

When it's time for problem solving, the teacher will look at the agenda and ask Jon to explain the problem of bugs to the others. Because Jon felt listened to when he was angry and placed his item on the agenda, he can now discuss the problem calmly. Jon's teacher will watch to see that the group focuses on the treatment of insects—not on who killed the beetle or how he should be punished.

Solving Problems

It may come as a surprise, but young children can be remarkably creative when it comes to solving problems. One afternoon, the following note appeared near the sign-out sheet at the Mountain View Preschool: "We are having a small bake sale this Thursday afternoon. We are learning to be responsible by replacing a ripped-up library book. We will bake cookies at school and sell them for twenty-five cents each. The children would also like to earn twenty-five cents at home by doing a special job. The bake sale idea came out of our class meeting discussion about a damaged book. We also discussed and demonstrated how to carry books and how to turn pages at the edge."

Over the course of the next week, the children prepared several batches of cookies during class time, learning new skills (and having a great time) in the process. On Thursday, the sale took place and was so successful that even after subtracting the cost of the cookie ingredients, the children had raised enough not just to replace the damaged book but also to buy another new one. They spent time at the next class meeting discussing what type of new book they wanted for their classroom.

Imagine if the teacher had scolded the children and taken away their book-corner privileges. The opportunity to learn and practice these vital life skills would have been missed.

Class meetings can also provide valuable opportunities to learn social skills.

One morning at meeting time, Candace, who is four, said that another child had called her friend Dylan a bad name. The teacher asked Dylan if this was a problem he would like the group to address. (It is important that children learn to be responsible for their own needs.) After Dylan told his story, the teacher asked whether anyone else had ever been called names. "How does it make you feel?" she asked. A lively discussion followed, and the children agreed that it hurt to be called names. They then came up with a list of possible solutions.

"Maybe the name-calling person could control himself." "Walk away." "Say, 'Don't say that!'" "Get a teacher to help." "Tell them you don't like it." "Ask them to take a cool-off." "Say, 'Stop!'" "All walk away and discuss it somewhere else."

The suggestions may have sounded similar, but all were honored and written down. Dylan and his classmates could now talk about the possible results of each choice (with some gentle help from their teacher) and decide ways they might respond to name-calling in the future. Remember, preschoolers are still refining their social skills; suggestions like "Call him a worse name" or "Punch his lights out" would provide opportunities to learn about more appropriate responses.

Planning Future Activities

When young children are asked about fun activities they might do as a group, not all of the suggestions will be practical: "We could all go to Disneyland." "I suggest we go to the beach." (Never mind the snow outside.) "We can go on an airplane trip. My daddy will take us with him." Once children start offering improbable suggestions, they tend to get on a roll, so it is helpful for the teacher to guide them by offering some practical, fun ideas for activities and outings.

There are dozens of ideas. Trips to the police station, fire station, zoo, and park may be possible field trips, depending on your program. Remember that a field trip can be a wonderful opportunity to invite children to solve problems in advance. Ask them what problems they had on their last field trip or what they think some good rules for the group would be. If the children can't think of anything, the teacher can make suggestions, such as discussing expectations about crossing streets, pushing and shoving, running around, or not listening quietly and respectfully when the fire chief talks. The children can then brainstorm solutions. Children are far more willing to follow rules when they've had a part in making them.

More immediate activities can also be planned. Classroom treats such as ice cream or popcorn are fun and easy to provide. If an expenditure of money is involved, the children can work out plans to raise the needed funds. They can earn money at home through special tasks or do so at school as a group. One bunch of enterprising youngsters decided to sell baked potatoes at the end of the day to tired and hungry parents. The aroma as parents entered the school was wonderful, and needless to say, this fund-raiser was a rousing success.

The group may set a goal, such as throwing a pizza party when all of the shelves and toys have been washed. The teacher can provide buckets and sponges, and the children can pitch in. One program has an occasional floor-scrubbing day during which the furniture is cleared away and there are sponges and mops for all. The children love the water play, training, and social interest, all rolled up into one activity. Remember that involving children in planning an activity, whether in art or cooking or play, will make that activity more successful. When children are invited to feel capable and creative and involved, they almost always respond with enthusiasm.

SPECIAL TIPS FOR EFFECTIVE CLASS MEETINGS

Keeping a few ideas in mind will ensure the success of your class meetings.

Be Aware of Timing

Class meetings for preschoolers may require that you be flexible. Depending on the children's mood, abilities, and attention span, you may need to keep meetings short or focus on only one element each time. Your meetings don't need to be long to cultivate belonging and encouragement. Many preschools find that one meeting each week is ample. Others like to have a short meeting every day so that children can practice giving and receiving compliments, listening with empathy, and focusing on solutions regularly. Trial and error will help you find just the right balance.

Use Special Signals

Young children love special signals, such as the same song being sung each day to signal cleanup time. A ringing bell could mean that everyone should freeze and listen to an announcement from the teacher. It also works well to develop a special signal to open and close class meetings. In one classroom, the kids sit on the floor in a circle and each child places his or her arms together with the elbows bent. To begin the meeting they slowly move their arms apart, like opening a book, and announce, "Class meeting is open!" At the end of the meeting, they reverse the process while saying, "Class meeting is closed!"

> **Tips for Effective Class Meetings**
>
> - Be aware of timing.
> - Use special signals.
> - Include voting (when appropriate).
> - Take notes.
> - Use a "talking stick."

Include Voting (When Appropriate)

In preschool, children can vote when the choice involves everyone, such as whether to have a popcorn party, have a pizza party, or make homemade ice cream. At this early age, children can learn that people think and want different things, and they can learn to give and take. (It is not appropriate to allow children to vote on a solution for another person. The person with the problem should be allowed to choose the solution she thinks will be most helpful for her.)

Take Notes

Keeping track of what happens in a meeting can be helpful, especially when your class needs to remember just what it was they decided! Because most preschoolers can't write, an adult will need to take the minutes. At the beginning of each meeting, you can review the previous meeting's notes and see how your plans and decisions are working out. Evaluate what did not work about the solution that was tried. Look over the other suggestions that were not used and come up with new ideas as well. If a problem persists, it is important to encourage a child to put it back on the agenda and discuss it again.

Use a "Talking Stick"

A decorated stick, a magic wand, or a small toy can be passed around the circle. Whoever holds the object has permission to speak. (We suggest you avoid stuffed animals since preschoolers have a tendency to rub their noses on the stuffed animal when it is their turn—a good way to spread cold germs.) A physical symbol can help young children learn to listen respectfully and speak in turn, and may encourage shy children to contribute to the group discussion when they have the object in their hands.

FAMILY MEETINGS WITH PRESCHOOLERS

If you have older children, you may have already discovered the many benefits of having family meetings. If your children are preschoolers, the concept may be new; you may even question the value of having family meetings with young children. You may wonder, "What can my preschooler possibly learn? Will she be able to sit still? How can a little child solve problems?"

Very little effort is required to adapt the material presented at the beginning of this chapter on class meetings to family meetings, and the benefits and blessings are well worth the time and energy you spend. Family meetings teach children that they are valuable, capable members of the family, and you may be amazed at your preschooler's resourcefulness and creativity. Preschoolers can offer compliments, help solve problems, plan family fun, and learn to express their needs and get help in positive (and surprisingly enjoyable) ways. Regular family meetings will help you and your children build a sense of mutual respect, trust, understanding, and love—and that can lay the foundation for the many years that lie ahead.

Here are a few ideas to keep in mind when beginning family meetings with preschoolers:

- **Be realistic.** You can have worthwhile, entertaining family meetings with children as young as three years old, but remember that the younger the child, the shorter the attention span is likely to be. Keep your meetings short and to the point; that way, no one will get tired of them.

- **Make family meetings a priority.** Our busy lives have a tendency to get in the way of even our best intentions. If you want your family meetings to work, set a regular time to get together, and stick to it. Older children often have commitments such as sports or music lessons, the timing for which cannot be controlled. It may be helpful to create a family calendar that shows each member's upcoming activities, and to use it to plan future meetings. Remember, it is easier for everyone to practice the skills when meetings happen consistently. Don't allow telephone calls, chores, or other distractions to get in the way. Making the time you spend as a family a priority will help you build a sense of unity and will let your young children know that you value them and the time you spend together.

- **Begin each meeting with compliments and appreciations.** This can feel awkward at first, especially if you have siblings who are more comfortable putting each other down, but looking for and commenting on the positive will encourage everyone and will get your meeting off to a friendly start. A variation some families prefer is to end the meeting with appreciations instead of beginning with them. When difficult issues are dealt with or strong emotions emerge, ending with appreciations and compliments can set a healing tone.

- **Post an agenda board in a handy place and help your preschoolers use it.** Even young children can "write" their problems and concerns in an agenda notebook or make a mark to indicate they have something to talk about. Taking these concerns seriously (and being careful not to immediately squelch your little one's sometimes unrealistic ideas) will show your children that you value them. The mere act of writing down a problem can be the first step to finding a peaceful, effective solution.

- **Leave time for fun.** Make sure part of your meeting is devoted to just enjoying each other, perhaps by playing a game, watching a video together, planning a family activity, sharing a special dessert, or reading a favorite story.

However you decide to do them, family meetings are one of the best habits you and your children can get into and will help you stay tuned in throughout the increasingly busy years ahead. For more information on family meetings with children of all ages, refer to *Positive Discipline* by Jane Nelsen, Ballantine, 2006, and *Top Ten Preschool Parenting Problems* by Roslyn Ann Duffy, Exchange Press, 2007.

A LEARNING OPPORTUNITY

Class and family meetings are astonishingly productive, teaching many life skills while helping children develop a strong sense of belonging. Adults sometimes underestimate the ability of young children to be creative and responsible, and class and family meetings allow this learning opportunity for everyone. You may discover that the youngsters in your care not only learn self-esteem and cooperation but have a marvelous time as well!

As we have learned, preschoolers are capable of contributing to meetings, even when very young and without well-developed problem-solving abilities. If your child is participating in class meetings at preschool, you will be amazed at how quickly he applies his new abilities at home, and it may inspire you to hold the same kinds of meetings with your family. The reverse is also true. You may wish to encourage your child's preschool to begin class meetings. The gift of this book will provide an excellent blueprint for success. Family and class meetings are a wonderful way for children and adults to experience cooperation, compassion, and problem solving, and to have fun learning together.

17

THE WORLD "OUT THERE"

Dealing with the Influence of Technology and Culture

I t's hard to imagine, but there was once a time when television and computers did not exist and families entertained themselves by reading books, gathering around the piano to sing, or telling stories aloud. You may find yourself wishing for simpler times, but, like it or not, there is no going back. Television, computers, the Internet, digital music players, and video games are here to stay, and new devices are undoubtedly just around the corner. At some point in your child's early years, you must make a decision about the place these technological terrors will occupy in your home. (In this chapter, "screen time" refers to the time your child spends on television, computers, video games, and other electronic devices.)

Consider the following:

- The average American family has 2.75 television sets.

- Sixty-six percent of American children have a television in their bedroom (including 20 percent of children between two and seven years old).

- Average viewing time for children and adolescents in America is more than twenty-one hours per week, or nearly one-fifth of a child's waking hours.

- Television viewing may affect attention span by conditioning children to short bits of information delivered in rapid succession.

- American advertisers spend approximately $15 billion each year marketing products to children.

- Having a television on in the background appears to hamper a child's ability to learn language.

- Increased television viewing is directly linked to obesity; the more time children spend in front of a screen, the less time they spend running, using their imaginations, and learning social and life skills.

- Exposure to TV violence in childhood is linked to aggressive behavior in young adulthood for both males and females.

Many children learn to operate sophisticated remote controls before their third birthday. Preschoolers around the world learn how to use computers, video games, and handheld DVD players, and sit mesmerized in front of screens to watch a cartoon, view a video, or play a digital game. In many homes television is even part of a child's bedtime routine; few parents are aware that television viewing before bed may disturb children's sleep patterns. Some children routinely fall asleep on the floor in front of the television screen rather than in their own beds.

Software designers are quick to promote "educational" programs for very young children, urging parents to start early to teach computer literacy to their small fry. One British study reported that the number of hours devoted to children's programming had increased ten times in the decade from 1995 to 2005. Wise parents learn to thoughtfully consider whether they will have the strongest influence in a child's life—or whether that influence will be handed over to television and advertisements. Who is most likely to have your child's best interests at heart?

CONSUMER KIDS

Children's television characters jump off the screen and onto lunch boxes, cuddly plush animals, and T-shirts, and children clamor for toys and products (often junk food, candy, or sugary beverages) bearing the image of their favorite television or video characters. Where is the demarcation line between marketing to kids and entertaining them? Unfortunately, there isn't one. It costs a lot to produce children's programming, but unlike adults, children don't have checkbooks, nor will a thirty-second ad have as much staying power in their minds as do the characters they have come to admire. The program itself must become the advertisement—and that is exactly what happens.

Marketing to children is a very deliberate process. Children as young as one to four years old are studied in focus groups to determine their play patterns. After being shown a sample program, they are watched to determine the type of play they will engage in. Will they want to look like that character? Then maybe dress-up clothing spin-offs are called for. Do they want to play a nurturing mommy or daddy game? Then maybe a plush toy conducive to cuddling.

These are rather benign examples of commercialism aimed at young children. The less savory examples involve merchandise that disregards children's needs. These include sugar-laden snack products, sexualized or stereotyped toys, or equipment that promotes violent play. Issues about commercialism are relevant to parenting and caregiving because they affect what children learn and the decisions children make. Children's growth also is affected physically (through poor nutrition and less active or outdoor play), emotionally (through the limiting nature of stereotypes), and intellectually (by superceding creative pursuits or time spent reading and being read to).

There is another subtle but insidious way in which the media influence children and adults alike. Advertising often creates dissatisfaction over things they don't have. Whether you have to deal with a meltdown at the mall over a toy princess doll, call a halt to a breakfast conflict over the cereal, or find yourself separating two children on the playground who are reenacting a cartoon battle, media's messages and modeling affect us all.

It is no accident that advertisers target children for their products. Young children may not have much spending money, but they certainly know people who do—and children are often able to whine, beg, and manipulate parents into buying the toy, product, or snack food of the moment. In addition to other safeguards, consider becoming more proactive by letting advertisers know when you object to their marketing to young children. Your voice does count.

TELEVISION: FRIEND OR FOE?

Q. My four-year-old twins watch television most afternoons. They also love to play video games with their older cousins. We try to make sure they aren't exposed to really violent things, but it seems harder than ever to screen out the images that are scary or that model aggressive behavior. Yesterday one of the twins jumped onto his brother's back and aimed a karate-like chop at his neck. I was horrified. I feel I have lost control over the harmful influences that my boys are being exposed to, but I can't simply lock them away from the world. What can I do?

A. Experts have spent a great deal of time over the past decade or two studying the effects of television and video game violence on young children. (For examples, as well as ratings for games and other programs, check David Walsh's excellent Web site, www.mediawise.org.) They have discovered that television and video violence may have a stronger effect on young children than previously thought. A forty-year longitudinal study funded by the National Institute of Mental Health and conducted by the Institute for Social Research at the University of Michigan found compelling evidence linking a child's exposure to media violence to a lasting tendency for violent and aggressive behavior later in life.

Children learn a great deal about behavior and attitudes by imitating others. Remember, young children cannot tell the difference between reality and fantasy in the same way older children and adults can. They also may be more likely to imitate aggressive behavior, especially aggression that goes unpunished or is performed in the service of "good" (as in superhero cartoons or movies). One recent study found that between 60 and 90 percent of the most popular video games have violent themes. Children who see screen violence are less likely to develop empathy for others; after all, if people on TV get shot and kicked and punched and are still okay (and they usually are), what's the problem? As one young child explained to his dad, "I was only killing him."

The best ways to deal with the effect of video and television violence on your child is to limit his exposure and to do lots of teaching. Watch programs or games *with* him and be sure you teach him the values you want him to adopt. Television viewing encourages passivity; critical thinking and learning occur only when dialog takes place. Let your child know kindly but firmly that kicking, punching, or hitting is not acceptable in your family and that real people suffer pain and harm when they are kicked or punched. Most important, put a cap on the time he spends in front of the screen—any screen—and substitute active play and conversation.

THE CULTURE OF DISRESPECT

Television, music, movies, and the culture in general have a subtle but pervasive influence on family life. Not too many years ago, the after-dinner hours were considered "family time"; programming was intended for children as well as adults, and profanity, sexual innuendo, and other adult influences were forbidden. And up until the 1990s, children's programming was designed only for children older than three.

Think about the programs that are broadcast regularly in prime time. What messages do they teach about respect for adults, courtesy, and cooperation? Even the evening news programs routinely deal with subject matter that most parents find inappropriate for young children. Certainly there are exceptions, but a great deal of the music, movies, and television available to young people fosters an attitude of disrespect toward others. (Remember, even if you limit your child's exposure to media, he will undoubtedly encounter a great deal of it in the company of other children at his child care center, the neighbor's house, and family get-togethers.)

GOOD PARENTING IN A TECHNOLOGICAL WORLD

It is essential that you stay aware and that you actively teach the character values and skills you want your child to practice. Limit screen time; question what he sees happening in a program and discuss whether or not those actions are appropriate. Encourage him to question what he sees, too.

Here are some ways to manage television and technology for young children.

Monitor Your Own Habits
It is difficult to limit your child's exposure to television, video games, and the computer when you never turn them off yourself. In fact, most adult relationships would improve if the screens were turned off more often. Be sure the television is off during family meals and conversations. (Consider recording the news so that adults can view disturbing events after children are in bed.) If you rely on the computer to work at home, make an effort to do as much of that work as possible during times when your child is occupied elsewhere. You are your child's most important role model; be sure you practice the values you expect your child to learn.

Allow Televisions, Video Games, and Computers Only in Common Areas of the House

We can think of no reason for a child younger than eight to have a television in his room—yet we know many who do, complete with video recorder and DVD player. Your child does not yet have the ability to choose his own viewing material—no matter how well he operates the remote. Be sure that all screens are located where you can easily view them along with your child. Supervision is essential, especially at this age, because screen time is addictive. A television located in a child's room encourages isolation instead of connection. When you combine addiction and isolation, you have a child who is developing habits of life numbness instead of life enjoyment. When the TV is in a common room (such as the family room), family members have the opportunity to negotiate what to watch and when.

Limit Time Spent in Front of the Screen

There is increasing evidence that screen time before the age of eight can negatively influence brain development. (The American Association of Pediatrics recommends that children two years old and younger watch no television at all.) You may choose to allow your child to watch a favorite program or video, but far too many children spend *hours* each day in front of the screen. Remember, your little one needs active play, time outdoors, conversation with you, and things to manipulate and explore far more than he needs the "educational" programs on television. Intellectual, emotional, and physical development all require activity and practice with other humans; the most important factor in healthy development is connection with parents and other

> **Dealing with Television, Video Games, and Technology**
>
> - Monitor your own habits.
> - Allow televisions, video games, and computers only in common areas of the house where everyone can see them.
> - Limit time spent in front of the screen.
> - Watch or play *with* your child.
> - Actively teach the values you believe in.
> - Spend time building a real relationship with your child.

caregivers. Children who feel connected to important others in their lives are less likely to engage in serious misbehavior. (We say "serious" because so much misbehavior is developmentally appropriate as part of the individuation process of testing and discovering boundaries.)

Watch or Play with Your Child

There is no better way to monitor the content of programs or videos (and to observe their effect on your child) than to watch or play with him. Invite your little one to teach you his favorite video game; settle down next to him to watch his special cartoon. You can ask curiosity questions to learn more and to engage your child in exercising his thinking skills. Curiosity is a great parenting tool and may help you understand your child's fascination with what he sees. You will also know when material is inappropriate for your child—and can turn it off.

Actively Teach the Values You Believe In

When parents don't teach, the culture will. Nature, it is said, abhors a vacuum, and the values and ideals of the mass culture will rush in to fill any empty space you leave in your child's education. Be sure you find opportunities to teach about respect, compassion, cooperation, and kindness. (Early experiences prepare the brain for future mastery.) When inappropriate behavior or attitudes occur in programs

you are watching together, use them as teaching moments to help your child learn a better way. ("What would you have said to that boy?" "How would you feel if that happened to you?") When all else fails, pull the plug and find something better to do. In fact, having the courage to pull the plug may be a good place to start. We know of one family who purchased a small TV that could be hidden with a toaster cover. They would bring it out only for special programs that were planned in advance.

Spend Time Building a Real Relationship with Your Child
There is *so* much to do with young children. Your child craves real connection with you; when he has it, he is less likely to look for stimulation and company elsewhere. (And, as mentioned above, he is less likely to misbehave.) As your child grows, his peers and the culture will become increasingly important. Be sure you take the time each day to connect with your little one and to explore the world you share.

WHAT ABOUT THE COMPUTER?

Much has been said and written about the importance of computer literacy. In a rapidly changing world, Americans are being urged to interest their children early in math, science, and technology in order to keep up with the rest of the world. It probably isn't necessary to start your child on the computer too early, however; none of the authors grew up in the computer age but all of us have learned to use—and enjoy—them. (Well, at least most of the time.)

The choice is not between total abstinence or instant addiction; instead, consider creating a thoughtful balance. If your little one truly enjoys simple computer programs that help identify colors, letters, shapes, and numbers, some computer playtime every now and then may be fine. (Be sure you use passwords or otherwise protect your own important records and files.) However, you should be aware that many experts believe screen time of any sort (including the computer) does more harm than good, especially in these early years.

You must find ways to protect your child, but it is realistic to do so within the context of the world around you. Remember, your child will also be exposed to computer use at friends' homes, child care centers, and eventually school. You should begin early to teach your little one appropriate screen use skills. Learning comes in many forms during these early years, and true computer literacy will not be required until your child begins school. Don't push, and continue to limit time spent sitting in front of the screen. There will be plenty of time in the years ahead to master the keyboard.

What They Hear (or Someday Won't)

One side effect of the media that is rarely discussed is the potential for damage to a child's hearing. Many technologies today include headphones of various types. These devices deliver sounds at high decibel levels, and because they are positioned so close to the sensitive membranes within a child's ears, long-term hearing damage or future hearing loss pose a real danger.

It may be wise to ban portable listening devices from young children (and to monitor their use with older children as well). Your child will be able to hear you better—and for a whole lot longer.

DECIDE WHAT YOU WILL DO, BE KIND AND FIRM, THEN FOLLOW THROUGH

Television, computers, and the other trappings of modern life loom increasingly large as your child grows and moves into the world "out there." These early years are a good opportunity to practice the skills you will need as your child tests his limits and experiments with the world around him. Positive Discipline tools will help you remain calm, kind, and firm as you decide how to approach these complex issues in your own family. Educate yourself about the issues, then decide what *you* will do. Teach values and skills; say no when necessary. Then follow through with dignity and respect for yourself and your child. Like it or not, you and your child must learn to live in an increasingly complicated and challenging world. The lessons you teach now will build the foundation for the years to come.

18

WHEN YOUR CHILD NEEDS SPECIAL HELP

No two children are alike. All young children have both assets and liabilities, and all occasionally need extra encouragement or support. But some preschoolers have needs that go beyond everyday parenting. They are born with physical, emotional, or cognitive differences, and their parents and teachers must learn to provide kind, firm discipline, connection, encouragement, *and* special help for their unique needs.

There are children for whom life just seems harder. They struggle in school; they have trouble making friends; they can't seem to manage basic skills. Some never stop moving, bouncing off the walls and struggling to connect with adults and peers; others don't seem interested in much of anything. These children (and families) may need more than just good parenting skills. Attention deficit disorder (ADD), either with or without hyperactivity, fetal alcohol or drug syndrome, autism spectrum disorders, sensory integration disorder, metabolic disorders, dyspraxia, and other developmental delays are among the conditions preschoolers, their families, and their caregivers may encounter. How can you tell when your child needs special help?

TAKING A CLOSER LOOK

For some families, a child's preschool years are burdened by stress and anxiety.

> *Lisa will never forget those panicked midnight trips to the hospital as baby Sandy's small face took on a bluish tint. Asthma threatened to steal Sandy from Lisa throughout her infancy and toddlerhood. Now, as she watches her four-year-old daughter race across the playground and take a tumble in the dust, Lisa must learn to give her daughter room to explore and grow while continuing to care for her health.*

> *Carol and Brad agonize over their son's stuttering. No matter how many people advise them to ignore Jesse's tortured language, both parents feel fiercely protective when other adults and children hear him struggling to speak. Their pain only makes Jesse more anxious. Is his problem somehow their fault?*

Most parents are quick to blame themselves when their children encounter repeated problems. Special needs that involve behavior or development create anxiety, guilt, and confusion for families, and may require time-consuming and expensive treatments. Guilt will not help you or your child. Accurate information and support will help you let go of guilt and replace it with beneficial action. The first step, of course, should be a physical or neurological evaluation from a doctor who specializes in the area of your concern.

If it is your child's behavior that troubles you, it's usually best to start at the beginning. Take a moment to think about the information already presented in this book. Consider your child's age and developmental level. Evaluate your own parenting style and expectations.

Consider your child's temperament and his individual needs and abilities. And consider the possibility of coded messages in his behavior. It may be wise to write down your observations to share with a professional. Most parents will find clues to understanding their child's behavior somewhere in this information. But if you've carefully considered these things and you find that your child still seems to need more help than you can provide, it may be time to look deeper.

THE REALITY OF SPECIAL NEEDS

Carlos was a difficult baby from the start. He never stopped moving, overreacted to every noise, and had trouble nursing because everything distracted him. Richard, four years old, darts all over his preschool classroom and seems startled by the sound of the gerbil moving in its cage, even when he's sitting across the room coloring. Cassie just can't sit still or pay attention for more than five minutes, no matter how hard she tries.

These children may not be misbehaving; they may be struggling with things that are genuinely difficult for them. The set of symptoms known as ADD or ADHD (attention deficit disorder without or with hyperactivity) is a chronic lifelong cluster of behaviors. It does not appear overnight, nor is it limited to children.

Be careful in trying to diagnose your child yourself, though. According to some estimates, 5 to 10 percent of the population may have ADD, but symptoms such as difficulty sitting still and paying attention or acting impulsively are not conclusive evidence. (Remember that all of these characteristics can also simply be indicators of different temperaments and normal development; in fact, many medical professionals will not diagnose a condition such as ADD until a child is at least of school age.) ADD (or the fear of it) brings many desperate parents to counselors' offices, to parenting classes, and into the arms of would-be miracle fix-it claimants, and it is generally acknowledged that ADD is overdiagnosed. Many children are being medicated because they can't sit still at an age when they aren't *supposed* to sit

Is My Child Okay?

Pediatricians have learned that parents are often the best judge of a child's development. Because early intervention is essential in the treatment of many developmental delays and disorders, your instincts—and concerns—about your child are always worth paying attention to. The incidence of autism and autism-related disorders has risen dramatically in recent years, now occurring in approximately one out of every five hundred births. While only a trained specialist can diagnose autism, you might look into getting a specialist's opinion if you answer no to many of the following questions.

- Does your child recognize and respond to familiar faces?
- Does he use his finger to point or show you something?
- Does your child turn his head toward you when you say his name?
- Does he imitate your actions, gestures, and facial expressions?
- Does he make eye contact with you?
- Is your child interested in other children, people, or objects?
- Does he respond to your smiles, cuddles, and gestures?
- Does your child try to attract your attention to his own activities?
- Is your child acquiring language and learning to communicate with you?

Other things to watch for include rocking, bouncing, spending long periods of time staring into space, and being unusually insistent on routines, predictability, or specific objects. Of course, symptoms do not necessarily indicate a problem; however, early intervention is critical for many developmental disorders. If you suspect that your child is not developing on schedule, do not hesitate to talk to your pediatrician.

still. Sometimes parents and teachers invite power struggles by being too demanding and controlling. They don't offer choices or get children involved in problem solving. Often children calm down when parents and teachers learn age-appropriate expectations and discipline methods.

Of course, there are many children for whom ADD is a real problem. Whatever special needs a child has, knowing that those needs are real and not the result of poor parenting, inadequate teaching, or a child's deliberate misbehavior brings a great deal of relief. Determining whether a child has a special need is a sifting process that begins with looking at all of the variables discussed throughout this book. In truth, even if a child is given a diagnosis, all of the Positive Discipline tools and skills will be helpful, in addition to whatever extra support a child may require.

All children, whether or not they have special needs, need to feel a sense of belonging and unconditional acceptance and will benefit from teaching, encouragement, and understanding. All can be helped to reach their fullest potential as capable, happy human beings. Parents of children with virtually any chronic condition experience a sense of frustration, sadness, and grief, as well as anxiety. They also need to develop specialized skills. Knowing that you're not alone works wonders; so does information about finding help and support.

LABELS: SELF-FULFILLING PROPHECIES?

Labels such as "clever," "clumsy," "shy," or "cute" all define who a child is in others' eyes, creating an image that may prevent that child from being appreciated and experienced for who she really is. On the other hand, some labels simply describe what is obvious. Labeling a child who wears glasses as "the little girl with glasses" doesn't necessarily cause people to prejudge her behavior. Sometimes a child's cluster or pattern of behaviors is equally obvious. Diagnosing such a child as having attention deficit disorder or sensory integration disorder can be helpful. Most parents and teachers find it easier to encourage and support a child who has a diagnosed condition than one who has been labeled "disruptive," "squirmy," or "a troublemaker."

Adults often must struggle with their own attitudes and expectations about children who are different or special.

When Vanessa was told that her four-year-old daughter was going to need glasses, she went home and cried, grieving that her poor little girl was going to be disfigured with glasses.

Keeping the Balance

Q. I have twin boys. One of them was born profoundly deaf. Because of the special classes, doctor's appointments, and treatments this child needs, the one with hearing must put up with lots of waiting. He used to be very helpful, patient, and easy. Since their third birthday, though, things have changed—he's become defiant, whines all the time when he doesn't get his way, and is withdrawn. This is the opposite of his personality just a few months ago. I have racked my brain trying to find out what is different now in our lives, daily routines, or family situation. Do you have any suggestions, or is this just a phase and it too shall pass?

A. It takes a great deal of patience and sensitivity to raise children with special needs. We often say that children are wonderful perceivers but not very good interpreters, and children often believe that the special therapies, doctor's appointments, and treatment that their special needs sibling receives indicate more parental attention and thus (they mistakenly believe) more parental love.

It's also wise to remember that while children develop at different paces emotionally as well as physically, three-year-olds are often experimenting with what we call "initiative"—forming their own plans, wanting to do things their own way, and (occasionally) practicing that by becoming defiant, whiny, and generally less compliant.

You're probably right that some of this will pass, but be sure to include regular "special time" with each of your children. This doesn't mean spending money or huge chunks of time: fifteen minutes to go for a walk, throw the ball, or read a story is usually all it takes. The key to each child's behavior lies in what he believes about himself and his place in his family.

Abruptly, she stopped and listened to what she had just told herself. She had described her daughter as "poor" and the glasses as "disfiguring." Vanessa asked herself whose problem this was. Her four-year-old would want and need her mother's support and acceptance. In fact, the glasses would help her to see better and would enable her to grow and develop normally.

Vanessa realized that the real problem was her own attitude. If she wanted to provide her daughter with the help she needed, Vanessa had to recognize the value of that help. From that moment on, she chose to support her daughter and obtain whatever care she might need, including glasses. Her daughter's "disability" had existed only in her mother's own mind.

In the same way, identifying a problem by way of a diagnosis does not define who a child is. It is simply a convenient word for that child's uniqueness and special abilities. If your child is diagnosed with a special need, you will undoubtedly feel some distress and will need to find ways to deal with any associated problems. But it is equally important (if not more so) to look at the assets and attributes your child possesses. Children who have attention deficit disorder, for example, are often highly intelligent and creative; their brains simply process information differently. Understanding those differences can be helpful rather than hurtful.

When a child lacks one ability, growth is likely to occur in other areas. A person who cannot see often develops acute hearing. Everyone has both strengths and weaknesses. What are your child's special gifts? A gentle spirit, a lively sense of humor, or a tender heart often will outweigh the liabilities that accompany "differentness"—if you choose to let them.

DENIAL AND GRIEF

A fear of labels or denying a child's special needs does not help anyone. A parent may feel more concerned about his own ego (or what people will think) than about what is best for his child. It requires a brave heart to accept and parent your children as they really are, to give them what they really need.

Leann taught parenting classes in churches and schools and was well respected as an educator in her community. She was also a skillful and effective parent who had raised three children. Imagine how embarrassed and despairing she felt when her fourth child came along and reacted differently to everything her mom did. By the time Grace was five, things were getting out of control. Three out of five days each week, Leann would carry a screaming child who was throwing a wild tantrum out of the preschool, trying to ignore the knowing glances and stares of the other parents. She tried everything she knew, but nothing seemed to work with Grace.

Finally she decided that she simply had to accept Grace for the child she was. When Grace threw a tantrum at the preschool, her mother took her to the car and read a book until the tantrum was over. Then she drove home without lecturing. Grace still wasn't able to control her behavior, but Leann quit worrying about what others were thinking, learned a new set of skills, and put her child's needs first.

Parents of special-needs children may also feel a deep sense of grief. After all, a child with developmental differences or disabilities is rarely what they dreamed of when they were planning the birth of their baby. Remember, you will do a more effective job of parenting your child when you are able to deal honestly and gently with your own needs and feelings. You may find a support group, your pastor, or a therapist helpful as you learn to parent your unique child.

LEARNING TO ACCEPT

It is often easier for adults to respond to children who have a highly visible disorder or who behave in extreme ways rather than children whose disorder may be less obvious. If Patsy, whose limbs are contorted with cerebral palsy, accidentally bumps into a classmate while struggling to maneuver the stairs on her crutches, a teacher probably will not tell Patsy that she must stay in from recess for pushing her classmate.

Nor will Patsy's mother be called in for a conference and told that if she would just improve her parenting skills and be more firm, Patsy would not have to struggle so to feed herself or learn to walk. Unfair as it seems, parents of children with ADD, fetal alcohol syndrome, sensory integration disorder, and dyspraxia often receive such criticisms and advice because these conditions are not as obvious, clearly defined, or well understood as physical disabilities.

While learning Positive Discipline parenting skills will help both you and your child, parenting is not the cause of your child's special need or condition. Parents and caregivers are, however, all too human, and it is sometimes easy to scapegoat a child whose behavior or appearance is different. Adults and other children need to learn and practice the art of offering respect, rather than blame, to those who are different. Tolerance, patience, and encouragement will go a long way toward helping all people (including children) live together peacefully.

INVISIBLE DIFFERENCES

Let's look a bit more at the case of children with ADD. Because children with ADD are often impulsive and find it difficult to sit quietly, their behavior is typically labeled "misbehavior" (especially in child care and other group settings) and others are quick to suggest remedies, including medication. Parents find themselves accused of ineffective parenting; they also feel considerable guilt and may believe they have failed as parents. Perhaps most difficult of all, they are living with a child whom they love dearly but with whom they struggle a great deal of the time.

When accurate, a diagnosis of ADD can be an enormously healing step for both parents and child. It establishes that this child is not merely disruptive or defiant. Difficult behavior can be understood as a symptom to be overcome rather than a series of intentional misdeeds. An ADD child is not a troublemaker, even when her behavior gets her into trouble.

Imagine that you are a small child and sometimes, for reasons you don't comprehend, you become terribly upset and begin to scream and kick. Wouldn't your loss of control be frightening? Your parents might decide your tantrum occurred because you couldn't have a toy when you wanted it, or you didn't want to turn off the TV when you were told to, or you thought the teacher had scolded you unfairly. They might also imply that you are somehow at fault or "bad." It's not hard to understand why a child may begin to see herself as "bad." The reality—that she has little ability to control her behavior regardless of the circumstances—is scary. (Keep in mind that all young children struggle to identify and manage their emotions; adult expectations often are unrealistic to begin with.)

Learning to understand the difficulties a child may face does not mean you should condone inappropriate behavior. In fact, having clear, reasonable expectations and following through with kindness and firmness is essential. Parents and teachers can learn to respond in ways that are productive and do not reinforce a child's image of himself as a "bad kid." Again, all children need connection and encouragement, regardless of their special needs or circumstances.

"GETTING AWAY WITH" MISBEHAVIOR

Dee has two daughters. The younger daughter, Mikayla, is six years old and has been identified as having ADD. Sheila, her older sister, is nine and does not have ADD. Before they go shopping, Dee takes the time to discuss her expectations with her two daughters. She has found this especially helpful for Mikayla, who has difficulty with transitions (a common characteristic of children with ADD—and of children with a "slow to adapt" temperament). They discuss the behavior that is expected as well as what is on the shopping agenda.

Late one Friday afternoon, Dee follows the usual pre-shopping routine with her daughters. Mikayla remembers their agreement that this is not the day they will get ice-cream cones, and she proudly reminds her mother of this fact. At the store, however, Mikayla sees a child happily licking an ice-cream cone. In Mikayla's mind, seeing another child with an ice-cream cone means she wants one herself. Soon a tantrum is

Misbehavior or Special Need?

Q. My daughter, now four years old, has had an ongoing problem with getting dressed. She complains that her clothes "hurt." She takes about fifteen minutes to put on socks, pulling them on and off, often dissolving into a tantrum because she claims they are painful. The same goes for underwear. I have tried buying all different types of underwear and socks, as well as allowing her to pick them out in the store and make her own choices in the morning. She asks me to cut all the tags out of her clothes because the tags hurt. I have tried helping her get dressed, I have tried ignoring her as she throws a fit over her socks, but what else can I do?

A. Some children struggle with the way their bodies process sensory information. While your daughter's complaints seem trivial or imagined to you, they may be quite real; she really may feel that the socks are hurting her. There is a condition known as sensory integration disorder that might affect your child. Although there is no consensus as to the specifics of this diagnosis, there are treatment options that might help. Consult an occupational therapist or a pediatric neurologist for further information. You may also find useful support on the Internet.

Most important, accept that your child really does feel pain, and resist the temptation to engage in power struggles with her. Treating her behavior as a parenting problem will not be helpful; accepting the validity of her complaints and finding help and support will.

under way. What happened to Mikayla's agreement that there would be no ice cream today?

The characteristic impulsiveness of attention deficit disorder translates *wants* almost immediately into *needs*, but it is important to remember that this is also developmentally appropriate for preschoolers. It is a matter of degree. All children behave impulsively at times, and most show other traits symptomatic of ADD on occasion. But ADD is suspected when the traits show up consistently, the child can't control them, and there is no psychological cause for them (John Taylor, Ph.D., *Helping Your Hyperactive/ADD Child*, second edition, Prima Publishing, 1997).

Dee stops shopping and asks Mikayla if she can regain control by herself or whether they should leave the store. The tantrum continues, so mother and daughters leave the store, with Mikayla hitting and screaming. The tantrum rages on in the car; when they arrive home, Mikayla runs into her room and slams the door. By now Dee is struggling to maintain her own control. She is angry, discouraged, and exhausted. Sheila, hurt and disappointed, is thinking, "I didn't do anything to spoil the shopping trip. Why did I have to miss out on the fun?" It's hard not to resent a little sister who behaves this way.

It's important to note that Dee does not spoil either of her daughters. She does not respond to unreasonable or demanding behavior by abandoning agreements she has made. There was nothing wrong with her parenting.

"Well," some parents might say, "if my child acted that way in a public place, I'd sure let her know how I felt about it. That mother should have spanked her daughter, or refused to let her have ice cream for a month!" But think for a moment. Has Mikayla "gotten away with" misbehavior? Will punishment or humiliation help her to change her behavior in the future? Did Mikayla *want* to lose control? Did she intend to misbehave?

It may be hard for her mother, who is experiencing a seething (and very human) mixture of anger, guilt, and blame, to keep this in mind, but Mikayla may not have consciously chosen to defy her mother. She was proud of remembering her agreement with her mother, and she knows that her mother follows through on those agreements. Dealing effectively with Mikayla's behavior means recognizing her special needs.

What can Dee do? When she and Mikayla have calmed down, they can discuss what happened in the store. They might also discuss ways Mikayla could help her sister feel better. Maybe Mikayla could offer to do one of Sheila's chores or play a game with her. Sheila, too, has needs that should not be ignored.

Mikayla almost always feels terrible when she loses control of her behavior; she can feel her mother's exasperation and disappointment, and it's hard for her to bear. Perhaps the most important thing Dee and Mikayla can do now is to work on ways Mikayla can cope with those out-of-control feelings. ADD is something they can acknowledge and face together; they can choose to be a family, loving and supporting one another.

It would be easy to allow Mikayla to feel that she is "bad" or "difficult," and because her mother is human, she will sometimes make mistakes and say or do things she later regrets. But as we've seen before, mistakes aren't fatal. And Mikayla's behavior may not change anytime soon. Facing reality, learning coping skills, and getting support will help both mother and daughter survive the difficult times.

DESPAIR OR PRIDE

Finding out that your child does not fit your ideal comes as an emotional blow. But once adults move beyond their fear of labels and their own denial, they can stretch their horizons wider to see the wonderful gifts their child has, not in spite of learning or behavioral differences but sometimes because of them. It undoubtedly takes time and determination, but you can learn to celebrate the very things that cause your child to require special help. People with asthma and diabetes have competed in the Olympics and become professional athletes; Temple Grandin, autistic herself, shed new light on autism and became famous for designing new systems of animal management; and Thomas Edison (along with scores of other famous people) is believed to have had ADD. What would the world be like without the invention of electricity?

WHAT ABOUT TREATMENT?

Robert had struggled with his son, Charles, to the point of desperation. When Charles was five years old, his teacher sus-

pected Charles might have some borderline ADD characteristics. Robert was horrified and not a little offended by this suggestion. He signed up for parenting classes, bought piles of books, and did his best to be a better father.

But Charles' problems continued. By the age of seven, he was having trouble with schoolwork and friendships, and his difficulties were affecting the entire family. Everyone seemed tense and touchy; arguments were frequent. Finally his dad decided it was time to look for help.

This time, Charles' doctor made a clear diagnosis of ADD. After months of counseling and trying various approaches, Robert agreed to try medication. Within a week, Charles' behavior was much improved. It was difficult for Robert to believe that those tiny pills could have such an influence on behavior—and equally difficult to admit that his son might need this kind of help. But whenever Charles missed his medication over the next few months, his behavior deteriorated dramatically. Robert began to see his son in a different light and enjoy the calm, interesting child he was becoming. Charles, too, was changing; finally he could be himself, rather than a desperate little person always struggling with the effects ADD had on his daily life.

Medication can be part of a comprehensive and loving approach to helping a child with ADD. However, even we three authors have differing opinions regarding medication. This only emphasizes the importance of doing your own research and deciding for yourself what works best for you and your child.

Again, listen to your inner wisdom; trust your knowledge of and love for your child. Be sure he understands what ADD is (one youngster informed his therapist that he was a "psycho" because he had something called ADD) and that it does not mean he is sick or bad. Be willing to change what doesn't work for your family. Build a supportive team of family, friends, and helping professionals who can give you and your child the help you need. And learn all you can about encouragement, kind and firm discipline, and other Positive Discipline tools. Confidence in your parenting skills will help you and your child immensely.

THE IMPORTANCE OF SELF-CARE

Eventually, most children with special needs will leave home and embark on life as independent adults. Just as you teach your child to set the table and do other age-appropriate tasks, you can allow him to understand and learn to maintain his own body.

Marcus was born with a metabolic disorder that required him to maintain a special diet. Eating his special dinner was easy when Marcus was a toddler, but when he got older and went off to preschool, he began wanting to eat the same food his friends enjoyed. Unfortunately, pizza, sandwich meat, and other common foods posed serious risks for Marcus. Darrel and Kemah, Marcus' parents, became overprotective and controlling, packing his lunch each day and giving him stern and scary lectures about what would happen if he ate the wrong foods. His preschool teachers worried that he would eat something forbidden while in their care and watched his every move like anxious hawks.

Like most preschoolers, Marcus chose the issue that most pushed his parents' buttons to demonstrate his personal power. He began trading lunches with friends at school. They found Marcus' special food intriguing, while Marcus was delighted to finally eat "like a normal kid." When Marcus went in for his periodic blood test, however, his deception was discovered.

The specialist and nutritionist sat down with Marcus' frightened parents and offered some ideas. Rather than trying to control or frighten Marcus, they suggested, his parents could involve him in caring for his own special body. Kemah and

Darrel began focusing on teaching Marcus about his disorder. They bought a small set of measuring tools and taught Marcus to measure and mix his special meals—with careful supervision, of course. They let him know that they understood his curiosity about other foods and his resentment of the disorder that made him different and required regular blood tests; they spent special time with him to strengthen the connection between them.

Most important, Kemah and Darrel recognized that someday Marcus would need to care for his own health. They gave him appropriate information, taught him skills, supervised without lecturing, and expressed their faith in his ability to make wise decisions. While food-related mistakes still occurred from time to time, the power struggles ended and Marcus began to focus on skateboarding with his buddies rather than sneaking food.

Preschoolers should *never* be left to handle or take medications without supervision. But they can learn to recognize the signals their bodies and emotions send them. Even young children with asthma or other conditions can be aware of their body's needs, accept the special treatment they require, and help maintain their own health. When parents allow children to become involved and responsible (in age-appropriate ways, of course), they not only help ensure their child's future health and well-being but also build self-confidence and a sense of capability.

LOOK FOR THE POSITIVE

Whatever the physical, behavioral, or emotional challenges you and your child face, focusing on your inadequacies as parents or caregivers will not help. Find support for yourself, take care of your own needs, and accept and learn from your mistakes. Educate yourself, your child, and your caregivers about the condition affecting her, practice applying both humor and hope to each day's struggles, and get help for any child who needs it. Above all, make every effort to discover and celebrate the qualities that make each child special, unique, and wonderful. Those qualities are always there—you only have to look.

19

GROWING AS A FAMILY

Finding Support, Resources, and Sanity

No matter how charming your preschooler is and no matter how delighted you are to be a parent, these early years can be lonely, exhausting, and challenging. Mothers (or fathers) staying at home with a young child often find that the job is tougher than they expected. It's not unusual for stay-at-home parents to find themselves longing for adult conversation and entertainment, while working parents quickly grow weary of the daily hassle of getting everyone off to child care and work. Sleep can be hard to come by, and the battles prompted by energetic little ones who are exercising their initiative can test even the most devoted mom or dad. A spouse or partner may find blow-by-blow descriptions of your child's new achievements and adorable moments enthralling, but many people will not. Most parents have occasional moments when they wistfully remember their pre-child days and long for a moment of quiet and solitude.

It is essential for parents of preschoolers to seek out support during these important early years of parenting. Connection with other adults will support, encourage, and nourish you and, through you, your children and other family members.

LEARNING FROM THE WISDOM OF OTHERS

While people seldom agree on every detail of raising children, building a support network, a circle of friends who've been there, provides an invaluable source of information about raising and living with children. It can be amazingly helpful to have people to call when things happen that you weren't expecting. Make an effort to build relationships with folks who have children the same age as yours—or who have recently survived the stage you're going through. Don't be afraid to ask lots of questions; finding out that other people's children have done the same strange or appalling things can help you relax.

Some options for support networks include church- or community-based parent-child groups, community college parent-child classes, Positive Discipline parenting classes, and friendships with neighboring parents. Perhaps your parenting group, with dinner out beforehand, can be part of a night out with your partner. Some groups meet at the park and discuss parenting challenges and successes while keeping a watchful eye as their children play. Some parents have started book study groups where they get together and take turns discussing the concepts in this and other Positive Discipline books and learn together how to use Positive Discipline tools. Some parents have even attended the two-day Teaching Parenting the Positive Discipline Way workshop so they could learn to facilitate parenting classes, knowing that teaching (and having the courage to be imperfect) is the best way to learn. (For information, see www.posdis.org.)

If you live in an isolated area or have no parents of preschoolers nearby, the magic of the Internet offers chat groups, question-and-answer boards, and lots of general information. If you go online after your children are asleep, you'll find many parents chattering away, seeking support and encouragement through the Internet. Even without home computer access, such services are available at local libraries. Ask a librarian or computer-literate friend to help you do a search for parenting resources; you'll be astonished at what you discover.

Consult your pediatrician, too. Family doctors see and hear a great deal as they go about the business of helping young patients and parents. They can often provide support as well as practical information and advice. No matter where you find support, however, remember that in the end you must decide what feels right for you and your child. Gather all the wisdom and advice you can, then listen to your heart before you choose what will work best for you.

YOUR RELATIONSHIP WITH YOUR PARTNER

PEPS and MOPS

One successful model of a good parenting support group is PEPS, a community-based program in the Northwest. PEPS groups form right after a baby's birth and consist of people whose children are born within days or weeks of one another. These families meet regularly in each other's homes or in family centers. The goal is to reduce isolation and create a network of support, resources, and encouragement. (PEPS, the Program for Early Parent Support, can be contacted at www.pepsgroup.org.) Another popular group is Mothers of Preschoolers (www.mops.org), which offers get-togethers and parenting support through neighborhood churches. Look for similar programs in your area, or consider initiating one of your own.

Many parents of preschoolers are single parents who face both the challenges and blessings (yes, there are many) of raising a child alone. But if you are parenting with a partner, your relationship establishes the foundation for your family and sets the tone for your home. In fact, there are a number of studies that show just how much young children learn and decide by watching the relationships parents have with each other. It is well worth your while to make sure your partner doesn't get lost in the chaos of raising an active preschooler and that your relationship remains vital and enjoyable.

Parents sometimes believe that once they have a child, that child should become the center of the family universe. But as you have

Make Room for Daddy

Q. My husband and I have a four-year-old son who is the joy of our lives. I am a stay-at-home mom but I want my husband to be actively involved in raising our son. At first, he got up with me to feed him at night, changed his diapers, and gave him baths. Lately, however, he has been "too busy" to help me. When I asked him about this, he told me he tries but he never does things right. He says I insist that he do things my way. I feel bad (because I think he's probably right), but I do believe the way I discipline and care for our son is the best way. What should I do?

A. Many husbands and fathers feel edged out by the close bond between a mother and her child, especially in the early years. It may help you make room for your husband to know that children benefit from the active involvement of *both* parents in their lives, even when those parents don't do things in exactly the same way. Studies have shown that fathers and mothers have different styles of play and interaction with children—and that children learn valuable skills from both styles.

Your son needs a close and loving connection with both his parents. Take some time to sit down with your husband and make a plan about discipline, daily routines, food, and other issues. It may be helpful to take a parenting class together, or to read this book together and discuss what you have learned. Then relax and allow him to do things his own way. You can use the time when he is in charge to take care of yourself or spend time with friends. Your son will be happier and healthier when he feels close to both of you—and when you feel close to each other.

learned, pampering a child is not healthy or effective, for you or for your child. You and your partner should have time on a regular basis to spend together, whether you go out for dinner and dancing, take a walk together, or simply curl up to watch a good movie. You will also need couple time to explore and resolve the many issues raising a child together will present.

AND BABY MAKES . . . FOUR

If you have a preschooler and are planning to have another child, you should know that the arrival of an infant can throw even the most delightful and confident preschooler into something of a tailspin. Most preschoolers claim with disarming honesty to love their new baby brother or sister; they offer to help fetch diapers and binkies, want to cuddle their new sibling, and gaze with utter fascination into the crib. So why does that same preschooler often resort to tantrums, insist on a pacifier herself, "lose" her toilet training, or whine for attention?

Well, take a look at the world through the eyes of a dethroned preschooler. Let's say you're almost four years old when Mom and Dad come home from the hospital with a noisy, squirming bundle in a blanket. Suddenly, *nothing* is the same. Mom and Dad tell you that you shouldn't cry or whine because you're a "big girl now." Visitors come to the house and walk right past you to coo at the new baby; they bring interesting gifts and toys (which you can't remember having received yourself) for the baby. Worst of all, your parents are completely enthralled by this noisy, messy little person. They're up all night, they tell you to play quietly because the baby is sleeping, and they constantly rock, cuddle, or carry the baby. They're always too tired and don't have time to play the old familiar games you enjoy. It's no wonder that after a week or two, even the most patient big sister is ready to send the intruder back to the hospital!

There are ways to smooth out the process of adding a baby to your family. Here are some suggestions:

- Begin early to prepare your child for a baby's arrival. You can explain in simple terms the process of pregnancy and let your child know when the baby will arrive. A wall calendar can be used to check off the days until the baby's birth. Talk honestly about what life is like with a new baby; it can be helpful (and fun) to get out photos of your child's own infancy and talk together about what those days were like.

- Invite your child to help prepare your home for the baby. You can allow her to make suggestions about colors and designs for the baby's room; she can go with you to purchase items for the baby's layette. She may even want to put some of her own toys in the baby's room as a welcome gift.

- Show her pictures of what you did to prepare for her birth, such as fixing up her room and buying tiny baby clothes for her. Let her know that many people brought her presents and fussed over her, just as they will do with the new baby. Ask if she would like to be in charge of receiving and unwrapping gifts for her new baby brother and then thanking the givers (since her baby brother can't talk). The more she is included, the less she will feel left out.

- When the baby comes home, be sure your older child is included in making the baby welcome. Set safety rules and supervise carefully, and then let your child hand you diapers and wipes at the changing table, sing songs or "read" stories to the baby, and bring you things as you nurse. Remember, self-esteem comes from having skills and making a contribution; your preschooler can be a tremendous asset at this busy time in your family's life.

- Recognize that your preschooler's perception of how and where she belongs in her family will have to change—and her behavior may change, too. It may be helpful for you to review the information on birth order in Chapter 3.

In spite of everything you do, do not be surprised if your preschooler still feels dethroned by the birth of a new baby. She will have many feelings that she can't name and doesn't understand herself. It's not unusual for an older child to mimic baby behavior in a mistaken effort to gain the same sort of attention the baby receives. Don't take this behavior personally; instead, focus on restoring your child's sense of connection and belonging. Spending special time one-on-one with her will help.

Grant and Margo waited for just the right time to tell their four-year-old twins, Tyson and Toby, that there was going to be an addition to their family. Still, the twins weren't thrilled with the news.

"You're going to have a baby?" Tyson said. "Why? Aren't Toby and I enough?"

"We don't need any babies around here," Toby chimed in.

Margo took a deep breath and smiled at her sons. "Come here, guys," she said. "I want to tell you a story about our family."

Toby and Tyson reluctantly sat down next to their mother on the sofa and watched as she lit a tall blue candle. "This candle is me," she said, "and this flame represents my love." Then Margo picked up a tall green candle. "This candle is your dad," Margo said, with a warm smile for Grant. She lit the green candle using the blue candle. "When I married him, I gave him all my love, but I still had all my love left.

"Then, five years ago I got news just like this—except that time, boys, it was you coming to live with us." Margo lit two smaller candles, one purple and one red, with her tall blue one. "When you were born, I gave both of you all my love, but your dad still had all my love, and I still had all my love left." Toby and Tyson gazed, fascinated, at the flickering candle flames.

Then Margo reached into her pocket and pulled out a tiny birthday candle. "Guess what this candle is?" she asked her boys.

"The baby?" they answered.

"That's right. And when this baby is born, I'll give it all my love. Your dad will have all my love, and Tyson will have all my love—"

"And I will have all your love!" Toby shouted out with a grin.

"That's right," Margo laughed. "And I'll still have all my love left. That's how love is—the more we share, the more we have. See how much bright love we're going to have in this family?"

They sat in silence for a moment. Then Tyson tugged at his mother's elbow. "Mom, can I light the baby's candle with my candle? I want to share my love."

Margo nodded and blew out the birthday candle, and Tyson carefully picked up his candle and lit the tiny one. Toby took a turn lighting the candle, as did Grant.

Margo looked at her two boys and put her arm around her husband. "This will be our baby," she said, "and your dad and I will need your help to take care of him or her. Will you help us, guys?"

The next months passed quickly. The arguing didn't disappear, but both Toby and Tyson enjoyed shopping for baby things, helping their parents fix up a room for the new baby, and thinking about names for boys and girls. They were thrilled when they got to hear the baby's heartbeat at the doctor's office. Tyson provided the crowning touch when he placed the tiny birthday candle on the baby's new dresser.

"We're a family," he said proudly, "and there's lots of love to go around."

Having a new baby in the house is both joyous and challenging. Remember, though, that children can be dethroned at any age. One doesn't need to be a firstborn to know the dismay of feeling replaced by a newcomer. This experience also occurs when families blend and stepsiblings are added to the family, or even when a niece or nephew arrives and the former baby of the family is faced with a challenge to his claim to cuteness. Remembering to get into your child's world to experience life from her perspective will help all of you adjust and grow together.

REFILLING THE PITCHER

Q. I am a young mother with three children who are younger than five years of age. They are my greatest joy and I dearly love being a mother! Lately, though, I'm really overwhelmed. My husband works long hours and attends evening school. I do the housekeeping, work part time, pay the bills, and raise the children. They are smart, nice, talented kids, but they are all strong-willed children as well. I feel like I'm pulled in so many directions, and no matter what I do, it's never enough. From the time I wake up until late at night, I never get more than a minute to myself. I'm always tired and sick, and I get terrible headaches. The bottom line is that I've been losing my temper a lot lately. Then I'm even more upset because I feel so guilty.

A. What's wrong with the picture you describe? You are not working part time or even full time, but overtime! No one flies around wearing a supermom cape, but it sounds as though that is what you are trying to do. The person you are not taking care of is *you*—and everyone suffers because of it. It is easy to get so busy with all of life's demands that your own needs get shoved not only to the back burner but completely off the stove. The best thing you can give to your family is a calm, rested you.

Consider getting a high school student to help with the housework. Be creative if money is short; perhaps you can barter something. Trade babysitting hours with someone else so you can go for a walk, take a yoga class, or get in a swim and sauna at the local Y once or twice a week. Your family will notice the difference, and of course, so will you.

Being a parent is a great deal like pouring water from a pitcher: you can only pour out so many glasses without refilling the pitcher. All too often, parents and other caregivers suddenly realize they've poured themselves dry for their children—the pitcher is empty. Effective, loving parenting takes a lot of time and energy. You can't do your best when

Caring for Yourself

It is just as important to take care of yourself as it is to take care of your child. Consider the following:

- Budget time wisely.
- Make lists.
- Make time for important relationships.
- Do the things you enjoy—regularly.

your pitcher is empty, when you're tired, cranky, stressed out, and overwhelmed.

How do you refill the pitcher? Taking care of yourself—filling up your pitcher before it runs dry—can take any form. If you find yourself daydreaming in a quiet moment about all the things you'd like to do, that may be a clue that you should consider some ways to take care of yourself.

Budget Time Wisely

Most parents find that they must adjust their priorities as their child grows. It can be extremely helpful—and quite a revelation—to keep track for a few days of exactly how you spend your time. Some activities, such as work, school, or tasks directly related to raising your children, can't be changed much. But most parents spend much of their time on activities that are not truly among their top priorities.

For instance, if you're often up during the night with a young child, make an effort to nap when your child naps. It is tempting to fly around the house doing all that "should" get done, but cleaning the bathroom and dusting the furniture will wait for you; you'll be happier and more effective if you get enough sleep.

Rula did not have the luxury of large blocks of free time. Between her evening classes at the community college and her daytime work at an espresso stand, she managed to spend only a couple of hours each evening sharing dinner with three-year-old Abdu and getting him ready for bed before his grandmother arrived to watch him. Their short periods together too often were eaten up by hassles that left Rula feeling both impatient and short-tempered. She recognized that she needed a way to nurture herself if she was going to succeed at any of the roles she was trying to fill.

Rula thought about the forty-five minutes she spent crawling along in rush-hour traffic after dropping Abdu off at his child care each day. She decided to try riding the bus instead and to use this time for herself. She would read a novel, enjoy a magazine article, or even close her eyes to practice meditation and slow breathing as the bus wove through the crowded roads. This small change made a big difference in lowering her stress level. Rula felt refreshed and the calming effect lasted throughout her day. She even found she enjoyed her time with Abdu more since she was less overwhelmed and could look forward to their time together with additional energy.

Time is precious and all too short when you share your life with young children; be sure you're spending the time you do have as wisely as you can.

Make Lists

In a quiet moment, list all the things you'd like to do (or wish you could get around to). Then, when your child is napping or with a caregiver, spend those precious hours working your way down your list. Don't list chores and duties; instead, write down activities that nurture you, like curling up with a good book, soaking in the tub, or having a cozy telephone chat with a friend. Taking time to write your needs on a list may make you more likely to honor them.

Make Time for Important Relationships

It's amazing how therapeutic a simple cup of tea with a good friend can be, and sometimes a vigorous game of racquetball can restore a positive perspective on life. Conversation with caring adults can refresh you, especially when your world is populated with energetic little people. You and your partner may trade time watching the children so that each of you has time for friends, or you may choose to spend special time together with other couples whose company you enjoy. A date night, when you go out together, should be on your list as well.

Meeting friends at the park can give parents (married or single) and children time to rest and relax together. Keeping your world wide enough to include people outside your family can help you retain your health and balance.

Do the Things You Enjoy—Regularly

It is important that you find time for the things that make you feel alive and happy, whether it's riding your bicycle, playing softball, singing with a choir, tinkering with machinery, working in the garden, or designing a quilt. Hobbies and exercise are important for your mental and emotional health—and you'll be a far more patient and effective parent if you're investing time and energy in your own well-being. Yes, finding time for these things can be a problem, and it is tempting to tell yourself, "I'll get around to that later." All too often, though, "later" never arrives. Even twenty minutes a day for something you love is a good beginning. Self-care really isn't optional because without it, everyone suffers. Parents often see taking time for themselves as "selfish." Nothing could be less true. Taking time to care for yourself benefits everyone in the long run.

Trust us: your children will survive without constant attention from you. In fact, they'll thrive all the more with healthy, well-supported parents. Remember, children sense emotional energy; exhaustion and resentment will not help your child grow and may drain the joy out of family life for all of you.

GROUPS AND MORE GROUPS: AVOIDING OVERSCHEDULING

Most parents do all they can to provide a rich and stimulating environment for their young children. After all, they're learning and developing important skills during these early years. Many young children find themselves enrolled in a surprising number of groups, often before the age of five. There are gymnastics groups, soccer leagues, and swim classes. There are preschools and playgroups.

There are music and educational classes for preschoolers. Parents often discover that they are living in their vehicles, rushing their children from one activity to another.

While these activities can be enjoyable and stimulating for a young child, it is wise to limit the number you sign up for. Researchers have noted that time for families to relax and just hang out together has become scarce; everyone is busy rushing off to the next important group, and relationships suffer as a result. Mothers and fathers are irritable and tired; children have little or no time to exercise their creativity, learn to entertain themselves, or simply play.

Remember, your child needs connection and time with you far more than she needs stimulation. Time to cuddle, crawl around on the floor together, or read a book is far more valuable than even the most popular group.

LEARNING TO RECOGNIZE—AND MANAGE—STRESS

Clenched teeth and fists, tight muscles, headaches, a sudden desire to burst into tears or lock yourself in the bathroom—these are the symptoms of parental stress and overload, and it's important to pay attention to them. Most parents—especially first-time parents—occasionally feel overwhelmed and exhausted and even angry or resentful. Because parents want so much to be good parents, they may find it difficult to discuss these troubling thoughts and feelings with others.

Mariam loved being a mom, even though it was sometimes hard to juggle parenthood with her job selling real estate. Five-year-old Lexey was bright, loving, and curious, and Mariam always looked forward to picking Lexey up from her caregiver and heading for home. Normally, the evening routine went smoothly and mother and daughter enjoyed being together. Tonight, however, Mariam was irritable and overwhelmed; her biggest deal of the year looked like it might fall through any moment and she really needed to spend some time at the computer going over the paperwork.

Unfortunately, Lexey was recovering from the flu and was still cranky and tired. Mariam tried to take shortcuts through their evening routine: she served a frozen meal, left the dishes in the

sink, and rushed Lexey through her bath and evening playtime. Lexey grew quieter as the evening went on, sensing her mother's distraction and annoyance. Finally, when Mariam read only one story instead of the usual two at bedtime, Lexey snapped.

With her arms crossed on her chest and her chin out defiantly, Lexey stomped her foot. "You're rude, Mom," she said angrily. "You don't want to be with me tonight—I can tell. You just want to sit at your old computer."

Stung by the accuracy of her daughter's words, Mariam lost her temper. "I'm tired, Lexey. I've had a difficult day and I work hard to provide for you. Just get into bed and let me work, okay?"

Lexey's face crumpled; angry tears sprang to her eyes. "I hate you!" she shouted. "Why don't you just go back to your stupid office and stay there?"

Mariam felt the blood rush to her face and she drew back her hand. There was a moment of complete silence as mother and daughter glared at each other. Suddenly Mariam realized how close she'd come to slapping her daughter's face and she took a step backward in shock.

"Oh, Lexey," she said. "Oh, honey, I'm so sorry. It's not

your fault—I'm grumpy and tired." Mariam got down on her knees and held out her arms. "Can you forgive me?"

Lexey could. Mother and daughter had a long cuddle in the armchair and Mariam read a second story. By the time she turned the lights out, peace and connection had been restored and all was well. It took Mariam a while longer, however, to deal with the unexpectedly strong feelings the encounter had created in her.

As we've mentioned before, there's a difference between a feeling and an action. It's not unusual for parents of young children to be frustrated, overwhelmed, and exhausted, and most parents feel terribly guilty when they feel anger or resentment toward their children. The feelings are quite normal—but you need to be careful what you do with them.

If you find yourself wanting to snap or lash out at your children, accept those feelings as your cue to do something to care for yourself. Make sure your children are safely occupied and take a few minutes of time-out (it usually works better for parents than for kids anyway). Better yet, arrange for some time to do something to nurture yourself. Exhaustion and frustration can lead even the best parents to say and do things they later regret; it's far better to invest the time it takes to help yourself feel better.

> ### Emergency Relief
>
> In the event you feel completely unable to cope with stress, do not hesitate to seek help. Most communities offer a crisis line for immediate phone assistance. Some hospitals provide similar services; a few moments speaking to an understanding, reassuring adult may make a world of difference.
>
> If you ever feel your child might be at risk, check to see if respite care is available in your community. It is not wrong or shameful to need help; it is true wisdom to ask for it.

REACH OUT AND TOUCH SOMEONE

Rose looked back at the front window, where her friend Caroline and three-year-old son, Vince, were waving good-bye.

As she slipped behind the wheel of the minivan, Rose smiled at the two good friends who shared the backseat.

"Boy, am I ready for this," she said.

Adele and Joleen laughed. "Us, too!" Joleen said. "And you'd better enjoy yourself—next week, the kids are all at your place."

Rose, Adele, Joleen, and Caroline had been sharing their "moms' day out" for about six months, and none could imagine how they'd survived without it. Each Saturday morning, one of the four women cared for the group's six children. Lunches were packed, activities were planned, and the three moms who had the day off had four blissful hours to shop, play tennis, take a walk, or just share conversation and a cup of coffee. All had felt a bit guilty at first, but they quickly learned to wave bye-bye and drive away, knowing their children were well cared for and would be happy to have a calm, cheerful mother pick them up. Because the women were careful always to return at the designated time, no one felt taken advantage of.

Support comes packaged in different ways. Whatever works for you and wherever you find it, accept it with gratitude. Parenting is too big a job to tackle alone. Children and their families need a community of support. The face that community wears may be that of a familiar relative, a parenting class, good friends, or even words floating through cyberspace. The important thing is that it is there. Use it—for everyone's sake.

CONCLUSION

The years of early childhood are often overwhelming for parents. Preschoolers have an amazing capacity to take center stage in a family's life, often leaving the adults around them breathless with laughter—or exhaustion. Each day seems to bring a new discovery and, sometimes, a new crisis. It may seem as though the kitchen counter will never be cleared, the laundry will never be done, these years will never end.

But they do. Our job as parents and teachers is to make ourselves unnecessary. From the first moments of our children's lives, we steadily guide them toward independence—loving and supporting them when they falter, keeping constant faith that they will grow and bloom. We hover nearby as inconspicuously as we can, holding our breath when they stumble, rejoicing when they continue on their way.

Yes, the preschool years are busy ones for parents and teachers. These years of testing and exploring can sorely try our patience, and we may catch ourselves longing for the day when our child is older and needs us less. But if we are wise, we will take time to enjoy and savor these years that pass so swiftly.

Far sooner than you think, you will look across the room and stare in amazement at the stranger you see. Gone will be the preschooler with the chronically runny nose; in his place will be a grinning youngster, ready for school and new friendships, ready to move farther and farther from the circle of your arms.

Our children will face life equipped with whatever love, wisdom, and confidence we've had the courage to give them. There will surely be struggles, bumps and bruises, and tears, yet if we've done our job well, our children will know that mistakes are opportunities to learn and that life is an adventure to be enjoyed.

There is a beautiful fable about two little girls who discovered the value of struggle and perseverance. They found two cocoons hanging from a branch, and as they watched in awe, two tiny butterflies emerged. The little creatures were so damp and fragile that it seemed impossible they could survive, let alone fly. The girls watched as the butterflies labored to open their wings. One girl, fearing that the butterflies would not survive, reached for one and gently spread its delicate wings. The second girl offered the other butterfly a twig to cling to; then she carried it to the window ledge, where the sun could warm it.

Both butterflies continued to toil valiantly, testing their new wings. The one on the ledge eventually opened its wings, paused for a moment in the sun's gentle warmth, then flew gracefully away. But the butterfly whose wings had been pried open never found the strength to fly and perished without ever taking wing.

It can be painful to watch your young ones struggle, to know that you cannot always save them from trouble and pain no matter how vigilant you are. But wise parents know that, like butterflies, children gather strength and wisdom from their struggles. It takes a great deal of courage—and a great deal of love—to refrain from lecturing and rescuing and to allow our children, with our encouragement, teaching, and love, to taste life for themselves and learn its lessons.

We can't fight our children's battles. And even the most loving parent cannot guarantee that his children will never know pain. But there is a great deal we can do. We can offer our children trust, dignity, and respect. We can have faith in them and in their ability to learn and grow. We can take the time to teach them: about ideas, about people, about the skills they will need to thrive in a challenging world. We can nurture their talents and interests, and encourage each small step they take. We can help them discover the gifts of capability, competence, and responsibility.

Best of all, we can love and enjoy them, laugh and play with them. We can create memories they—and we—will cherish all our lives. We can steal into their rooms at night and feel again and again that overwhelming tenderness as we gaze on our children's sleeping faces. We can draw on that love and tenderness to give us the wisdom and courage it takes to do what we must as parents and caregivers.

This book is all about learning from our mistakes and celebrating our successes. As authors and as parents, we hope you have found it useful. But the ultimate answers will always be found in your own wisdom and spirit; you will parent (and teach) best when you do so from your heart. Take a moment now and then to savor this special time of childhood despite the inevitable hassles and frustrations; enjoy your children as much as you possibly can. These are precious, important years, and we can only live them once.

SUGGESTED READINGS

Adler, Alfred. *Social Interest*. New ed. Oxford: Oneworld Publications, 1998.

———. *What Life Could Mean to You*. New ed. Oxford: Oneworld Publications, 1992.

Chess, Stella, M.D., and Alexander Thomas, M.D. *Know Your Child*. Northvale, N.J.: Jason Aronson, 1996.

———. *Temperament: Theory and Practice*. New York: Bruner/Mazel, 1996.

Copple, Carol, and Sue Bredekamp. *Basics of Developmentally Appropriate Practice: An Introduction for Teachers of Children 3 to 6*. Washington, D.C.: National Association for the Education of Young Children, 2006.

Dreikurs, Rudolf, and V. Soltz. *Children: The Challenge*. New York: Plume Books, 1991.

Duffy, Roslyn Ann. *Top Ten Preschool Parenting Problems*. Redmond, Wash.: Exchange Press, 2007.

Erikson, Erik H. *Childhood and Society*. New York: Norton, 1993.

Erwin, Cheryl. *The Everything Parents Guide to Raising Boys*. New York: Adams, 2006.

Frieden, Wayne S., and Marie Hartwell Walker. *Family Songs*. Available as downloadable MP3 files at www.focusingonsolutions.com.

Glenn, H. Stephen, and Michael L. Brock. *7 Strategies for Developing Capable Students*. New York: Three Rivers Press, 1998.

Glenn, H. Stephen, and J. Nelsen. *Raising Self-Reliant Children in a Self-Indulgent World*. New York: Three Rivers Press, 2000.

Greenman, Jim, and Anne Stonehouse. *What Happened to the World: Helping Children Cope in Turbulent Times*. New South Wales, Australia: Pademelon Press, 2002.

Greenspan, Stanley I., M.D. and Serena Wieder, Ph.D. *The Child with Special Needs: Encouraging Intellectual and Emotional Growth*. Cambridge, Mass.: Perseus Publishing, 1998.

Healy, Jane M. *Endangered Minds: Why Children Don't Think and What We Can Do About It*. New York: Simon & Schuster, 1990.

Karoly, Lynn, Rebecca Kilburn, and Jill Cannon. "Proven Benefits of Early Childhood Interventions." RAND Corporation Research Brief, www.rand.org, 2005.

Kohn, Alfie. *Punished by Rewards*. New York: Houghton Mifflin, 1999.

Kvols, K. *Redirecting Children's Misbehavior*. Seattle: Parenting Press, 1997.

Lott, Lynn, and Jane Nelsen. *Teaching Parenting the Positive Discipline Way: A Manual for Parent Education Groups*. Lehi, Utah: Empowering People, www.empoweringpeople.com.

Nelsen, Jane. *Positive Time Out: And Over 50 Ways to Avoid Power Struggles in Homes and Classrooms*. New York: Three Rivers Press, 1999.

———. *Serenity: Eliminating Stress and Finding Joy and Peace in Life and Relationships*. Lehi, Utah: Empowering People, 2005, e-book available at www.positivediscipline.com.

Nelsen, Jane, and Cheryl Erwin. *Parents Who Love Too Much*. New York: Three Rivers Press, 2000.

———. *Positive Discipline for Childcare Providers*. New York: Three Rivers Press, 2002.

———. *Positive Discipline for Stepfamilies*, Lehi, Utah: Empowering People, 2005 e-book available at www.positivediscipline.com.

Nelsen, Jane, Cheryl Erwin, and Carol Delzer. *Positive Discipline for Single Parents*. 2nd ed. New York: Three Rivers Press, 1999.

Nelsen, Jane, Cheryl Erwin, and Roslyn Duffy. *Positive Discipline: The First Three Years*. Second ed. New York: Three Rivers Press, 2007.

Nelsen, J., C. Erwin, M. Hughes, and M. Brock. *Positive Discipline for Christian Families*. Lehi, Utah: Empowering People, 2005, e-book available at www.positivediscipline.com.

Nelsen, Jane, Linda Escobar, Kate Ortolano, Roslyn Duffy, and Deborah Owens-Sohocki. *Positive Discipline: A Teacher's A–Z Guide*. New York: Three Rivers Press, 2001.

Nelsen, Jane, R. Intner, and L. Lott. *Positive Discipline for Parents in Recovery*. Lehi, Utah: Empowering People, 2005, e-book available at www.positivediscipline.com.

Nelsen, Jane, and Lisa Larson. *Positive Discipline for Working Parents*. New York: Three Rivers Press, 2003.

Nelsen, Jane, and Lynn Lott. *Positive Discipline in the Classroom: Teacher's Guide*. Lehi, Utah: Empowering People, www.empoweringpeople.com.

———. *Positive Discipline for Teenagers*. New York: Three Rivers Press, 1997.

Nelsen, Jane, L. Lott, and H. S. Glenn. *Positive Discipline A–Z*. Third ed. New York: Three Rivers Press, 2006.

———. *Positive Discipline in the Classroom*. Third ed. New York: Three Rivers Press, 2000.

Owens, Judith, Rolanda Maxim, Melissa McGuinn, Chantelle Nobile, Michael Msall, and Anthony Alario. "Television-Viewing Habits and Sleep Disturbance in School Children," *Pediatrics* 104, 3 (September 1999): e27.

Patrick, Aaron. "Soft Sell: In Tots' TV Shows, A Booming Market, Toys Get Top Billing." *Wall Street Journal,* January 27, 2006.

Piaget, Jean. *The Origins of Intelligence in Children*. New York: International Universities Press, 1952.

Scarupa, Harriet J., ed. "Family Strengths Often Overlooked, but Real," summary of report from Annie E. Casey Foundation for Child Trends, Washington, D.C., January 2002.

Schulman, Karen. "Overlooked Benefits of Prekindergarten." National Institute of Early Education Research Policy Report, March 2005.

Shore, Rima. *Rethinking the Brain: Research and Implications of Brain Development in Young Children*. New York: Families and Work Institute, 1997.

Siegel, Daniel J., M.D., and Mary Hartzell, M.Ed. *Parenting from the Inside Out: How a Deeper Self-Understanding Can Help You Raise Children Who Thrive*. New York: Tarcher/Putnam, 2003.

Singer, Dorothy G., and Tracey A. Revenson. *A Piaget Primer: How a Child Thinks*. New York: Plume, 1996.

ADDITIONAL RESOURCES

CCFC: *Campaign for a Commercial-Free Childhood,* c/o Judge Baker Children's Center, 53 Parker Hill Avenue, Boston, MA 02120-3225, ongoing information available at www.commercialfreechildhood.org.

"From a Parent's Perspective," bimonthly column by Roslyn Ann Duffy, *Exchange* magazine, Exchange Press, Redmond, Wash., (800) 221-2864; information for parents and child care programs at www.childcareexchange.com.

Mothers of Preschoolers (MOPS), www.mops.org.

Program for Early Parent Support (PEPS), www.pepsgroup.org.

T.R.U.C.E.: Teachers Resisting Unhealthy Children's Entertainment, P.O. Box 441261, West Somerville, MA 02144; more information at www.truceteachers.org.

FOR MORE INFORMATION

The authors are popular speakers and workshop presenters for parents, elementary school teachers, preschool teachers, and child care providers. They are also available for parent and teacher coaching.

Contact Jane Nelsen by going to www.positivediscipline.com or
    jane@positivediscipline.com.
Contact Cheryl Erwin at www.posdis.org or at
    cheryl.erwin@sbcglobal.net.
Contact Roslyn Duffy at www.RoslynDuffy.com or by phone at
    (206) 527-9728.

ACKNOWLEDGMENTS

We are often asked, "Where do you get your stories?" We get them from so many people without whom this book could not have been written. We want to note that names and details in these stories have been changed to protect the privacy of the families who shared them with us; some are composites of several families. And that makes sense: parents and children everywhere experience many of the same challenges as they grow together, and we can all learn from one another.

We owe our biggest thanks to our children. They have provided us with personal family "laboratories." As you have seen, we believe that mistakes are wonderful opportunities to learn. Our children have put up with our mistakes—and have helped us learn from them. We love them and appreciate them.

We also have had many opportunities to learn from parents in our parenting classes and in our counseling offices. It is easy to play the expert with other people, but in truth, you are the only expert on your own children—no one knows them as well as you do. This book offers solid information and good suggestions, but in the end, you must trust your own wisdom and knowledge of your children to help you decide what to do. It isn't always easy. We often tell parents in our classes, "You help me when I get emotionally hooked, and I'll help you when you are emotionally hooked." Parents often tell us how much we help them; we want them to know how much we have learned from them—and how grateful we are.

We have had the opportunity to answer questions on www.positivediscipline.com as well as other venues, from radio call-in programs to parent and teacher groups to audiences at our various talks around the country and internationally. Such questions, and our answers, provided excellent material for this book.

We appreciate the many wonderful people everywhere who are so eager to give children the love and guidance they need. We also appreciate our colleagues and friends who continue to work tirelessly to create more respectful families, schools, and communities. You might not think parenting has changed much in recent years, but we continue to learn new ways of understanding both our children and ourselves. Some of the information in this book has been contributed and enhanced by other Adlerian professionals. We are grateful for them and for the work they do.

The birth order information we shared was wonderfully enhanced by the wise counsel we received from Jane Griffith, a past president of the North American Society of Adlerian Psychology and Professor Emerita of the Adler School of Professional Psychology in Chicago.

We have had excellent editorial help. We gratefully acknowledge Lindsey Moore, our project editor at Three Rivers Press. We can always count on Lindsey to be responsive and encouraging and to make our information clearer and more helpful. We also want to acknowledge Paula Gray for her wonderful illustrations, which add so much to this—and our other—books.

A special thanks to the Learning Tree Montessori Childcare for much of the background material for the chapter on finding quality child care and many of the examples in the chapters on class meetings and mistaken goals of misbehavior. Such insights helped bring deeper meaning to this work.

We will always be grateful to Alfred Adler and Rudolf Dreikurs, the originators of the philosophy upon which Positive Discipline is based. These psychiatrists left a legacy that has changed the lives of thousands—including our own. We feel honored to continue their legacy by sharing their ideas with others.

And oh, how we love our families. Instead of complaining about the time it takes for us to write books, they support and encourage us. They constantly demonstrate their ability to be self-sufficient instead of demanding. They are proud of us for sharing concepts that have helped us all enjoy each other so much. Although our own children are grown now and busy living their own, independent lives, we continue to love spending every moment we can with them and with the next generation, our grandchildren. May this book make the world a healthier and happier place for them, their peers, and the children they will one day parent.

INDEX

ABOUT THE AUTHORS

JANE NELSEN, Ed.D., coauthor of the bestselling Positive Discipline series, is the mother of seven children and grandmother to twenty—and still counting. She is a California-licensed marriage, family, and child therapist and an internationally known speaker. Jane and her husband, Barry, now divide their time between San Clemente, California, and South Jordan, Utah. She has appeared on numerous TV shows, including *Oprah, Sally Jesse Raphael,* and *CBS This Morning.* Her books have sold more than two million copies.

CHERYL ERWIN, M.A., is a licensed marriage and family therapist in Reno, Nevada, and is the author or coauthor of nine books on parenting and family life. She is a popular speaker, trainer, and parenting radio personality, and she is married and has a 22-year-old son.

ROSLYN ANN DUFFY founded and codirected the Learning Tree Montessori Childcare, and she has written adult and children's texts, including *Top Ten Preschool Parenting Problems* as well as the internationally circulated column "From a Parent's Perspective." She lectures and trains in numerous cultures, is a parent to four and a besotted grandma to three, and lives and practices counseling in Seattle, Washington.